THE
RENAISSANCE
IN PERSPECTIVE

LONDON / G. BELL & SONS, LTD.

To Istanbul Colleagues and Friends

PREFACE

This study of the European Renaissance of the fourteenth, fifteenth, and early sixteenth centuries attempts to place the Renaissance in the perspective of the Western historical experience. The Renaissance was essentially a phenomenon of Italian urban communities, but the Italian Renaissance did not develop in isolation. It had deep roots in the European cultural heritage, it profoundly influenced countries beyond the Alps, and, above all, it encompassed and highlighted a crisis affecting the whole European community. Therefore, while attention is necessarily directed chiefly to Italy, significant aspects and key figures of the Renaissance in northern and western Europe are also kept in view.

The book is intended for students in the broadest sense of the term. Avoiding technicalities and a formidable catalogue of names and events, it seeks to encourage awareness, appreciation, and understanding. Enough factual background is presented to enable even the beginning student to follow the discussion, and a chronological guide has been included for reference. But the book is less a compilation for the memory bank than an invitation to expand one's thinking. Some figures have been omitted altogether from the discussion to permit detailed analysis of those who most fully illuminate the nature and significance of the period. Brief critical bibliographies attached to each chapter (except the final summarizing chapter) serve as a guide to the body of scholarly writings now available on all aspects of the Renaissance.

Although there is a rich and abundant literature devoted to the history and culture of the Renaissance, there are few works that give concisely both a broad description and an interpretation of its essential character and its relevance for succeeding ages. Aiming at such an interpretation, the present study carefully examines social and political trends but stresses the intellectual forces—the underlying assumptions, ideals and aspirations, the vision of man and his position in the universe and his destiny—that motivated the creative spirits of the Renaissance. Ideas and ideals, the highest achievements of a civilization, are the key to its strengths and its limitations.

While endeavoring to avoid dogmatic judgments, this survey incorporates a point of view—one that is neither radical nor entirely new, although it does involve a shift in emphasis from the usual interpretation. In relation to the overly long controversy as to whether the Renaissance was "medieval" or "modern," it regards the Renaissance as a product of the Middle Ages, not simply in the retention of vestiges of belief and behavior patterns, but in its most striking and triumphant achievements. The Renaissance evoked the fullest and most articulate expression of concepts that had stimulated the medieval imagination but had never before been developed to their full potential. In breaking with the Middle Ages, the modern age broke with the Renaissance as well. The result has been both gain and loss.

Aspects of modernity can be detected in the Renaissance, but these grew slowly, unattended. The dominant traits of the modern age—and of our own "post-modern" era—were mainly recessive during the Renaissance. They appear as crosscurrents, generally unrecognized, or looked at askance, although ultimately potent enough to shatter the foundations of the older civilization. The monumental products of Renaissance art, literature, and philosophic thought offer the final statement of a long-enduring cultural, moral, and spiritual tradition. The abandonment of this tradition led not to a decline in creative powers but to a decisive change in the purposes to which they were put—to new departures continuing unbroken to our own day. The real significance of the Renaissance is that it represents a great divide in Western history, perhaps in world history. It marks a point of no return.

The Renaissance was the ripest fruit of the prescientific age. Our own age was shaped by the impact of science and its accompanying industrial and technological revolutions. These forces brought not only sweeping material changes but an equally great transformation in values and goals. Interest shifted from what can be imagined to what can be measured; from harmony with nature and the cosmos to conquest of nature and the cosmos; from the flavor, color, and quality of life to its quantity, extension, and control. Where the Renaissance sought to understand man, our age seeks to manipulate him. A vast expansion of knowledge has brought us powers that men of the Renaissance could scarcely conceive. They dreaded the influence of the planets on people's lives; we dare dream of peopling the planets.

The problems and anxieties of contemporary civilization, no less than its proudest accomplishments, have their origin in forces operating over many centuries. We can better understand them through exploring their early manifestations in that transitional era of magnificence and tragedy known as the Renaissance.

I would like to acknowledge the many Renaissance scholars and specialists whose work has been invaluable to me in writing this book. I am indebted to Leslie Fairfield and J. Kelley Sowards for their reading of my manuscript and for their many insightful suggestions and to Wilma Ebbitt for her editorial skill. I am also deeply grateful to my colleagues and to my students for their stimulation, challenge, and encouragement, and to my wife for her patience and support throughout the enterprise.

Holland, Michigan   P. L. R.
October, 1972

CONTENTS

*A photo essay of Renaissance art
begins on p. 182*

I

INTRODUCTION

*The sixteenth century, in its full and legitimate extension,
runs from Columbus to Copernicus, from Copernicus
to Galileo, from the discovery of the earth to that of
the heavens.*
  That is when man found himself.
  —Jules Michelet, HISTORY OF FRANCE—THE RENAISSANCE

*The differences between classical and Christian ways of
life and thought were too great to be brought into
harmony. The effort to do so caused a state of uncertainty
in which old standards of faith and morals were
undermined and nothing stable was put in their place.*
  —Cecilia Ady, LORENZO DEI MEDICI AND RENAISSANCE ITALY

In the popular imagination the Renaissance is a glamorous epoch,
something of a golden age. It may be thought of as a time when
masterpieces of art were being produced in every studio and when
the cultural level reached such a height that the artist's life was a
secure and happy one. Or it may be identified with an intellectual
awakening that revolutionized every field of thought and that was
all the more remarkable because it followed close on the heels of
the "Dark Ages"—an undefined era sometimes carelessly confused
with the whole of the medieval period, the nine or ten centuries that
followed the "fall" of the Roman Empire in the West. The period
may even be viewed as the starting point of everything that goes
to make up the modern age. This assumption makes the Renaissance
synonymous with the birth of science, the emancipation of the individual from arbitrary authority, the rise of efficient governments and
the secularization of the state and society—in short, with the beginning of all real progress.
  It is not difficult to account for the enthusiastic estimate of the
Renaissance that has embedded itself in popular tradition. The very

name commonly applied to the era induces an admiring response. No historical epoch has been more fortunate in the title bestowed upon it by posterity. A "rebirth," the renewal of life and resurrection of the spirit after a long winter of hibernation—this is a figure to stir the most sluggish imagination.

The prestige of the Renaissance has been enhanced by the widespread influence of several of its ardent admirers in the world of scholarship. Jacob Burckhardt, a Swiss historian, whose *Die Cultur der Renaissance in Italien* was first published in 1860, inaugurated the cult of Renaissance worship in modern times. Actually it was not Burckhardt but the French historian Jules Michelet who first used the term to designate an epoch of European history, specifically the sixteenth century: he gave the title "The Renaissance" to the seventh volume of his *History of France* (1855). It was Michelet, too, who originated the famous phrase "the discovery of the world, the discovery of man." Burckhardt seized upon it and, as Wallace Ferguson aptly observed, "expanded an unforgettable epigram into a great book."

THE BURCKHARDT THESIS

The famous "Burckhardt thesis" provides a convenient starting point for the arguments of both admirers and detractors of the epoch. Buttressing his conclusions with solid research and enriching his commentary with vivid personality sketches and graphic illustrative anecdotes, Burckhardt saw the Italian Renaissance of the fourteenth and fifteenth centuries as a momentous turning point in the history of European civilization. Whereas during the Middle Ages, he said, human consciousness "lay dreaming or half-awake beneath a common veil," in Italy "this veil first melted into air; an *objective* treatment and consideration of the State and of all the things of this world became possible." [1] According to Burckhardt, not only did culture free itself "from the fantastic bonds of the Middle Ages" but the era witnessed the "perfecting of the individual." Even despotic governments in the Italian city-states, he argued, did not seriously

---

[1] Jacob Burckhardt, *The Civilization of the Renaissance in Italy*, trans. S. G. C. Middlemore (Oxford: Phaidon Press, 1944), p. 81. Other quotations from this edition are identified by page references in parentheses immediately following the quotation.

interfere with the attainment of full stature by the human personality; and, in spite of despotism, the trend in Italian society was towards greater flexibility and equality. The trend was inspired largely by reawakened memories of the Roman Empire, which "stood as a permanent ideal before the minds of Italians. From henceforth all the aspirations and achievements of the people were governed by a moral postulate, which was still unknown elsewhere in Europe" (p. 87).

In passages like these, Burckhardt paid generous tribute to the Renaissance Italian—"the first-born among the sons of modern Europe"—and to his latter-day descendants as well. He summarized his own main thesis in the proposition "that it was not the revival of antiquity alone, but its union with the genius of the Italian people, which achieved the conquest of the western world" (p. 104).

Fascinated though he was by the personalities, attitudes, and scope of the Renaissance, Burckhardt was by no means blind to its faults. His nineteenth-century moral sense recoiled again and again at the cruelties of princes and *condottieri,* the assassinations, diabolical intrigues, and crimes of passion which he recorded without dissembling. He noted, and perhaps exaggerated, the strong currents of religious skepticism, agnosticism, and atheism that manifested themselves in the thought of the period. He interpreted the Italian Renaissance as essentially pagan in spirit, explaining this characteristic as a natural consequence of the combination of individual self-assertiveness, the cult of pagan antiquity, and the failure of the contemporary Church to satisfy either moral or intellectual demands. Neither ignoring nor defending the vices of the age he so greatly admired, he regarded them as incidental to the emergence of a freer society, comparable to the growing pains of an adolescent. And he observed, not unreasonably, that men of the nineteenth century no less than those of the Renaissance were still uncertain of the paths leading "back to God" after the advance of factual knowledge and the discipline of objective inquiry had shattered the naive faith of an earlier age of ignorance (pp. 304–305).

Numerous writers after Burckhardt contributed to the process of glorifying and idealizing the Renaissance. Notably influential was John Addington Symonds, who incorporated the Burckhardt thesis in his seven-volume study, *Renaissance in Italy,* and who—while providing literary and artistic criticism of a high order—went even farther than Burckhardt in asserting that the Renaissance embodied a complete break with the Middle Ages and in hailing it as the dawn of the modern world. For the Middle Ages Symonds could find nothing good to say:

The arts and the inventions, the knowledge and the books, which suddenly became vital at the time of the Renaissance, had long lain neglected on the shores of the Dead Sea which we call the Middle Ages. . . . The mental condition of the Middle Ages was one of ignorant prostration before the idols of the Church—dogma and authority and scholasticism. . . . The reason, in one word, was not awake; the mind of man was ignorant of its own treasures and its own capacities.[2]

Viewed against this dismal background, the Renaissance, in Symonds' version, was indeed a "new birth." It appeared as

a natural movement, not to be explained by this or that characteristic, but to be accepted as an effort of humanity for which at length the time had come, and in the onward progress of which we still participate. The history of the Renaissance is . . . the history of the attainment of self-conscious freedom by the human spirit manifested in the European races. . . . The force then generated still continues, vital and expansive, in the spirit of the modern world (pp. 3–4).

Such a remarkable transformation from death to life demanded an explanation. "How was it," Symonds queried, "that at a certain period, about fourteen centuries after Christ, to speak roughly, the intellect of the Western races awoke as it were from slumber and began once more to be active?" He turned away from the question as too difficult to answer: "The mystery of organic life defeats analysis." But in the next paragraph he offered what would seem to be an extremely simple explanation, at least for the geographical location of the miracle: "The reason why Italy took the lead in the Renaissance was, that Italy possessed a language, a favorable climate, political freedom, and commercial prosperity, at a time when other nations were still semi-barbarous" (pp. 4–6).

Symonds was reluctant to admit any debt of the Renaissance

---

[2] John A. Symonds, *Renaissance in Italy*, Vol. I: *The Age of the Despots* (New York: Holt, Rinehart & Winston, 1888), pp. 4–6. Other quotations from this source are identified by page numbers in parentheses.

to the Midlde Ages; the two were as different as day and night. To quote one of his most striking invidious comparisons:

During the Middle Ages man had lived enveloped in a cowl. He had not seen the beauty of the world, or had seen it only to cross himself, and turn aside and tell his beads and pray. Like S. Bernard travelling along the shores of the Lake Leman, and noticing neither the azure of the waters, nor the luxuriance of the vines, nor the radiance of the mountains with their robe of sun and snow, but bending a thought-burdened forehead over the neck of his mule; even like this monk, humanity had passed, a careful pilgrim, intent on the terrors of sin, death, and judgment, along the highways of the world, and had scarcely known that they were sightworthy or that life is a blessing. Beauty is a snare, pleasure a sin, the world a fleeting show, man fallen and lost, death the only certainty, judgment inevitable, hell everlasting, heaven hard to win; ignorance is acceptable to God as a proof of faith and submission; abstinence and mortification are the only safe rules of life: these were the fixed ideas of the ascetic mediaeval Church. The Renaissance shattered and destroyed them, rending the thick veil which they had drawn between the mind of man and the outer world, and flashing the light of reality upon the darkened places of his own nature. For the mystic teaching of the Church was substituted culture in the classical humanities; a new ideal was established, whereby man strove to make himself the monarch of the globe on which it is his privilege as well as destiny to live. The Renaissance was the liberation of the reason from a dungeon, the double discovery of the outer and the inner world (pp. 13–14).

THE REACTION OF THE MEDIEVALISTS

In the twentieth century a reaction set in against the thesis that the Renaissance constituted a uniquely brilliant epoch of civilization and the point of departure for the modern age. Quite understandably, the reaction was promoted especially by students of the medieval period, who acquired a sympathetic appreciation of the culture of the era that had seemed so barren to Burckhardt and Symonds. Medieval scholars denied that the Renaissance had really made a sharp break from the immediate past. They identified it simply as the final stage of the Middle Ages; or they alleged that, if the salient features of the Renaissance are fundamental to the modern age, their origins can be discovered as far back as the twelfth and thirteenth centuries. Some medievalists went so far as to claim that the characteristic thought and expression of the High Middle Ages was actually superior to that which flourished in the Italian cities of the later and more celebrated period.

A landmark in this revisionist movement was Charles Homer Haskins' *The Renaissance of the Twelfth Century*. While not belittling the Italian Renaissance, and while accepting the conventional assumption that humanist attitudes were inspired primarily by a revival of interest in ancient Latin authors, Haskins discovered in twelfth-century Europe a widespread knowledge and appreciation of the Latin classics. This appreciation went far beyond mere drill in the rules of grammar and rhetoric; the classics, Haskins emphasized, were enjoyed and valued as literature and exerted a significant effect upon men's orientation toward life. He cited the case of John of Salisbury (d. 1180), in whom the Ciceronian tradition had fused with a ripe knowledge of the Bible and the Latin Church Fathers to produce "a well rounded Christian humanism"; he remarked the popularity of Ovid, a most nonascetic poet; and he pronounced the twelfth century "a great age, probably the culminating age, of religious poetry." [3] Haskins concluded that the intellectual quickening evident in the twelfth century continued uninterrupted and that "there is no real break between the mediaeval renaissance and the Quattrocento" (p. 9). In any case, aside from the question of continuity, "the very century of St. Bernard and his mule, was in many respects an age of fresh and vigorous life" (p. viii).

The scholars who rendered the valuable service of rehabilitating the Middle Ages tended to exaggerate the medieval achievement and to do less than justice to that of the Renaissance. Some found in Scholastic philosophy—which has repelled many lively intellects of ages more recent than Petrarch's—not only an impressive synthesis of medieval experience but an unrivaled source of truth and wisdom. The great French intellectual historian Etienne Gilson wrote in his *Philosophy in the Middle Ages* (1922):

It is necessary, then, to relegate to the domain of legend the history of a Renaissance of thought succeeding to centuries of sleep, of obscurity, and error. Modern philosophy did not have to undertake the struggle to establish

---

[3] Charles H. Haskins, *The Renaissance of the Twelfth Century* (Cambridge, Mass.: Harvard University Press, 1927), pp. 100–101, 107–109, 166.

the rights of reason against the Middle Ages; it was, on the contrary, the Middle Ages that established them for it.[4]

A few reputable medieval scholars have forthrightly denied the originality of Renaissance contributions to any significant field of human endeavor. It had been assumed that science was the region of knowledge most woefully neglected during the medieval "age of faith," of superstition, and of contempt for the world, and that impressive scientific advances indicative of progress in the European mentality should be credited to the Renaissance. But several historians of science deny the Renaissance any substantial role in the emergence of modern science. Lynn Thorndike has called the fifteenth century scientifically inferior to the fourteenth and characterized even the sixteenth century as "not an age of scientific specialization but marked by a somewhat amateurish literary interest." For this deficiency he blamed "the emphasis upon eloquence, humanism and the classics." Humanism, he said, emphasized "style rather than science, and show rather than substance." [5] According to a more recent critic, "The early or 'pure' Renaissance, 1450-1500, stands in the front rank of competition for the most sterile half-century of Western mathematics and physics." [6] Perhaps the severest stricture of all was pronounced by George Sarton, in 1929: "From the scientific point of view the Renaissance was *not* a renaissance" but "a sort of anticlimax between two peaks." He scored the "antiscientific tendencies of the humanists" and accused the men of the Renaissance of an "instinctive resistance to any kind of scientific enlightenment." [7]

---

[4] Wallace K. Ferguson, *The Renaissance in Historical Thought* (Boston: Houghton Mifflin, 1948), p. 340 (Ferguson's translation).

[5] Lynn Thorndike, *A History of Magic and Experimental Science*, Vol. V: *The Sixteenth Century* (New York: Columbia University Press, 1941), pp. 4–5, 8.

[6] C. A. Truesdell, "Leonardo da Vinci, The Myths and the Reality," *The Johns Hopkins Magazine*, XVIII, 2 (Spring 1967), 32.

[7] George Sarton, "Science in the Renaissance," in James Westfall Thompson *et al.*, eds., *The Civilization of the Renaissance* (New York: Frederick Ungar, 1929), pp. 75–95. Later, however, Sarton reached diametrically opposite conclusions, as indicated by the eulogy he pronounced in 1952: "In the field of science, the novelties were gigantic, revolutionary. . . . The Renais-

CHANGING CONCEPTIONS OF THE RENAISSANCE

Estimates of and attitudes toward the Renaissance have oscillated widely over the centuries. The term itself came into general use only gradually; not before the nineteenth century was it adopted as the conventional name for a period of European history. Still, the notion that some sort of a cultural rebirth took place at the close of the Middle Ages can be traced back to the Italian humanists themselves. Giorgio Vasari, a Florentine painter and architect most famous for his *Lives of the Great Painters, Sculptors, and Architects* (1550), was apparently the earliest writer to adopt the name "rebirth" (*la rinascita*) for the epoch he represented, but he was designating—and honoring—an epoch in the history of art.

Petrarch, who is usually credited with initiating the "revival of learning" through his fervent championing of classical Latin authors, might have been pleased to know he was destined to go down in history as the "father of humanism," but he probably would have viewed with mixed emotions the label which posterity fastened upon his era. Petrarch conceived a very simple and drastic division of European history, into "ancient" and "modern." But the "modern" he dated from the adoption of Christianity by the Roman emperors, and he characterized this whole stretch of time down to his own day as an "age of darkness." He was far from enthusiastic about the attitudes prevalent among his contemporaries and wished he had been born in the glorious days of ancient Rome. Petrarch's quarrel with his own time was provoked largely by his impatience with the arid academic tradition and the scarcity of like-minded scholars, and by his own deep enchantment with the world of Cicero, Vergil, and Seneca—to whom he addressed long and impassioned letters adorned with as much of the classical Latin style as he was able to master.

The flowering of Greek as well as Latin scholarship during the century and a half after Petrarch, accompanied as it was by

<hr>

sance scientists introduced not a 'new look' but a new being. The novelty was often so great that one could hardly speak of a Renaissance or rebirth; it was a real birth, a new beginning." "The Quest for Truth: Scientific Progress during the Renaissance," in Wallace K. Ferguson *et al.*, eds., *The Renaissance: Six Essays* (New York: Harper & Row, 1962), p. 57.

brilliant achievements in painting, sculpture, and architecture, brought a justifiable sense of accomplishment. But even though men of the Renaissance boasted of the rebirth of art and of literature, they did not think of themselves as inaugurating a new civilization. If they had, they would have been hard pressed to define the character of their age in view of the variety of life styles, the shifting moods, and the contradictory currents running throughout the Renaissance. It is true, as is generally asserted, that the early period displayed a spirit of hope and confidence, while the High Renaissance was burdened with doubts and harassed by unresolved conflicts. Yet Petrarch, honored as the father of humanism, was so torn between a craving for fame and feeling of guilt over his vanity that he toyed with the idea of renouncing the world—even the world of letters—for the cloister; while Benvenuto Cellini, who lived in and beyond the High Renaissance, accepted with relish all the claims of his animal and human natures.

During the four centuries of the post-Renaissance or "modern" era, conceptions of the Renaissance have shifted in accordance with successive changes in dominant interests and beliefs. The religious Reformation of the sixteenth century, while it represents a more complete break with medieval institutions than does the Renaissance, was hostile both to the spirit of humanism and to its expression in the fine arts, and it rejected out of hand the concept of man's self-sufficiency and intrinsic worthiness. Long after the Reformation it was common in the Protestant tradition to interpret the Renaissance not only as having prepared the ground for the revolution launched by Luther and Calvin but also as an allied and kindred movement; but this interpretation obscures the most salient characteristics of both the Renaissance and the Reformation.

In contrast to the era of the Reformation with its bitter theological disputes and its wars of religion, the period of the seventeenth and eighteenth centuries known as the Enlightenment brought a renewed confidence in man's potentialities, even to the point of affirming the dogma of human perfectibility. Not surprisingly, exponents of the Enlightenment viewed the Renaissance sympathetically, according it the honor of having begun the age of progress by striving for emancipation from the brutishness, ignorance, and superstition of the "barbarous" Middle Ages. But eighteenth-century liberals were much less interested in the past than in the future, and they believed their own age was the first to possess enough wisdom to make possible the realization of an ideal society. Voltaire, for example, while commending men of the Renaissance for repudiating their medieval religious heritage (he mistakenly assumed they had done so), reproached them for not having replaced this burdensome ecclesiastical system with a religion founded on reason and the truths of science. To Voltaire it seemed obvious that such a religion was a necessary basis for morality and human felicity. He could not foresee that to nineteenth-century tastes, Deism—the "natural religion" of the philosophers of the Enlightenment—would seem more lifeless and unappealing than the religious traditions the Renaissance had inherited from the Middle Ages.

By the early nineteenth century, rationalism and neoclassicism gave way to romanticism. Romanticism inculcated a sympathetic attitude, approaching reverence, toward the past, and stimulated its exploration in depth. Writers of the Romantic period found in the Renaissance a certain fascination, often a morbid fascination. They were captivated by the towering personalities, by the wickedness, the blood and violence. Victor Hugo, in his popular play *Lucretia Borgia* (1833), embellished the legends of intrigue, poison, and incest surrounding this notorious woman to present her as a monster of lust and cruelty typifying her age. Somewhat earlier Johann Goethe, whose intellectual grasp embraced both romanticism and classicism, chose as the most representative figure of the sixteenth century the egotistical, neurotic artist Benvenuto Cellini in preference to the majestic Raphael. The influential mid-Victorian English critic John Ruskin condemned the art of the High Renaissance as pagan, irreligious, immoral, and characterized the spirit of the Renaissance as generally evil. Not surprisingly, the qualities, real or imagined, that repelled a moralist like Ruskin were the very ones to attract the romantic arch-individualist Friedrich Nietzsche in the late nineteenth century. Nietzsche praised the Renaissance because to him it represented a revolt against Christian humility and an affirmation of the natural, instinctive, and pagan will to live—an age of unbridled Superman.

Despite its emphasis upon emotion, however, the era of romanticism did not draw its chief inspiration from the Renaissance nor assign it a lofty position in the historical scheme. This was partly because many of the romanticists sought to reaffirm religious values and condemned the reputed paganism of the Renaissance, and partly because they were more interested in the origins and distinguishing traits of the European nationalities than in the remnants of a classical heritage. More important still was the fact that the romanticists had discovered the Middle Ages and preempted it as a kind of fairyland, delighting to invest its scenes and characters with radiant colors and extracting from it any idea that suited their fancy.

Strangely enough, the full exploitation of the rich vein of historical lore in the Renaissance was a phenomenon of the later nineteenth century—a highly unromantic epoch crowded with solid, prosaic material achievements. Probably rapid industrial expansion, the growth of large anonymous corporations, and the mounting pressures of an increasingly mechanized environment help account for the vogue of the Renaissance during this period. Burckhardt, in his *Civilization of the Renaissance,* stressed as one of its central contributions the concept of individualism, and entitled one section of his book "The Development of the Individual." In *The Revival of Classical Antiquity* (1859) and later writings, the German historian Georg Voigt, while aware of the limited intellectual scope of Italian humanists and critical of their naive infatuation with the classics, at the same time commended them for giving free play to individual personality. He attributed this bold new departure to the example of Petrarch, in whom "for the first time individuality and its rights stood forth strong and free with a claim to the highest significance." Liberals, romantic individualists, even patriotic nationalists of the nineteenth century could cherish the Renaissance as the starting point of Western progress and also envy it as a time when man was still free from the burdens of a complex and more and more standardized industrial society. And then, somewhat unkindly, the dissecting knife of twentieth-century scholarship—in an age even more harassed by the machine but somewhat disillusioned concerning the possibilities of human freedom—proceeded to cut away the magic wrappings from the Renaissance, robbing the epoch of its uniqueness and threatening to reduce it to a mere bridge between medieval and modern times.

It is doubtful whether even the most devastating attack can destroy the concept of the Renaissance. After the last rites have been performed and the corpse consigned to decent burial (whether pagan or Christian might be disputed), it will be found still very much alive in people's consciousness. Debate over its nature and significance has produced an extensive body of literature devoted to interpretation of the Renaissance, and probably will continue. The Burckhardt thesis, in spite of its documented deficiencies, still elicits qualified support. In his brilliant and sensitive study, *The Genius of Italy* (1949), Leonardo Oschki, like Burckhardt before him, paid tribute to the unique qualities of the Italian mind and spirit and explained Renaissance civilization as one of the successive manifestations of Italian genius. Hans Baron, a commanding figure in modern Renaissance scholarship, finds Burckhardt's main emphasis still valid. "Recent scholarship," he wrote in 1943, "has been developing the Burckhardtian thesis that at the basis of the fifteenth-century Renaissance there was a fundamental change in man's outlook on life and the world—the coming of the 'first-born among the sons of modern Europe.' " [8]

The harshest critics of Burckhardt have gone to such extremes in correcting a faulty perspective that they have substituted one equally distorted. Perhaps Giuseppe Toffanin may be placed in this category despite his persuasive erudition. In *What Humanism Was* (original Italian edition 1919) he flung down a challenge by reversing practically all the dicta customarily applied to Renaissance culture. While he lauded humanism, he interpreted it not as the harbinger of individualism inspired by contact with the pagan classics but as a rallying of Catholic orthodoxy to defend the faith and conserve universal spiritual values against the heretical forces of materialism, undisciplined individualism, particularism, and modernism. In his view the Latin language, universalism, and the Roman Church stood as allies in the cause of truth and civilization, in opposition to such evils as divisive vernacular literatures, late medieval communal democracy, and scientific materialism. Toffanin's radical reassignment of traditional roles, while uncovering several grains of truth, confounds rather than clarifies judgment. But though the clash of divergent opinion may perpetuate discord, at least it reinforces the conviction that the period in dispute was a crucial one, of lasting importance to the destiny of Western society.

---

[8] "Toward a More Positive Evaluation of the Fifteenth Century Renaissance," *Journal of the History of Ideas*, IV (1943), 22–49.

INTERPRETATION AND JUDGMENT

The problem of understanding and evaluating the Renaissance lies in the fact that while it is too complex and many-sided to fit neatly into any single conceptual category, it seems to cry out for interpretation. The term "Renaissance" is itself a proclamation and a challenge. The culture to which the metaphor is applied—bound with so many subtle ties both to the past and to the future—can be appreciated only by attempting to view it in the perspective of Western civilization as a whole. This means making a subjective judgment, which, though it can make no claim to omniscience, can serve to highlight salient features and bring them closer to the viewer's own experience.

It is legitimate to classify the Renaissance as a period of transition between the medieval and modern ages, but though such a classification is convenient, it is not very illuminating. On the one hand it suggests that the era lacked distinction of its own, which is not true. On the other hand it calls for clarification of what is meant by "Middle Ages" and "modern age," both of them vague elastic terms, subject to a variety of definitions. Certainly the Renaissance was a period of transition—what age is not?—but the important questions are whether the currents of change were moving in the same direction or at cross purposes, whether the changes were merely incidental or were essential elements in determining the character of the age, and whether they were consciously perceived or were taking place without the intention and even against the wishes of the people involved.

The Renaissance was an era of ferment and movement—both social and intellectual—and in certain respects was changing in a direction that has continued with variations into our time. This category of change, chiefly external and material—the increasing predominance of urban society and capitalist enterprise, an expanding interest in travel and discovery, widening knowledge of the physical world and its inhabitants—had begun long before the Renaissance and did not constitute its most distinctive features. Far more important were changes in personal and social goals, in thought and imagination—elements that, though intangible were given expression in literature and art. And the dominant themes in art and literature were not those most congenial to the modern temper. To a considerable extent they were opposed to what have become the distinguishing traits, interests, and commitments of the post-Renaissance centuries. They embraced assumptions and reflected values that have been largely abandoned, not only in practice but in the realm of the imagination as well.

The Renaissance was least successful in dealing with those aspects of civilization that relate to the dawning modern age—technological innovation and exploitation of the discipline of science (a field long neglected, even viewed with hostility by many Renaissance thinkers). Above all, it failed to meet or even recognize the needs of the unprivileged workers and unemployed paupers, whose numbers increased along with a tightening concentration of wealth. It was most successful in cultivating its heritage from the waning Middle Ages—the hopeful promise of a union of faith and intellect; a fervent vision of human destiny; and the tradition of using art and literature to articulate the noblest concepts of the mind. The inability of Renaissance thinkers to convert their motivating ideals into effective instruments for alleviating the inequities and callous cruelties in their own societies goes far to explain the fragility and ultimate failure of Renaissance civilization. Before the close of the Renaissance, sensitive intellects were aware—if only dimly—that their cherished values had suffered erosion. They found the available human material, shaped as it was by contemporary institutions, insufficiently responsive to their vision of what man can and should be, and their ideals too sharply at odds with the society in which they had been propagated.

In the conventional tripartite division of European history the Renaissance is commonly treated as a definite period, although one with flexible dates—a segment of time occupying three centuries or more. The term becomes meaningful, however, only when used in a narrower sense, as applying to a constellation of cultural factors, manifest primarily in Italy although influencing countries beyond the Alps, and limited approximately to the period 1300–1550. Federico Chabod admirably defined the most useful approach when he called the Renaissance "a mobilization of ideas, an artistic, literary and cultural 'period' which is first and foremost an 'intellectual' reality." In explaining points of contrast between medieval and Renaissance civilization, he observed:

The Renaissance does not find its expression in practical activity, which is incidental to the existence of the individual—in the gay life of a citizen of Florence, the self-indulgence of a Mantuan gentlewoman, the unrestrained ambition of a *condottiere* or the amorous intrigues of some member of the Court of Naples—but rather in the manner in which human designs and actions conform to an ideal system and are elevated from the plane of mere practical, instinctive activity to the status of a spiritual creed, a programme of life.[9]

The judgment and the assumptions that underlie the present study can be briefly summarized: The Renaissance, both in form and spirit, was far more medieval than modern; but this dictum— on which there is now wide but not universal agreement—is a relatively trivial point. To affirm it may give more due to the Middle Ages than is customary, but it by no means downgrades the Renaissance. While leaders of the Renaissance revived, admired, and employed the forms of classical antiquity, the classical tradition served them chiefly as an "energizing myth" (Chabod's term). They retained and embellished medieval conceptions and formulas. They remained within the framework of medieval civilization—not as prisoners but as legitimate heirs enthusiastically redecorating the old family mansion. While the medieval social and political order was beginning to crumble, and even while fascination with the golden age of Roman antiquity incited an anti-medieval bias, creative talents sought to give vivid expression to ideals and aspirations that had been active or latent all through the medieval centuries. These ideals, the product of a long philosophical and religious tradition, received new treatment. In a sense they were "secularized," drawn more directly into the orbit of individual consciousness and experience. What the boldest spirits of the Renaissance attempted was to bring to full realization the promise inherent in the wisdom of the ancients and in the Christian tradition—to transform this promise from a distant hope to a present reality to be enjoyed by living men and women.

The leading exponents of Renaissance culture—known by the general term "humanists"—were indeed man-centered. But they

---

[9] Federico Chabod, *Machiavelli and the Renaissance*, trans. David Moore (Cambridge, Mass.: Harvard University Press, 1960), p. 163.

were convinced that man is both the child of nature and the creature of God, and that through his twin heritage he can reach a station of dignity and benevolence. A late Renaissance figure, Erasmus of Rotterdam—who was at the same time one of the greatest, and one of the most devotedly Christian, scholars of his age—went so far as to claim that "God hath ordained man in this world, as it were the very image of Himself, to the intent, that he, as it were a god on earth, should provide for the wealth of all creatures." [10]

The Italian Renaissance cannot be understood as a purely peninsular affair, detached either in time or space from the larger community. And although it may be described as a "mobilization of ideas," it shows significant differences between its earlier and later stages. The early Renaissance exhibited a confident, often ebullient spirit. The late, or High, Renaissance—which includes the last half or last third of the fifteenth century and the early sixteenth, and which brought forth magnificent and powerful works of art—was troubled by feelings of frustration, disillusionment, and despair. The Renaissance reached its climax about the middle of the second decade of the sixteenth century. It is remarkable, and surely no coincidence, that several of the most memorable products of artistic, literary, and philosophical genius were conceived or executed about that date: Michelangelo's Sistine Chapel ceiling frescoes, 1508-12; Erasmus' *Praise of Folly*, 1511; Machiavelli's *The Prince*, 1513; More's *Utopia*, 1516; Ariosto's *Orlando Furioso*, 1516; Castiglione's *The Courtier*, ca. 1518, to name the most striking examples. In 1517 Martin Luther posted his *Ninety-five Theses* in Wittenberg. Thus the apogee of the Renaissance almost coincides with the beginning of the Reformation, a movement destined not only to shake the Church to its foundations but also to stifle the Renaissance. Within a generation of its fullest outburst, the affirmative spirit of the High Renaissance had largely subsided in Italy, yielding to the somber and inhibitive mood of the Counter Reformation. The European mind retreated from the lofty summit which its imagination had commanded—descending to concern itself with necessary and fruitful enterprises on the plain below, but resigned henceforth to surveying human destiny with lowered sights.

---

[10] Quoted in Douglas Bush, *The Renaissance and English Humanism* (Toronto: University of Toronto Press, 1939), p. 68.

A dichotomy pervades the life and culture of the Renaissance, incipient in the early optimistic period, conclusive and disruptive in the later stage, when it imparted a tragic quality to some of the greatest masterpieces of art. This dichotomy needs to be examined, not only because it plagued the Renaissance but because it has never been resolved and, under different guise, continues to afflict our own civilization.

REFERENCES AND SUGGESTIONS FOR FURTHER READING

Burckhardt, Jacob, *The Civilization of the Renaissance in Italy*, trans. S. G. C. Middlemore (Oxford: Phaidon Press, 1944). The Harper Torchbook edition of the Middlemore translation (2 vols., New York, 1958) includes a valuable introduction by Benjamin Nelson and Charles Trinkaus. Insisting that Burckhardt's central insights "remain essentially unimpaired," they direct attention to the prescribed limits within which he conceived his great essay and the respects in which he has often been misunderstood, and relate Burckhardt's account of Renaissance individualism to the predicament of contemporary man: "To read Burckhardt's pages is to look into a mirror."

Haskins, Charles H., *The Renaissance of the Twelfth Century* (Cambridge, Mass.: Harvard University Press, 1927). Reprinted in Meridian Book edition (New York, 1957).

Symonds, John A., *Renaissance in Italy*, 7 vols., London, 1875–81. References are to Vol. I: *The Age of the Despots* (New York: Holt, Rinehart & Winston, 1888).

For the evolution of the concept of the Renaissance and changing interpretations of it, the indispensable study is Wallace K. Ferguson, *The Renaissance in Historical Thought: Five Centuries of Interpretation* (Boston: Houghton Mifflin, 1948). A masterpiece of analysis and narration.

Convenient brief compilations of extracts from sources and essays illustrating the wide variety of viewpoints and interpretations are: Karl H. Dannenfeldt, ed., *The Renaissance: Medieval or Modern?* (Lexington, Mass.: Heath, 1959). Denys Hay, ed., *The Renaissance Debate* (New York: Holt, Rinehart & Winston,

1965). Peter Burke, ed., *The Renaissance* (New York: Barnes and Noble, 1964). W. J. Bouwsma, *The Interpretation of Renaissance Humanism,* American Historical Association Pamphlet Series (Washington, D. C., 1959). Includes both commentary and bibliographical citations.

Among many interpretive essays on the nature or significance of the Renaissance, the following are especially recommended: Federico Chabod, "The Concept of the Renaissance," in *Machiavelli and the Renaissance,* trans. David Moore (Cambridge, Mass.: Harvard University Press, 1960). Examines contrasting viewpoints and offers a fresh and vigorous statement. Douglas Bush, *The Renaissance and English Humanism* (Toronto: University of Toronto Press, 1939). Chapter I, entitled "Modern Theories of the Renaissance," is perceptive, warm, and witty. Peter Munz, in the Introduction to his translation of Eugenio Garin, *Italian Humanism* (New York: Harper & Row, 1965), ably summarizes the problem of interpreting the Renaissance and examines contrasting approaches, including Garin's argument for the elements of modernity in the thought of the humanists.

II

RENAISSANCE POLITICS: THE ACTUALITY

*How sad to see noble Italy, whose right it is to rule other
nations, itself suffer slavery!*
—Coluccio Salutati, LETTER TO THE ROMANS, 1376

*In Italy princes become tyrants because here there is an
abundance of spirit and intelligence, which is not
the case in the countries beyond the mountains.*
—Girolamo Savonarola, SERMON OF DECEMBER 28, 1494

THE PARADOX OF MACHIAVELLI

Consideration of Renaissance politics inevitably brings to mind the
Florentine diplomatist and political philosopher, Niccolò Machiavelli. It is appropriate that he was a native of Florence, because
this Tuscan town epitomized the Italian Renaissance in almost all
its aspects. Florence easily established a preeminence in humanist
scholarship, in literature, and in the fine arts that was for long unchallenged. At the same time, the town was continually in the
maelstrom of power politics, and her citizens were forced to concern themselves with public affairs. Among their number Machiavelli
(1469–1527) had the sharpest intellect of those who recorded their
political reflections. *The Prince,* his small book of hardly one hundred
pages, has become one of the most famous works in the history of
Western thought.

The argument of Machiavelli's *Prince,* with all its bluntness
and apparent straightforwardness, immediately suggests a strange
contradiction in the Renaissance view of things. For the most part,
Renaissance humanism delighted in what it discovered concerning
human nature. Nourishing itself on the chronicles of illustrious

Greeks and Romans and resurrecting the language in which the exploits of these heroes had been celebrated, it awakened hope for a new heroic age. In their own eyes—and, to a considerable extent, in the eyes of posterity down to the present—humanist scholars were endeavoring to reveal man's potentialities for a fuller and more satisfying existence. *The Prince*, however, reflects a startlingly pessimistic view of human nature. It offers one of the most caustic appraisals of man ever to win a permanent place in the libraries of the world.

Here, in a famous passage of *The Prince*, is Machiavelli's verdict on the human race:

> For it may be said of men in general that they are ungrateful, voluble, dissemblers, anxious to avoid danger, and covetous of gain; as long as you benefit them, they are entirely yours; they offer you their blood, their goods, their life, and their children . . . when the necessity is remote; but when it approaches, they revolt.[1]

Again, "men are so simple and so ready to obey present necessities, that one who deceives will always find those who allow themselves to be deceived" (Chap. 18). Thus, Machiavelli's judgment on the majority of mortals seems to be that they are both wicked and stupid, and he warns the would-be ruler to remember that "men will always be false to you unless they are compelled by necessity to be true" (Chap. 23).

Machiavelli was, of course, addressing his remarks not to the general public but to one in a position to command, to the potentially successful ruler or "prince." Nevertheless, he grounded his teachings on what he conceived to be the salient traits of human character and behavior as demonstrated by experience. In order to cope with the fickleness, avarice, and short-sighted egoism of the multitude, the ruler, in Machiavelli's view, must be not only intelligent and forceful but also a master of the arts of deceit. Understanding what men are really like, the prince "must know well how to use both the beast and the man." He "must imitate the fox and the lion"

---

[1] Machiavelli, *The Prince and the Discourses,* trans. Luigi Ricci (New York: Modern Library, 1940), Chap. 17. Other quotations from this edition are identified by chapter references in parentheses immediately following the quotation.

(Chap. 18). While carefully presenting the appearance of all virtues, he must "learn how not to be good" (Chap. 15), because a prince is "often obliged, in order to maintain the state, to act against faith, against charity, against humanity, and against religion" (Chap. 18). Machiavelli concludes that if a choice is necessary between being loved and being feared, it is better for the prince to be feared by his subjects, because though the chain of love is easily broken, "fear is maintained by a dread of punishment which never fails." He does add the significant point that the ruler should avoid being *hated*, but he believes this can easily be managed without any particular tenderheartedness on the ruler's part. Most of the people, he says, will be relatively contented under an efficient despot as long as neither their own persons, their women, nor their property are molested: "for men forget more easily the death of their father than the loss of their patrimony" (Chap. 17).

Machiavelli's depressing vision of the nature of government and the governed was not something spun out of his own warped psyche. Close before him—perhaps too close—he had the evidence of contemporary Italian statecraft. To illustrate his concept of the ideal prince, he chose Cesare Borgia, Duke of Valentinois, a notorious adventurer who, with the backing of his father, Pope Alexander vi, had hammered out a sizable principality in central and northern Italy by methods that shocked even an age inured to cruelty and treachery. Machiavelli was no sadist and did not idolize brutality. His official reports on Borgia, prepared while serving as Florentine ambassador, are not entirely flattering and warn of the possible danger to Florence in the duke's aggressive designs. But by 1513, when Machiavelli was writing his stinging essay, whatever threat Borgia posed had been removed by his death, and his extraordinary career provided an object lesson in the need for a coherent political program in Italy and of the difficulties in implementing such a program. What Machiavelli praises is Cesare's effort to establish an effectively centralized state in one of the worst governed sections of Italy, an effort that almost succeeded despite seemingly impossible odds and the perfidy of Cesare's own agents.

It is easy to sympathize with Machiavelli's impatience with the capriciousness of Italian city-state politics, but his denunciations cut very deep, and it might be argued that his implied remedy is worse than the disease. What cannot be questioned is the author's concern; the tone of studied detachment and cool irony does not conceal Machiavelli's anguish. But his is not the anguish of despair. It is joined to the belief that a turning point has come in the political firmament, presenting an opportunity that should not be allowed to slip by.

THE EUROPEAN POLITICAL SCENE

In order to understand the purport and relevance of Machiavelli's doctrines, it is necessary to survey the political trends of the age, not only in Italy but in Europe as a whole. Though the political scene was less confused than it had been during the period of the barbarian invasions of the fourth and fifth centuries or following the breakup of Charlemagne's empire in the ninth and tenth, European politics were still decidedly turbulent. But turbulence is not always a calamity. Its underlying cause in this period was the decay of feudalism as a political force and the necessity for devising new instrumentalities of government to take its place.

At its height, feudalism—in spite of crude beginnings and inherent absurdities—had provided a fair degree of stability for western European society. A hierarchy of allegiances, strung together by the personal responsibility of each man to his immediate superior, created an unbroken chain from the lowest to the highest rank. Many of the larger feudal principalities developed into relatively peaceful states, equipped with reliable judicial machinery and a reasonably clear-cut legal code. But the feudal system could be effective only so long as social and economic conditions remained static. And, as so often happens in the history of institutions, at the very time when the feudal machinery of government was becoming perfected, its bases were being undermined by changes in the economy and, ultimately, in the structure of society. In the eleventh and twelfth centuries the revival of trade, the growth of towns, the rise of a middle class of manufacturers, traders, and bankers all tended to promote a greater social mobility and threatened the supremacy of feudal magnates. The towns and their inhabitants could not fit comfortably into the feudal scheme of things, and as commerce expanded, even the larger and better governed feudal territories were inadequate to provide the protection and facilities that merchants required. The nobles, in spite of their lingering influence and privileges, became less essential politically at the same time that their economic preeminence was challenged by the bourgeoisie and by the gradual shift from a landed to a capitalist economy.

Although the decline of feudalism produced disturbances, it was not a trend in the direction of anarchy. On the whole, political bonds were becoming tighter rather than looser. The problems resulting from the increasing complexity and mobility of society created a demand for more effective central government, while the accumulation of wealth, by making a system of taxation possible, promised to supply the government with its necessary resources.

From the eleventh century onward, the growth of population, an increase in wealth, and the simultaneous development of a diversified economy and of means of communication and exchange between formerly isolated regions made it certain that governmental operations would expand far beyond their previous role. Because the trend was toward bigger and more authoritative political units, the stakes of rulership became more tempting. Therefore, as old feudal allegiances dissolved, a struggle for power ensued among towns, great territorial lords, ecclesiastical administrators, and kings. Formerly representatives of dynasties held in check by the feudal contract binding them to their vassals, the kings now conceived themselves as progenitors of a new political order.

Although prospects seemed bright in areas where feudalism was decaying most rapidly, there was still no clear indication as to what new political pattern would replace the old feudal one. The nation-state—grounded in a common language, common interests, or a consciousness of a common destiny—which it is so easy for us to think of as the inevitable next step, was at the time only dimly sensed, if at all. In some parts of Europe, partially or completely self-governing cities flourished without any feeling of loyalty to a larger national entity and sometimes in opposition to the titular territorial ruler. During the Renaissance era Germany had its "free cities," owing fealty directly to the emperor, who was seldom able to interfere decisively, and some of these were long able to resist absorption into neighboring kingdoms or duchies. Italy of course offers the most striking examples of independent cities with many of the attributes of sovereign states.

In a few countries, notably England and France, a process of unification under the leadership of hereditary monarchs was well under way by the thirteenth century; but the interest of the kings lay in nothing so vague, so sentimental, so mercurial as nationalism. Nationalism in the modern sense had not yet been invented; and in any case the kings were not the instruments of popular sentiment. They created the territorial state—where they were able to—as a domain for the exercise of their own will. The logical culmination of their program was the maxim attributed to Louis XIV in the seventeenth century: "I am the State." The kings could not have succeeded in their efforts at territorial expansion and consolidation without the support of important elements within the population, but they frequently used ruthless means to secure their objectives, and they did not submit their decisions to popular referendum. Only very gradually, after centralization had been achieved and the power of the state demonstrated—and not until this power had begun to be resented and resisted—did the great body of subjects experience any deep sense of personal identification with the state. During the Renaissance, while the framework of the modern nation-state was taking form, nationalism was no more than embryonic.

Among the larger European countries Germany was making least progress toward the modern type of territorial state, while Spain's progress was perhaps too precipitate. A spectacular increase in the strength and prestige of the monarchy moved Spain into the front rank of the great powers, but without really liquidating feudalism and through measures that spelled ruin for the middle classes and thus left the country deprived of the foundations on which her rivals built so successfully in the seventeenth and eighteenth centuries. Though confusing on the surface, the situation in Germany shows most strikingly the difficulties of transition from an antiquated political structure to a new one of radically different character.

Theoretically Germany was well equipped to achieve unity under a common administration. The legal and philosophical basis had already been provided, not by some adventurous dynastic upstart but by that venerable medieval institution known as the Holy Roman Empire, the roots of which were believed to reach back to Charlemagne and beyond him to classical antiquity. A "Roman Empire of the German Nation" was a bold and ambitious concept, suggesting a bridge between the ancient and modern worlds. But the impressive title was deceiving, the formula little more than a figure of speech. The imperial office by no means represented "Caesarism"—either in the legitimate old Roman sense or in the perverted sense imparted by despotic rulers in more recent times.

The German nobles successfully whittled away at the emperor's authority, assuming sovereign rights of their own and ultimately reducing Germany to a mere conglomeration of rival states of various shapes and sizes. The imperial office, bearing the most illustrious pedigree in Europe but actually only a kind of courtesy government, could not stand up against strong opposition, could not compete on equal terms with small states that were well organized. The emperor had to entreat, cajole, or bribe the princes because he could not coerce them, nor could he go over their heads to reach the common people. If the emperors had been shrewder, they might have allied themselves with the townsmen, using them as the French and English kings did to thwart the feudal nobles. But too frequently they neglected the towns, leaving them to organize their own regional leagues for protection against robber barons. Emperors bartered away valuable properties and revenues for dubious promises of allegiance from their haughty vassals. They left Germany without a unified body of laws or a system of courts to enforce the laws, without an army controlled by a single responsible authority, and without taxation to support a central government. When the Hapsburgs recovered the imperial title in the fifteenth century, they found it a financial liability. Simply to ensure the election of another member of the family whenever the throne became vacant entailed such an outlay of funds that it threw them on the mercy of the moneylenders. Emperor Maximilian I, continually frustrated in his twofold ambition to reform the German Reich and play a dominant role in European politics, argued with the Diet and the princes, stormed, fumed, and threatened to throw the crown at his feet "and stamp upon it"—but to no avail. Maximilian's grandson, Emperor Charles V (1519–56), appeared for a while to be the strongest ruler in Europe; however, his strength was derived not from the imperial crown, which had cost him a fortune, but from the series of lucky events that had given him possession of the Netherlands, Spain and her possessions in the New World, and the kingdoms of Sardinia, Sicily and Naples.

The impotence of the Holy Roman Empire was demonstrated during the very climax of Hapsburg power, under Charles V: it was helpless in the face of two great crises of the sixteenth century— the Turkish invasions and the Protestant Revolt. By heroic efforts Charles managed to defend his family's possessions in Austria and Hungary against Ottoman attacks, but even with papal support he failed completely to enlist the European sovereigns in a general crusade against the Turks. He was unable either to conciliate the Lutherans or to crush their revolt, and when he abdicated his throne to spend his last days in monastic retirement, he left a Germany irreconcilably divided.

In contrast to Germany, the trend in France and England was toward a strong national monarchy. The Hundred Years' War had been a miserable and exhausting affair, but it brought each of the two warring countries closer to unification on a nonfeudal basis. Although the war had been fought on French soil and temporarily reduced parts of the country to barren wilderness, the French king finally triumphed over the English invaders and capitalized on his success. Louis xi (1461–83) by force, craft, and intrigue won submission from most of the territory comprising modern France. This "spider king" has also been called a "bourgeois king" because he chose middle-class advisers, allied himself with the cities to check rebellions of the nobles, and also showed callous indifference to the sufferings of the poor peasants and artisans from whose labor his wealth ultimately derived. While relying heavily on spies and bribes to obtain his objectives, he laid such a solid foundation for absolutism in France that it was not seriously imperiled either by his own blunders or by those of the incompetent kings who succeeded him.

England too was moving rapidly away from the medieval political pattern. In the thirteenth century the great nobles had been able to coerce a formidable tyrant like King John into signing Magna Charta. In the late fifteenth century they were discrediting themselves—and eliminating some of their own number—by the melancholy "Wars of the Roses." The firm rule of the Yorkist Edward iv (1471–83) and the accession of the Tudor dynasty in 1485 brought welcome relief from the civil wars and a willingness to accept a king who could fill the role of "Big Policeman." Henry vii was crafty, miserly, but effective. Although he had never read The Prince, he had no need to, he was a true Machiavellian. His expansive son Henry viii, in spite of an apparent affability, displayed a remarkable capacity for getting what he wanted. He brooked no opposition at home and, in molding the English church to his liking, defied with impunity both the pope and the mighty Hapsburgs.

Of course, there is another side to "Tudor despotism." By catering to their material interests, the Tudor sovereigns won the loyalty of the middle classes, both mercantile elements and country gentry. And, while the French Estates General sank into disuse, the importance of the English parliament increased. Modern constitutional historians can surefootedly trace throughout the Tudor period the development of the parliamentary initiative that was to culminate in revolution and the execution of a king in the seventeenth century. But it would have been difficult for a contemporary observer to prophesy such an outcome. The obvious lesson from the example of England no less than of France seemed to be that the *sine qua non* of a durable state is a powerful monarch.

DEMOCRACY AND DESPOTISM IN ITALY

The political scene in Italy presents something of a paradox. During this era and far beyond, Italy failed signally to achieve statehood or even formal unity. At the end of the Renaissance the peninsula remained divided, partitioned, occupied by foreign powers—destined to remain "a geographical expression" until late in the nineteenth century. But it is evident that despite the retarded political condition of their country, Italians were the most politically mature of all Europeans. They were the first to establish embassies and employ regular ambassadors, the first to create efficient fiscal and administrative machinery. Just as they pioneered in developing modern methods of merchandising, bookkeeping, banking, and insurance, so they invented or discovered the techniques of the modern art of politics. Their problem was not ignorance or lack of astuteness. It almost seems that their excessive versatility was responsible for their failure to unite effectively.

During the Renaissance era Italy was anything but stagnant politically, and many of the changes taking place could, at least in a limited sense, be interpreted as progress. Feudalism, never deeply entrenched in Italy, was easily supplanted. The growth of cities began earlier and advanced more rapidly than in the rest of Europe. The leading northern Italian cities were exchange centers of a vast interregional commerce. Such powerful city-states as Genoa and Venice, enriched by the transport services they had developed during the Crusades, possessed far-reaching empires. Ironically, the kingdoms of Naples and Sicily, although approaching closest to the political pattern that was to predominate in Europe during the next several centuries, were the most backward regions

THE STATES OF ITALY ABOUT 1450

SWITZERLAND

CARINTHIA

TYROL

Rhone R.

Trent

Drave R.

Danube R.

MONTSERRAT

SAVOY

MILAN

V E N E T I A

CARNIOLA

Save R.

Verona

Milan

Padua

Venice

CROATIA

Pavia

Cremona

Adige R.

Mantua

Po R.

Parma

Modena

SALUZZO

Ferrara

FERRARA

MODENA

Genoa

Bologna

Ravenna

GENOA

Lucca

Pistoia

Prato

Pisa

Florence

Livorno

Arno R.

FLORENCE

Urbino

Arezzo

Ancona

PAPAL STATES

R E P U B L I C

Nice

Siena

Perugia

Assisi

SIENA

Adriatic Sea

Elba

Orvieto

Spoleto

CORSICA
(to Genoa)

Viterbo

Tiber R.

Ostia

Rome

N A P L E S

SARDINIA

Naples

Amalfi

Tyrrhenian Sea

Mediterranean Sea

Palermo

N

SICILY

Elba

0   50   100
Scale of Miles

Malta

culturally and economically; the brilliant promise of a highly cosmopolitan society resulting from a fusion of Greek, Arabic, and Norman elements had not been fulfilled. The Hohenstaufen Emperor Frederick II, acclaimed by his thirteenth-century contemporaries as a veritable "wonder of the world," had almost succeeded in anticipating history by establishing an efficient despotism on the foundations of the old Norman kingdom. But his ambition infuriated the popes, who finally managed to exterminate the "viper brood" of Hohenstaufen and in doing so opened the land to pillage and to a succession of French and Spanish overlords.

Rome and the Papal States constituted a special case but tended to follow the general pattern manifesting itself over most of Italy. During the period of residence in Avignon (the "Babylonian captivity" of 1309–77) the popes had been unable to keep a firm grip on their estates in Italy. When they returned to Rome they worked assiduously to consolidate and tighten the administration of their territories. The popes of the fifteenth century were much less interested in the universal papal monarchy of medieval inspiration than they were in establishing a solid temporal monarchy in the sections of Italy nominally under their control. They imposed taxes to supplement reduced "spiritual" revenues, struggled to subjugate local despots and self-governing communes, and hired mercenary armies to defend and extend the patrimony of St. Peter.

During this period Italy presented the greatest variety of political types in Europe, perhaps in the world. It was a political laboratory where experiments were conducted continually—not, however, in an atmosphere of academic detachment but under social pressure and the spur of personal ambition. This epoch of Italian history offers a striking parallel with ancient Greece. The norm, in northern Italy, was the independent city-state, both large and small, with diverse constitutions and traditions. As in the case of classical Greece, a general pattern of evolution can be detected. In both instances democracy emerged as one of the possible forms of government. But whereas in ancient Greece, with Athens the supreme example, the sequence ran from monarchy through aristocracy to democracy, in Renaissance Italy it typically descended from a partial democracy to oligarchy and from thence finally to tyranny.

Italian communes in their early, more democratic phase owed nothing at all to the example of ancient Greece. On the contrary, they were a late medieval phenomenon. Townsmen had banded together to protect their persons and possessions against depredations by ecclesiastical or feudal lords and to nourish the commercial enterprise on which their strength rested. Towns emerged as corporate entities before the end of the eleventh century and won autonomy by taking advantage of the recurring struggle between pope and emperor, joining with one to fight the other, switching allegiance without compunction. Following the collapse of the Hohenstaufen dynasty in the mid-thirteenth century, a number of northern Italian towns achieved complete independence. As long as town populations remained small, they preserved a fair degree of equality within and among the several corporate guilds. A drift toward oligarchy set in with the growth of specialization and the expansion of commerce from a local to a regional basis. The rise of an export trade gave a commanding position to guilds supplying foreign markets. The richer merchants gradually constituted a new kind of aristocracy, dominating the town government and closing their ranks against additional members from among smaller businessmen. With a widening gap between haves and have-nots and the aggravation of class animosity, the step from oligarchy to dictatorship became fairly easy. The successful despot was one who could hold class strife within bounds, conciliating the lower orders by occasional favors while insuring continued prosperity for the wealthy minority and maintaining sufficient military forces to defend the state. As early as the fourteenth century, the sovereignty of Italian communes was passing from the people to the rule of one man or one family, and in succeeding centuries genuine republics became even rarer.

Constant rivalry between cities and tensions within them created unprecedented opportunities for adventurers to make their political fortunes. The phenomenon of the rise and fall of despotisms, built on the craft, daring, and naked force of strong personalities, inspired Burckhardt's definition of the plastic Renaissance state as "a work of art." A key figure in this process, particularly in its later stages, was the *condottiere,* the professional commander of mercenary troops, upon whose services practically all of the Italian states came to rely. Calculating his profits and losses with the prudence of a tradesman, the *condottiere* was both the hope and the despair of his employers. He sold his services to the highest bidder, changed sides without warning if it seemed to his advantage, and sometimes overthrew the government he had been hired to defend.

Among the numerous instances in which the career of *condottiere* served as stepping-stone to political power, the most famous example is that of the Sforza family, who founded a dynasty in Milan. But in fact, the rise of the Visconti family, who preceded the Sforza, had already illustrated the typical stages in the transformation of the government of a rich and populous city into one-man rule. As early as 1287 a politically ambitious archbishop secured the election of his grandnephew, Matteo Visconti, to the office of "Captain of the People." Although this office had been originally conceived as a popular bulwark to protect the common citizens against the nobles, it served as an entering wedge for the Visconti dictatorship, which reached a climax in the late fourteenth and early fifteenth centuries. Giangaleazzo (1385–1402), ablest of the Visconti rulers, though naturally timid was ruthless enough to seize and poison his uncle and, in enlarging the territory of Milan, carried out such extensive conquests that he threatened to dominate all of northern Italy. But Giangaleazzo was struck down by the plague, and his two sons could not hold his state together or control the various military commanders he had kept employed. In the confusion the citizens of Milan attempted to revive their ancient republic, but, faced with an attack from Venice, they engaged the ablest of the *condottieri*, Francesco Sforza, as commander in chief. After checking the Venetian threat, Francesco promptly turned back and subdued Milan. Already married to the illegitimate daughter of the late Duke Filippo Maria Visconti, Francesco set himself up as Duke of Milan in 1450 and passed on the title and territorial claims to his descendants.

THE ARISTOCRATIC REPUBLIC OF VENICE AND THE PSEUDO-DEMOCRACY OF FLORENCE

The two most powerful and influential city-states that maintained their republican form throughout the Renaissance were Florence and Venice. Although often regarded as representing contrary social and political types, they actually showed certain parallels in their development. Facing similar problems, they attempted somewhat different solutions. Venice was outwardly, and for a longer period, more successful; Florence, in its failure, compiled an illuminating record of experimentation and produced a considerable body of speculative thought.

Though founded upon the sands, Venice became not only the richest and most imposing of the Italian city-states but apparently the most stable. The "Queen of the Adriatic" was a blend of Byzantine and Roman, of medieval aristocracy and commoners solidly united into a kind of joint-stock company for the pursuit of profit. Her political constitution evolved gradually, not painlessly but with remarkably little violence and always in the direction of efficient centralization. Formally a republic, the government was controlled by great merchant families. The doge, nominal head of the state, had been originally the appointed representative of the Byzantine emperor in Constantinople, later an elected president chosen by and responsible to assemblies of free citizens, and finally the agent of a closed mercantile aristocracy. By the opening of the fourteenth century the supremacy of the Great Council of nobles was firmly established. It absorbed the functions of the ancient popular assembly, determined the selection of the doge, and in 1311 created a subsidiary Council of Ten as a kind of committee of public safety to ferret out any latent opposition to the dominant oligarchy.

The history of Venice provides a rare example of an ancient nobility adapting itself to the conditions of a commercial society and to the hazardous task of building and defending a maritime empire. Venetian nobles relinquished feudal pretensions, cast their lot with citizens of the islands, and tamely submitted to the jurisdiction of civic authorities. Operating within the legal framework of the republic, they were able to convert it into an instrument of their own ambitions. In order to achieve this objective the nobles had to sacrifice the traditional aristocratic privilege of fighting among themselves, develop a corporate sense, and agree to concentration of power in small committees capable of disciplining their own obstreperous members as well as restraining the proletariat. But the material rewards were enormous, especially during Venice's golden age in the fourteenth and fifteenth centuries. The city's commercial ascendancy, her luxurious establishments, the acuity and finesse of her ambassadors became proverbial. And the apparent unshakability of the Venetian constitution awakened the envy of contemporary statesmen.

Although the Venetian system was authoritarian, it embodied both a deep-rooted respect for law and an unusual concern for the public welfare, even for the welfare of those excluded from political life. And the Venetian nobility acquired a character very different from that of the European feudal aristocracy. In the course of their rise to dominance in the state, they excluded some families of ancient lineage, admitted commoners to their ranks, and continued the practice of intermarriage with lower-class families. The "closing" of the Great Council in 1297 was not the seizure of power by a small clique but actually an enlargement of the ruling group. Although henceforth only those classified as nobles could participate in government, members of the Great Council enjoyed both legal and social equality, regardless of differences in wealth. Usually referred to as an aristocratic republic, Renaissance Venice is more accurately described as a republic of aristocrats. At least during the fourteenth and fifteenth centuries, the ruling body was probably no smaller a proportion of the population than in Florence, notwithstanding the democratic professions of the latter.

The republic of Florence provides another prime example of a city-state in the grip of a wealthy minority, but with economic strength founded principally upon manufacture and banking rather than upon the carrying trade. A more striking contrast with Venice, however, is seen in the process through which the oligarchy established itself. Venice witnessed the triumph of a business-minded aristocracy; in Florence a successful bourgeois revolution displaced or absorbed the nobility. The process was complex, and Florentine society long remained fluid, without a clearly separated nobility, middle class, or proletariat. Intense rivalries were always present among families and interest groups, and in competing with one another they seized upon class labels as weapons.

Theoretically the Florentine republic and its constitution represented the triumph of *the people*—actually, members of the several guilds—over the feudal aristocracy. This had been achieved before the close of the thirteenth century with the establishment of the communal governing body (*signoria*). At the outset the commune was not a unitary state but an association of quasi-sovereign bodies, including the guilds, the Church, and the Guelph party—traditional defender of Florence's independence against the Holy Roman Emperor but now evolving into the political arm of an aristocratic faction. The looseness and complexity of Florence's constitution left the door open for a continuous internal power struggle. The Ordinances of Justice of 1293 specifically excluded a large number of noble families from office. However, many families that had risen to prominence in the span of a few generations through successful ventures in manufacture, commerce, or banking commanded more resources than feudal proprietors had ever enjoyed and posed at least as great a threat to the interest of the humbler folk. Rivalry persisted, therefore, between "the people" and their potential enemies, variously referred to as "the great," "the rich," "the wise," "the big houses," or "magnates." The dividing line between *popolani* and *grandi* or *magnati* was thin and elastic. During the heyday of Renaissance Florence most of her prominent figures, including the Medici, were of popular (*popolani*) origins, even though wealth and position made some of them in effect an aristocracy. On the other hand, "the people" was always a restricted category, generally applying to members of the twenty-one guilds, without taking into account the larger number of unorganized employees, small craftsmen, day laborers, and paupers. No serious thought was given to enfranchising the lowest classes. Political struggle, even when it veered in a democratic direction, was between men of great wealth and those of moderate wealth, each group claiming to represent the interest of the people, of the republic, and of liberty.

The turbulent contests that characterize the history of the Florentine republic produced democratic overtones chiefly in their formal attacks upon the aristocratic tradition. The term *magnate* became not merely a social stigma but a legal bar to public office, and *super-magnate* a synonym for traitor. A strange but well documented phenomenon of the fourteenth century is that of Florentine nobles petitioning to be granted *popolani* status; some who were successful in the attempt to become commoners changed their family names. Conversely, the government intimidated recalcitrant citizens by threatening to have them declared magnates. A powerful minority within the *popolani*—including rich merchants and international bankers—exploited the equalitarian instincts of the common people to oust their own enemies of whatever social stratum as they strove for ascendancy in the state. This aggressive group did not exterminate the nobility. They tamed it, assimilated it, aped it, and, more importantly, gradually created a new aristocracy based on wealth and a record of public officeholding.

The experience of Florence, which was typical of many other northern Italian cities, indicates that the Renaissance was a period of social mobility, with opportunities for a radical transformation of society, but that it also manifested a tendency to seek stability through rigidity, resulting finally in a stifling of social energies and a slackening of morale. The class struggle that continually jolted the Florentine republic cannot be fitted into either the classical model of plebes against patricians or the Marxist formula of proletariat against bourgeoisie. Proletarians there certainly were, and their lot was sorry enough to justify revolt, but they remained unorganized, unrecognized, and largely unchronicled. In Florence the most intense and persistent conflict was within the middle and upper ranks of society, primarily between established *popolani* families—fused with remnants of the old nobility—and new men of rising fortunes who were determined to win a place at the top. Although the older families were forced to give ground and share their prerogatives, the benefits did not trickle down very far.

The outlook for democratic progress in Florence was brightest during the middle years of the fourteenth century, a period of crisis and catastrophe, marked by bank failures, ravaging epidemics that included the Black Death of 1348, and external conflicts culminating in an exhaustive war with the papacy in 1375-78. Displaying extraordinary vigor and resilience in the face of these disasters, the Florentines undertook to strengthen the republic by broadening its base. In 1343, after expelling a *condottiere* who had attempted to convert the commune into a principality, they reformed the constitution to increase representation of the guilds in the government—for the first time admitting artisans and small shopkeepers from the fourteen lower guilds—and doubling the number of citizens eligible for membership in the *signoria*. That the social structure was still flexible is evidenced by the large number of "new people" admitted to Florentine citizenship during the early years of the century. All elements essential for the evolution of democracy apparently were present; but elements hostile to democracy were also present and proved to be stronger. The "new people" absorbed into the citizen body from the surrounding country districts were for the most part the wealthiest of the rural population. While retaining their country estates, they purchased property within the city, won membership in the guilds, and established a political base from which to advance their own business and financial interests. At the same time, by immigrating to the city they deprived the rural districts of effective leadership and left the poor and servile inhabitants subject to increasingly severe discriminatory legislation imposed by a mercantile oligarchy.

Indicative of the growing influence of an oligarchic faction is the republic's fiscal policy, which consistently favored the rich. New sources of revenue became necessary to meet rising expenses, especially military expenses, which because of the hiring of mercenaries increased by 1000 percent during the fourteenth century. But while the budget swelled to mammoth proportions, a minority of affluent citizens frustrated every attempt to impose direct taxes until the second decade of the fifteenth century. Even when an income tax was adopted (in 1427) it was not equitably applied. The very rich were as successful as today's millionaires in evading their fair share of the burden. Indirect taxes, bearing most heavily on the poor, were repeatedly revised upward. But the favorite money-raising device was the forced loan. As long as they were honored by the state as public obligations, loans constituted a profitable investment and enhanced the wealth of the class that was forced to provide them. As early as the mid-fourteenth century, a majority of Florentines active in civic affairs were large shareholders in the *Monte,* as the funded public debt was called, and the proportion of shareholders increased during the next hundred years. An official document of 1470 described the *Monte* as "the guard and most secure fortress and most certain establishment of the salvation of all the body and government of our state." In plainer language, the system was an association of men of substance for mutual profit, plunder, and exploitation of the weak and of subject territories.

The last significant attempt to impel the Florentine republic in a democratic direction occurred in 1378 with the so-called *Ciompi* revolt, named after the unorganized workers in the woolen industry. The movement had much wider support than the title suggests, and the uprising was serious enough to bring about another reform of the constitution, though only a very temporary one. Within four years the great families recovered control of the government, canceled the reforms, and forced the woolen workers back to their previous helpless condition. The revolutionaries' demands had been moderate, even conservative. They sought political recognition, the right to form their own guild with representation in the government —a program entirely consistent with the spirit of the original thirteenth-century commune. The revolution could have succeeded if it had not been for the defection of its early supporters—members of the established guilds. These corporate bodies, even the seven "greater" guilds, contained many men of humble station—armorers, grocers, doublet-makers, druggists, blacksmiths, furriers, hosiers— "little people" whose antagonism toward the "fat people" was of long standing. In a crisis, however, the *popolo minuto* feared the masses below them more than they feared the plutocrats above them, into whose ranks they might hope to penetrate. Themselves employers of labor, they were unwilling to combine with the unprivileged classes in a struggle for thoroughgoing reform because they profited from the workers' legal disabilities and lack of organization. By tolerating and actively assisting in the suppression of the *Ciompi*, the middle classes spurned an opportunity both to democratize the state and to heal a widening rift in society. Eventually they paid a high price for their shortsightedness.

The republic of Florence preserved the outward appearance and legal framework of popular government throughout its long and crowded history. The constitution was bewilderingly complex, an aggregation of wheels within wheels, of new organs added to old without any systematic reconstruction. It retained such democratic features as short terms in office and the selection of a majority of officials by lot. But by limiting and manipulating the lists of citizens eligible for office, it was possible for a small inner circle to retain control. The triumph of a mercantile and financial oligarchy, achieved by the late 1300s, not only shaped policies of the moment but also wrought permanent changes in the character of the city-state. A concentration of power gradually transformed Florence from a sprawling medieval commune into a coherent territorial state, surprisingly modern in structure and functions. Multiple associations with competing loyalties dissolved under the pressure of an active central administration. The *signoria* broke the power of the nobles, the Guelph party, the guilds, and even the Tuscan Church—successfully challenging the traditional right of sanctuary, the jurisdiction of ecclesiastical courts, and the tax-exempt status of the clergy. Fulfilling a positive role externally as well as internally, Florence in the late fourteenth century embarked on a course of territorial aggrandizement, and within the space of two generations subjugated almost the whole of Tuscany. But the process of expansion and centralization, while tightening the reins of government and foreshadowing the modern state system, also dissipated the medieval democratic tradition.

The most brilliant period of the Florentine republic began in the mid-fifteenth century when the city passed under the rule of the Medici. Only one of many families to reap large fortunes through banking and trade, the Medici exhibited political acumen far above the average. They insinuated themselves into the government of the city without disturbing traditional forms or repealing constitutional guarantees. They retained the status of private citizens, disguising their role of autocrat and refraining from excess in their style of living while holding firm control of Florence for three generations. Their accession to power was facilitated by the fact that the state authority and revenue were already lodged in a mercantile oligarchy possessing a recognized community of interest. Cosimo de' Medici, who initiated the epoch of Medici rule in 1434, did so as the leader of opposition to a rival banking family (the Albizzi), whose preponderance in the *signoria* had been accompanied by an insufferable display of arrogance and an unsuccessful military venture. After ousting the Albizzi, Cosimo effectively controlled the government for thirty years, until his death in 1464. He made only slight changes in the electoral mechanism (though sufficient to insure a perpetually pro-Medicean regime), avoided any appearance of personal ostentation, and devoted his talents to protecting the financial interests of the leading citizens.

While Cosimo has been likened to the boss of a modern political machine, he actually served as a kind of unofficial chairman of the board for the Florentine oligarchy. He held the state's highest office (*gonfalonier*) for a total period of only six months, but it is significant that he regularly allowed himself to be elected to membership on the *Monte* board, which administered the funded public debt. His constituents had little cause for complaint. Cosimo's realistic approach to foreign policy, as well as his sound grasp of finance, contributed to stability and prosperity. Reversing Florence's longstanding tradition of hostility to Milan, he helped the usurper Francesco Sforza to power in that city and formed an alliance with Milan and the kingdom of Naples to check the aggressions of Venice and the papacy, thus establishing a temporary equilibrium in the peninsula. He also patronized artists and scholars and contributed resources of his own to embellish the city—at the same time falsifying his income tax returns. Cosimo's epitaph proclaimed him not founder of the Medici dynasty—which might have been appropriate—but "Father of his country."

The apogee of Medici influence, and also of Florence's cultural preeminence, was reached under Cosimo's grandson, Lorenzo (1449–92). Lorenzo *Il Magnifico* seemed to embody in his own personality and career all the main currents of the Renaissance.

Highly intelligent, resourceful, and large-spirited, he was an astute critic and patron of the arts and at the same time a skillful political leader. Without the backlog of economic success on which his family had risen to greatness, Lorenzo would probably have remained undistinguished, but in him bourgeois rapacity had been refined to an urbane gentility. Ironically, the financial empire that undergirded the influential position of the Medici was beginning to collapse in Lorenzo's lifetime, partly because of his own ineptitude and indifference to business matters, which he left entirely in the hands of agents. Although he took pride in contemplating the amount of money his ancestors had spent in the city, the shrinking of the family fortunes meant that Lorenzo could not equal his grandfather's largesse, even though he secretly appropriated state funds for his own use.

In spite of his disdain for the trappings of authority, Lorenzo *Il Magnifico* fulfilled most perfectly the role of an ideal Renaissance prince. Refusing to be called lord or sovereign, though he was so regarded by other Italian *signori* and by many of his fellow Florentines, he continued the policy of indirect rule under the trappings of democracy, rewarding the citizens for their docility with artistic triumphs and lavish festivals; and he upheld in the face of continual intrigue Florence's strategic role in Italian interstate politics. His regime was so firmly grounded that it withstood the shock of an assassination attempt against his own person—the Pazzi Conspiracy of 1478—and he could let the pope, who had instigated the conspiracy, rage impotently at the execution of the frustrated ecclesiastical assassins.

Judged by any reasonable standard, Lorenzo de' Medici must be counted a capable ruler. Nevertheless, there was always something precarious and specious in his position and in the political climate of Florence even during its most brilliant epoch. The Medici dared neither to put the democratic constitution into full operation nor to replace it openly with a hereditary autocracy on the model of other despotisms in northern Italy, although after the Pazzi Conspiracy Lorenzo created a new Council of Seventy to control all branches of government. The peculiar kind of personally directed democracy that the Medici tried to maintain called for an almost superhuman political agility and also for a degree of dissembling and hypocrisy that ultimately corroded the integrity of the citizens. The recurrent crises that marked the forty years following the death of Lorenzo the Magnificent—and ended only with the final extinction of the old republican constitution in 1532—reveal the shallowness of Florence's republican foundations. And it is this period that coincides with Machiavelli's career both as participant and as political theorist.

Lorenzo's eldest son and successor, Piero, blundered into war with the invading French king Charles VIII and then made an abject surrender so infuriating to the Florentines that Piero and his brothers fled from the city. Nominally the uprising of 1494, which drove the Medici into temporary exile, aimed to restore civic liberties. Actually, it was instigated by members of the wealthy upper class, who hoped to recover the position they had enjoyed before the personal rule of the Medici, and it reopened the struggle between aristocrats and the middle class for control of the state. Neither faction was interested in fundamental reform or had a concrete plan for replacing the discredited Medici system. A constitution adopted in 1494 was essentially a reversion to the pre-Medicean pattern but with the addition of a Great Council of three thousand citizens, after the analogy of Venice, which it was hoped would provide greater stability. Stability, however, was a quality Florence never exhibited for very long, if only because of the rankling animosities within her population.

The man who healed the breach temporarily was no seasoned politician but the fanatical friar Girolamo Savonarola, who had joined the Dominican convent of San Marco in Florence in 1490 at the invitation of Lorenzo the Magnificent and who, with no resources other than his moral ardor and fiery eloquence, dominated the counsels of the Florentines during the crisis that followed the expulsion of the Medici. Although he had risen to fame as the prophet of impending doom, at the height of his career his message changed to one of hope and appealed to civic pride. He hailed Florence, repentant and regenerated, as a New Jerusalem, destined to be the center of a reformed Christendom, and also promised that as God's chosen city she would be rewarded with riches, power, and glory in this world and the next.

Spellbound by the wizardry of Savonarola's fevered preaching, crowds of Florentines cast jewelry, paintings, and other such vanities into the bonfire; and they thrilled as the monk, in his inspired rebellion against the world's wickedness, defied even the pope. But for all his deep sincerity and sense of mission, Brother Girolamo had no solution for the practical problems confronting the Florentine state. His religion was evangelism, his political principles derived rather hazily from the medieval ideal of a Christian commonwealth, with a distribution rather than concentration of power. He denounced the Medici dictatorship, which he regarded as corrupt and wicked. During the three and one-half years of his ascendancy he swayed the minds and wills of devoted followers from all ranks of society through his force of personality, his reputation as a prophet, and his capacity to invest the patriotic tradition of a great civic destiny—the "Florentine Myth" [2]—with the fervor of a moral crusade.

Inevitably the spell passed. The crowd grew weary of austerity and evangelism, and though Savonarola was far from being a democrat, the upper classes suspected his egalitarian bias. The "unarmed prophet" (Machiavelli's shrewd epithet), condemned by the pope as a heretic and deserted by many of his own supporters, was doomed. And the Florentines, who had applauded his earlier triumphs, seemed to derive almost as much satisfaction from watching him burn at the stake.

After Savonarola's execution in 1498 the republic maintained an uneasy existence for fourteen years. Machiavelli, who served as a secretary in the chancellery and undertook several important diplomatic missions, watched the republic suffer the strain of internal tensions and finally founder on the rocks of a disastrous foreign policy—clinging to a French alliance when Louis xii was pitted against the combined might of pope and emperor. With Spanish troops at her gates, Florence was forced to expel her officials, including Machiavelli, and readmit the Medici in 1512. Still deferring to the forms of republicanism, they reestablished their system of personal control; and during the reigns of two Medici popes—Leo x (second son of Lorenzo Il Magnifico) and Clement vii (illegitimate son of Il Magnifico's brother Giuliano)—the real decisions were made in Rome.

Amid the kaleidoscopic changes in the Italian situation the Florentine republic was "restored" for one more brief interlude (1527–30), when an invasion of Italy by troops of the Hapsburg emperor brought the fortunes of Clement vii to their nadir and

---

2 Donald Weinstein, *Savonarola and Florence* (Princeton: Princeton University Press, 1970), p. 77.

forced him to relax his grip on the Tuscan city. But as soon as the pope and Emperor Charles v came to terms, the fate of Florence was sealed. In view of the ambiguities in Florence's republican pedigree, perhaps it was poetic justice that she should now receive as her governor a pope's bastard son, betrothed to an emperor's bastard daughter. At any rate, Alessandro de' Medici made amends for his dubious credentials by stripping away the threadbare mask of republicanism. In 1532 he assumed the title Duke of Florence. Duke Alessandro—who seems to have been a sort of monster both in appearance and in character—succumbed to an assassin five years later; but this time no one lifted a finger to revive the dead republic. A younger branch of the Medici family promptly ascended the ducal throne and established a firm monarchical despotism. The republic of Florence disappeared in the grand duchy of Tuscany.

THE FATE OF ITALY

In their internal development the Renaissance city-states of northern Italy exhibited many modern characteristics, and in their dealings with one another they exhibited traits and practices that have become all too familiar in the foreign policy of sovereign states: expansionist ambitions, mutual suspicion, provoked and unprovoked assaults, betrayal of allies, and the sacrifice of long-range objectives to immediate advantage. While the old bonds of allegiance to a universal empire or Christian commonwealth dissolved, there emerged no new sense of community capable of inspiring a common loyalty. The ideal of a united Italy was seldom expressed, let alone consciously or widely shared. Patriotism was particular and local. Even Machiavelli, who came closer than most to visualizing an Italian state, remained above all else a partisan of Tuscany. Continual rivalry and aggression among Italian despotisms—unstable despotisms never free from the threat of disruption within themselves—led inevitably to intervention by outside powers.

When the great European kingdoms found respite from their own internal troubles, they willingly ventured into the arena of Italian politics. The northern and southern extremities of Italy appeared most vulnerable: Valois kings of France could produce historical claims both to Naples, from which the Spanish house of Aragon had ousted the French Angevins as recently as 1435, and to Milan (the dukes of Orléans were descended from a Visconti heiress). Undoubtedly European monarchs would have invaded Italy even without any legal pretext, but Italian rulers abetted the evil by inviting the foreigners in.

In 1494 Duke Lodovico Sforza of Milan, menaced by a combined attack from Naples and the papacy, encouraged Charles VIII of France to press his claim to the kingdom of Naples. A French force traversed the length of the peninsula, setting off a shock wave that toppled the Medici regime in Florence, lifted Savonarola to the pinnacle of his career, and drew another foreign ruler, the emperor Maximilian, into an anti-French coalition. Charles VIII was forced to withdraw without the slightest advantage for France, but his excursion provided a vivid demonstration of the vulnerability of Italian states. Charles' successor, Louis XII of France (1498–1515), bought the support of Pope Alexander VI for his depredations by conferring the duchy of Valentinois upon the pope's son, Cesare Borgia, and lent him troops for Cesare's campaign in the Romagna. Louis' troops seized the duchy of Milan, and the unfortunate Lodovico ended his days in a French dungeon. Pope Julius II (1503–13), who hated the Borgias and all their works and is usually credited as one of the most statesmanlike of Renaissance popes, was nevertheless so eager to despoil Venice of her mainland territories that he did not scruple to form an alliance embracing both the emperor and Louis XII. But when this aggressive combination proved too successful, Pope Julius made a separate peace with Venice, called for "liberation of Italy from the barbarians," and organized a "Holy League" (1511) to expel the French and, incidentally, to humble the Florentines.

One episode in the tedious struggle between France and the empire for control of the peninsula evoked a slight tremor of national feeling among Italians. In 1526 when Pope Clement VII was involved in another defensive league, this time with the French king Francis I against the emperor Charles V, he appointed to command his troops a popular and courageous *condottiere*, Giovanni "of the Black Band," descendant of a younger branch of the Medici family. Giovanni threw himself unreservedly into a cause that promised to transcend the selfish ambition of local princes. But his heroic sacrifice proved to be futile. The Medici pope did not trust the Medici general and withheld men and supplies, at the same time rejecting the advice of that peerless courtier Baldassare Castiglione, who was imploring him not to make war on the emperor. The betrayal and defeat of the brave Giovanni added the last dregs of bitterness to the cup of Machiavelli, who had hailed "Giovanni d'Italia" as the long awaited Liberator yearned for in *The Prince*. In 1527 German and Spanish troops that had invaded the peninsula perpetrated the hideous sack of Rome, a blow from which the Renaissance papacy never quite recovered and final proof of the paralysis of Italian political communities.

Historians have long pondered not simply the causes of the eventual partitioning of Italy but the broader problem of the decline of liberty in the Italian communes. Some contend that this decline—accompanied by an apparent decay in civic virtue and moral fiber—was an inevitable result of the division of Italy into so many sovereign units, continually feuding with one another and making impossible any effective defense against interference by the autocratic monarchs beyond the Alps. It is true that when the country became a battleground for foreign troops the results were highly demoralizing; but the theory is inadequate to explain the failure to develop and preserve political freedom. Most Italian states had become despotisms, open or disguised, before the French and Spanish invasions began. In the case of Florence it could be argued, on still narrower grounds, that her leaders made the fatal mistake of supporting France most of the time rather than the ultimately victorious Spain. By consistently betting on the wrong contestant they exhausted their patrimony and forfeited their city's independence. But no one could seriously maintain that the cause of freedom in Florence or anywhere else would have been strengthened by alliance with the houses of Aragon and Hapsburg.

The typical Italian despotisms were home grown, as indeed were those of northern Europe and the Iberian peninsula. They were apparently in harmony with the spirit of the times—but to say this is to dodge historical explanation. Every age has many manifestations of its "spirit," or many different spirits, and only a doctrinaire determinist could content himself with the assertion that things had to turn out the way they did.

It is noteworthy that the age of despotism in Renaissance Italy exhibits a great interest in liberty and a deep yearning for it. Liberty is a theme so prominent in the literature of the time that it must have figured palpably in contemporary thought. The Florentines were its fiercest partisans. They cherished the concept, personified it, and once during a war with the papacy staged a

tournament in honor of "Lady Liberty." Perhaps they came closer
to achieving liberty than most of their fellow Italians, closer indeed
than the great European monarchies of this period. Nevertheless, it
was in Florence that the ideal became most cynically abused,
bandied about as a party slogan, and corroded by the interests of a
self-serving class. In the external sphere it came to mean excluding
every possible rival from Tuscany, an end best assured by Florentine conquest of the region. What the citizens of Florence hailed
as *libertà* appeared as something very different to the inhabitants
of Pisa, Livorno, and other subjugated cities and indeed was indistinguishable from imperialism. In this early dawn of the modern
age, appeal to liberty was already becoming a hollow incantation
that obscured real issues even when there was no deliberate intention to deceive. The Church saw her "liberties" threatened by the
encroachment of state authority, while secular governments in expanding their jurisdiction claimed to be protecting the liberty of
their subjects. In the name of liberty the Medici were expelled from
Florence in 1494. They in turn justified the quelling of the republic
in 1512 by declaring that it was impossible "to preserve freedom
and to remove all obstacles to it without full, free, total and absolute authority and power." [3] Machiavelli's contemporary, the historian Guicciardini, recorded the warning, "Don't believe those who
so fervently preach liberty. Nearly all of them—probably every
single one of them—has his own particular interests in mind." [4] In
spite of Florence's pride in her free institutions and her distrust of
aristocratic Venice, Venice permitted at least an equal degree of
freedom of thought and expression and was preferred over Florence
as a haven for exiles.

While Florentines paid lip service to the principle of equality
before the law, the dominant oligarchy steadfastly refused equal
opportunity or minimal economic justice to the poorer elements of
the population, both rural and urban. The concept of individual

---

[3] Felix Gilbert, *Machiavelli and Guicciardini* (Princeton: Princeton University Press, 1965), pp. 132–133. This rationalization of autocratic rule may
be compared with *The True Law of Free Monarchies* of the seventeenth-
century Stuart king, James I of England, a famous exponent of the doctrine
of divine right.

[4] *Ibid.*, p. 278.

freedom was subtly transformed into submission to and adoration of a providentially guided state, lauded as the "new great city," "daughter of Rome," and renovator and savior of Italy. And among the privileged minority, liberty became synonymous with the health of the public treasury and the government's capacity to meet its interest obligations to wealthy bondholders. In Florence as elsewhere, liberty did not prove to be a happy consort for oligarchy: the natural offspring of such a misalliance was despotism.

REFERENCES AND SUGGESTIONS FOR FURTHER READING

GENERAL TREATMENT

Cambridge Modern History, Vols. I and II (1902, 1903). Though old, is still useful.

Ferguson, Wallace K., *Europe in Transition, 1300–1520* (Boston: Houghton Mifflin, 1962). An excellent text, reliable and readable.

Gilmore, Myron, *The World of Humanism, 1453–1517* (New York: Harper & Row, 1962). Excellent, although restricted to the later period; contains a critical bibliography.

Hay, Denys, *The Italian Renaissance in Its Historical Background* (Cambridge: Cambridge University Press, 1961). A series of interpretive lectures.

Jacob, Ernest F., ed., *Italian Renaissance Studies* (New York: Barnes and Noble, 1960). Sixteen brief scholarly monographs on various aspects of the Renaissance.

Lucas, Henry S., *The Renaissance and the Reformation*, 2nd ed. (New York: Harper & Row, 1960).

Lucki, Emil, *History of the Renaissance*, Vol. V: *Politics and Political Theory* (Salt Lake City: University of Utah Press, 1964).

Mattingly, Garrett, *Renaissance Diplomacy* (London: Jonathan Cape, 1955). Leading study of the development and practice of diplomacy in the fifteenth and sixteenth centuries.

New Cambridge Modern History, Vol. I: *The Renaissance, 1493–1520* (1957); Vol. II: *The Reformation, 1520–1559* (1958).

THE ITALIAN STATES AND THEIR POLITICAL HISTORY

Plumb, J. H., *The Italian Renaissance, a Concise Survey of Its History and Culture* (New York: Harper & Row, 1965). Lively sketch of history and politics; weak on cultural aspects.

Waley, Daniel, *The Italian City-Republics* (London: Weidenfeld and Nicolson, 1969), World University Library. Describes development of the communes from the late eleventh to the early fourteenth centuries.

Florence has been most fully treated, both because of its central role in the Renaissance and the extraordinary richness of its archives:

Ady, Cecilia, *Lorenzo dei Medici and Renaissance Italy* (New York: Macmillan, 1952), Teach Yourself History Library. A sympathetic account by a renowned scholar.

Becker, Marvin B., *Florence in Transition*, Vol. I: *The Decline of the Commune*, Vol. II: *Studies in the Rise of the Territorial State* (Baltimore: Johns Hopkins Press, 1967, 1968).

Brucker, Gene A., *Florentine Politics and Society 1343–1378* (Princeton: Princeton University Press, 1962). Treats in depth the semi-democratic interlude of the fourteenth century. *Renaissance Florence* (New York: Wiley, 1969), Historical Cities series. Brief but clear and well-documented description of Florentine politics, economy, and society during the fourteenth and fifteenth centuries.

Gilbert, Felix, *Machiavelli and Guicciardini: Politics and History in Sixteenth-Century Florence* (Princeton: Princeton University Press, 1965). Includes a clear description of Florentine government and politics during the period 1494–1512.

Martines, Lauro, *Lawyers and Statecraft in Renaissance Florence* (Princeton: Princeton University Press, 1968).

Rubinstein, Nicolai, *The Government of Florence under the Medici (1434–1494)* (Oxford: Clarendon Press, 1966). A detailed, balanced account of the Medici techniques of control, the extent and limits of their power.

Schevill, Ferdinand, *History of Florence*, rev. ed. (New York: Frederick Ungar, 1936). A substantial work, scholarly and readable but no longer adequate in the light of recent research. Also, Schevill's *The Medici* (New York: Harper & Row, 1960).

OTHER ITALIAN STATES

Ady, Cecilia, *A History of Milan under the Sforzas*, ed. Edward Armstrong (London: Methuen, 1907).

Bouwsma, William J., *Venice and the Defense of Republican Liberty: Renaissance Values in the Age of the Counter Reformation* (Berkeley: University of California Press, 1968). A fresh and far-ranging interpretation based on intensive research.

Herlihy, David, *Pisa in the Early Renaissance; A Study of Urban Growth* (New Haven: Yale University Press, 1958). *Medieval and Renaissance Pistoia: The Social History of an Italian Town, 1200–1430* (New Haven: Yale University Press, 1967).

Partner, Peter, *The Papal State under Martin V: The Administration and Government of the Temporal Power in the Early Fifteenth Century* (London: British School at Rome, 1958).

Schevill, Ferdinand, *Siena, the History of a Medieval Commune* (New York: Harper & Row, 1964), with critical Introduction by William M. Bowsky. Also for Siena, William M. Bowsky's articles: "The *Buon Governo* of Siena (1287–1335)," *Speculum*, 37 (1962), 368–381, and "Medieval Citizenship: The Individual and the State in the Commune of Siena, 1287–1355," in *Studies in Medieval and Renaissance History*, Vol. IV (Lincoln: University of Nebraska Press, 1967).

BIOGRAPHICAL STUDIES

For Machiavelli, see References for Chapter III.

An illuminating recent study of Savonarola is Donald Weinstein, *Savonarola and Florence; Prophecy and Patriotism in the Renaissance* (Princeton: Princeton University Press, 1970). Argues that Savonarola was as deeply influenced by Florence as Florence by him. Includes a critique of earlier biographers, notably Pasqualle Villari, *Life and Times of Girolamo Savonarola* (original Italian edition 1859–61). Also, Roberto Ridolfi, *The Life of Girolamo Savonarola*, trans. Cecil Grayson (New York, 1959).

Roeder, Ralph, *The Man of the Renaissance, Four Lawgivers: Savonarola, Machiavelli, Castiglione, Aretino* (New York: Viking, 1933). Somewhat impressionistic but engagingly written; provides an exciting introduction to Renaissance interests and issues through a study of four influential personalities.

III

RENAISSANCE
POLITICS:
THE IDEAL

*Every government is nothing but violence over subjects,
sometimes moderated by a form of honesty.*
    —Francesco Guicciardini, DISCORSO DI LOGROGNO

*It is the duty of a good prince to consider the welfare of
his people, even at the cost of his own life if need be.*
    —Desiderius Erasmus,
    THE EDUCATION OF A CHRISTIAN PRINCE

MACHIAVELLI'S FAILURE AND TRIUMPH

Machiavelli's political treatises can be properly understood only in
the context of the political realities he encountered, either directly
or vicariously. The dissonant tone of *The Prince* is explained partly
by the fact that the overthrow of the Florentine republic and restoration of the Medici in 1512 terminated his public career. The
downfall of the regime which he had served for some fourteen
years entailed suffering for Machiavelli; atlhough his term of im-
prisonment was brief, he was exiled from the city, and forced retirement from politics was a bitter pill to a man for whom statecraft
was the highest calling. Machiavelli's loss was the world's gain.
He used his unsought leisure to write his most important works.
The Prince is not merely a memorial to personal frustration, nor a
turncoat's attempt to ingratiate himself with despots, although, with
the hope that never quite dies in politicians, he did seek employment with his erstwhile enemies, the Medici. The most he was
able to procure was a commission from the University of Florence,
sponsored by Cardinal Giulio de' Medici, to write the *History of
Florence*. On this enterprise he labored for five years, not without

discomfiture because—with more conscience than he is usually given credit for—he had to steer a course between telling the truth as he saw it and risking the displeasure of his patrons.

Machiavelli had the Medici in mind when he wrote *The Prince,* hurriedly during the later months of 1513, and he hopefully dedicated the little book to a second Lorenzo the Magnificent, grandson of the real *Magnifico*—a youth whose utter insignificance had not yet been clearly demonstrated. At this particular juncture Machiavelli had reason to believe that vigorous leadership, which the Medici were in a position to exert, could repair the tattered fortunes of Italy, perhaps with permanent benefit to the peninsula. In March Giovanni de' Medici had acceded to the papacy as Leo x, after the stormy pontificate of Julius ii, whose "diabolical spirit" Machiavelli had regarded as likely to wreck Christendom as well as the states of Italy. Now that the Medici were in control of both Florence and the papacy and temporarily aligned with Spain and the empire, they commanded a rare opportunity to establish effective rule and promote peace and stability. Unfortunately for Machiavelli's expectations, the Medici lacked either the ruthlessness or the statesmanship to rise to the challenge.

As for its intended audience, *The Prince* fell on deaf ears, and later audiences have condemned it as a cynical betrayal of man's political birthright. The judgment is too harsh. Whatever its limitations, *The Prince* is not unalloyed cynicism. Indignant, scathing, sarcastic, it was intended as a prod to action, and it yields a kernel of hope. Only years later, when his hopes had been crushed again and again, did Machiavelli succumb to despair.

Neither in his governmental service nor in his writings was Machiavelli a detached and dispassionate observer of the contemporary scene. In this respect he differs from his compatriot and fellow historian Francesco Guicciardini (1483–1540). It is Guicciardini who approximates the coldly analytical recorder, faithfully dissecting the motives and behavior of human beings, plumbing the depths of callousness, hypocrisy, and greed without wincing. In what he set out to do—and this was a great deal—he was more successful than Machiavelli. He too participated in government as well as describing it, and, in contrast to Machiavelli, enjoyed a long and remunerative career as administrator and diplomat, mainly for the Medici popes, under whom he rose to the important and lucrative post of governor of the Romagna. A skillful and eloquent narrator, a master of rhetoric, Guicciardini was a historian of enviable stature. His *Florentine History* is far superior to Machiavelli's in the selection and discriminating use of sources, in accuracy and balance. Yet successive generations of readers have preferred Machiavelli. And with reason.

As a thinker and historian, Machiavelli had almost unforgivable limitations. He lacked the capacity for theoretical analysis or synthesis; he achieved no broad philosophical grasp of his material. His political judgments were often wrong; even on military policy, which he made his specialty, his conclusions were highly dubious. Why, in spite of these faults, is Machiavelli of enduring value? Doubtless it is because, in addition to seeing some things very clearly, he cared about what he saw. Bitterness, even cynicism is evident in Machiavelli; but he assumes greatness because he was—in spite of himself perhaps—concerned with the ends of human life and society. He belongs, however uncomfortable he would be to find himself there, in the tradition of European moralists.

Thoughtful reading of Machiavelli tends to invalidate most of the labels that have become attached to him. Hailed as the father of modern political science, he actually constructed no theory of the origins and nature of the state or of the science of government; he indulged more in exhortation, reproof, and sarcasm than in patient analysis; and he sought his models and maxims in the remote world of antiquity. *The Prince* is not a treatise on government but a manual for despots—and a stinging rebuke to Italian citizens for deserving nothing better than despotism. Neither is the *Discourses on Livy* a positive contribution to political science, although it is more sober and judicious in tone than *The Prince* and gives a clearer picture of the author's underlying republican convictions. Machiavelli is termed a realist, which he was in a sense; but there is something brittle and venomous about his realism that suggests an incompletely suppressed desire for the ideal. It has frequently been remarked that Machiavelli's unique contribution to modern political thought was his separation of politics from religion and ethics—that he performed the necessary hatchet job on the theocratic medieval tradition and thus cleared the way for the businesslike secular state. But insofar as he dissociated politics from morality (and certain passages in *The Prince* emphatically support the charge), he did it not casually, but deliberately, in ringing tones, making it clear that violence was being done to the normal and proper scheme of things.

The defects in Machiavelli's vision and judgment, as well as his shrewd insights, are largely a reflection of the age in which he lived, and they are an aid to understanding it. If his writings are full of inconsistencies and contradictions, so were the society and culture which engendered them. Machiavelli, in common with many of his contemporaries, was both fascinated and troubled by the emerging cult of power. With imagination and only a little distortion on the reader's part, *The Prince* could be interpreted as a caricature of the ruthless and unscrupulous despot, and it was so interpreted by some eighteenth-century critics of absolutism, including Jean Jacques Rousseau.[1]

It is difficult to delineate in precise terms Machiavelli's political philosophy because it has to be inferred—or even constructed— from his scattered observations on various matters. And in spite of his shrewdness he fell wide of the mark in appraising contemporary social forces. Instead of making a serious attempt to analyze the society of Florence, he fell back on formulas extracted from antiquity. While the Tuscan republic was openly and proudly proclaiming itself a city of merchants and artisans—though in fact it was in the grip of an upper bourgeois elite—Machiavelli continued to think in terms of the traditional opposition between nobles and commoners, which he equated with the struggle between patricians and plebeians in early republican Rome. Not only was his view of the contemporary class structure and its tensions a distorted one, but he never could quite make up his mind whose side he was on. At times he seems to show a deep-seated confidence in the judgment and probity of the common people. "The aim of the people is more honest than that of the nobility"; [2] "the best fortress [for a prince] is to be found in the love of the people." [3] But again he scorns the masses, and he attributes the ruin of the Florentine republic to the dissension caused by their ambition. In a forceful

---

[1] "He professed to teach kings; but it was the people he really taught. His *Prince* is the book of Republicans." *Social Contract,* Bk. III, Chap. 6.

[2] Machiavelli, *The Prince and the Discourses,* trans. Luigi Ricci (New York: Modern Library, 1940), Chap. 9.

[3] *Ibid.,* Chap. 20.

passage in the *History of Florence* [4] he laments the degradation and expulsion of the Florentine nobility, because it deprived the city of her natural leaders, caused the decay of "military virtue and generosity of feeling" ("the people not possessing these qualities"), and eventually made necessary the rule of a prince. Conversely, he commends the ancient Roman republic for having retained class distinctions and the preeminent position of the nobles, and he denounces the Gracchan agrarian laws of the second century B.C., citing the strife to which they gave rise as a prime cause of the ruin of the republic.[5] The decay of civic virtue and greatness in Florence he blames on the leveling of classes that resulted from the "insolent and unjust" demands of the lower orders.

But though he argued against political equality, Machiavelli did not actually endorse aristocracy. What he sought was a balance between the middle class and the nobility or patriciate, such as the ancient Romans achieved through a process of nonviolent adjustment and compromise during the early period of the republic. He saw these two opposing factions, the "nobility" and the "people," as permanent elements in the state and apparently as necessary for its survival. He believed an equilibrium between them could provide a safeguard against both princely tyranny and "the nauseous rule of the rabble." [6] To prevent the common people from endangering this precarious equilibrium, he would not hesitate to keep them at a low economic level: "In well-regulated republics the state ought to be rich and the citizens poor." Poverty produces better civil fruit than wealth, which brings ruin.[7] So incontrovertible was this principle in Machiavelli's view that he declared it advantageous to a republic to have laws deliberately designed to keep its citizens poor—surely gratuitous advice, to judge from the condition of the majority of Florence's inhabitants in the early sixteenth century.

Machiavelli is strangely ambivalent in his analysis of republican institutions and the prospects for their survival. He distrusts

[4] Machiavelli, *History of Florence and of the Affairs of Italy* (New York: Harper & Row, 1960), Bk. III, Chap. 1.

[5] Machiavelli, *Discourses on the First Ten Books of Livy*, trans. Christian E. Detmold (New York: Modern Library, 1940), Bk. I, Chap. 37.

[6] *History of Florence, op. cit.*, Bk. III, Chap. 4.

[7] *Discourses, op. cit.*, Bk. I, Chap. 37; Bk. III, Chap. 25.

equality as a dangerous idea, and he says the attempt to achieve it invites disaster. Yet he also asserts that equality among citizens is essential to the success of a republic. His own logic therefore would seem to rule out the possibility of a republic—to say nothing of democracy—for mortal men. But he cannot suppress his own republican instincts, even when they have been chilled by cold logic or bruised by experience. His imagination turns hopefully to Germany—that barbarous land derided by the humanists—and he discovers that there alone in all the world "probity and religion still exist largely among the people," who are so honest that they pay their proper taxes without any compulsion or supervision. In Germany, he reports, republics are flourishing—free, uncorrupted, and enjoying perfect equality. In this mood he identifies the nobles as the real stumbling block in the path of republics (the Germans have solved the problem by killing them). So, he concludes, where there are many nobles—as in Naples, Lombardy, and the Romagna —a republic is impossible. In Tuscany, by implication, the prospects should be brighter.[8]

In his political writings Machiavelli frequently appeals to the court of history to illustrate or vindicate his argument. Believing that one should "read carefully the history of the past and observe the course of present events," he deplores the lack of sound historical knowledge among his contemporaries. However, his own use of history is capricious, distorted, and sometimes myopic. He carelessly assigns trivial causes to great events: the collapse of the Roman Empire was "merely due to the hiring of Goth mercenaries."[9] He indulges in sweeping generalizations and clichés: national characteristics never change—the modern French are deceitful, just like the ancient Gauls.[10] If he has any philosophy of history it is simply the old Greco-Roman concept of cyclical recurrence, which was shared by most historians of the age.

It may be observed, that provinces amid the vicissitudes to which they are subject, pass from order into confusion, and afterward recur to a state of order again; for the nature of mundane affairs not allowing them to continue in an even course, when they have arrived at their greatest perfection, they

---

[8] *Ibid.*, Bk. I, Chap. 55.
[9] *The Prince, op. cit.*, Chap. 13.
[10] *Discourses, op. cit.*, Bk. III, Chap. 43.

soon begin to decline. In the same manner, having been reduced by disorder, and sunk to their utmost state of depression, unable to descend lower, they, of necessity, reascend; and thus from good they gradually decline to evil, and from evil again return to good.[11]

His work betrays no idea of progress, no conception of the evolution of institutions except for the endless recurrence of events in a closed pattern.

When Machiavelli sought an underlying cause for historical occurrences, he found it in Fortune—that is, blind chance—sometimes more circumspectly referred to as God. In this he reflects the contemporary climate of opinion, affected as it was by the classical view of man's precarious position in the cosmos. Machiavelli, however, firmly believed that within limits man can shape his own ends: "Not to extinguish our free will, I hold it to be true that fortune is the arbiter of one half of our actions, but that she still leaves us to direct the other half, or perhaps a little less." [12] In common with other humanist writers he placed *virtù* in opposition to Fortune or Necessity. Machiavelli used the term *virtù* loosely and with varying connotations—ranging from moral virtue to force of will or simply military valor—but always as an affirmation of some distinct quality in man which is not ruled by fate and which enables him to hold his own amid untoward circumstances. His affirmation rested on intuition rather than on demonstrable evidence; it was an article of faith. It helps to explain the nature of his "realism," which was neither the jaundiced view of the pessimist nor the unclouded vision of the scientist. Machiavelli was both "pitiless in his analysis of what is" and "untiringly optimistic with regard to what might be." [13]

A historian can attain stature in his craft without a philosophy of history. A far more serious defect in Machiavelli is his lack of historical perspective. He had little comprehension of the main contours of the European past. By a prodigious foreshortening of the historical landscape he saw the sixteenth-century Italian city-states operating in the same milieu as the Roman republic of the

---

[11] *History of Florence, op. cit.*, Bk. V, Chap. 1.

[12] *The Prince, op. cit.*, Chap. 25.

[13] John H. Whitfield, *Machiavelli* (New York: Russell & Russell, 1965), p. 62.

fourth century B.C. (although operating badly in contrast to the glittering success of the Romans); his perspective makes the entire Middle Ages disappear. Of course, it was characteristic of Renaissance humanists from Petrarch on, and characteristic as well of many later thinkers down to the present, to ignore or despise the Middle Ages. The point is not whether medieval civilization and institutions were worthy of respect. The point is that Machiavelli judged out of context the political organisms that had aroused his greatest interest and were the source of his own high hopes for the Italy that might be. The communes of the twelfth and thirteenth centuries—still relatively small, relatively poor, relatively equalitarian, still functioning in a medieval environment—exhibited the qualities Machiavelli admired and longed to see rehabilitated. The swollen city-states, principalities, and empires of the fifteenth and sixteenth centuries were vastly different. To them the medieval canons—the restraints imposed by guild and church and time-honored local customs, and the precarious balance between rival pope and emperor—no longer applied. Neither could the valor and *virtù* of the ancient Romans be implanted in their inhabitants, except superficially and sentimentally. These Roman attributes, whatever their original significance, had been irrelevant to the late medieval revival of municipal life without which the Renaissance could never have come about. Nevertheless, Machiavelli pleaded with his countrymen to recover the Roman virtues and to apply the lessons of Roman history. It is difficult to believe he could have retained his stubborn faith in the feasibility of free and successful republics on the basis of his reading—and misreading—of ancient history alone. On the contrary, imbedded in his memory as a model was an actual historical phenomenon, far closer to his own day than was ancient Rome:

Although nothing has subsequently arisen from the ruins of Rome at all corresponding to her ancient greatness . . . there was so much bravery and intelligence in some of the new cities and governments that afterward sprang up, that although none ever acquired dominion over the rest, they were, nevertheless, so balanced and regulated among themselves, as to enable them to live in freedom, and defend their country from the barbarians.[14]

---

[14] *History of Florence, op. cit.,* Bk. V, Chap. 1.

Thus does Machiavelli pay homage, though grudgingly, to the medieval communes, which had already become almost as anachronistic as the ancient Roman republic. It was not the failure of the political ideals embodied in the late medieval cities but their appreciable success during the twelfth and thirteenth centuries that engendered Machiavelli's dissatisfaction with the immediate present and his tenacious hope for the future. The most obvious and striking instance of his indebtedness to these late medieval communes is seen in his advocacy of a citizens' militia, a scheme he came to regard as a veritable panacea, calculated to rekindle patriotism and military ardor, provide better defense for the cities, and remove the curse of the *condottieri* from the land. Here, as Federico Chabod has pointed out: "Machiavelli becomes once again a municipalist, a descendant of the old *bourgeoisie* of the free Communes. He is not a prophet of the future, but simply an anachronistic evoker of a past that must be regarded as dead." [15]

Machiavelli was neither a reliable interpreter of the past nor an accurate forecaster of the future. He was a trenchant critic of the politics of his day, which he saw leading to weakness, chaos, and ruin. He did not offer any solution, least of all perhaps in the book put forward as a manual for princes. The reason he could find no solution is that he did not understand the scope and magnitude of the changes taking place around him—in the structure of society, in the stakes and dimensions of power politics. The specific advice he offered was largely unrealistic and futile. The communal militia system could not be revived, especially in the face of growing armies of mercenaries hired by national monarchs. The Italian city-states, instigators and beneficiaries of a commercial revolution, were not likely to heed Machiavelli's injunction to return to a virtuous poverty. Although by preference a man of action rather than a recluse and certainly no mystic, Machiavelli sought in his writings an antidote to the crass, intractable outer world. His perusal of history was a dignified form of escapism: ancient history supplied noble examples, modern history horrible examples—the sordid and petty events of "this wasted world." Even the theory of recurring cycles could be comforting: if things become bad enough they are bound to get better eventually. In an age of turbulence and flux,

---

[15] Federico Chabod, *Machiavelli and the Renaissance*, trans. David Moore (Cambridge, Mass.: Harvard University Press, 1960), p. 102.

churned by the capricious wheel of Fortune, Machiavelli longed for stability, sometimes to the point of being willing to sacrifice almost all other values to attain it. He praised the constitution of ancient Sparta and hailed its reputed founder Lycurgus as a supreme statesman—not for the intrinsic merit of his decrees but because he gave the Spartans "by a single act all the laws they needed" and because his constitution lasted "more than eight hundred years . . . without experiencing a single dangerous disturbance." [16]

Machiavelli can hardly be called a modern man in his outlook and attitudes. But he was modern in his rejection of any return to the medieval theocratic ideal. The *Respublica Christiana* was for him extinct, if not purely mythical. In this respect he was a realist, although by no means wholly original. In the ecclesiastical hierarchy as well as in the secular states, ideal goals had repeatedly been subordinated to other considerations. Political power has always been at odds with ethical imperatives, whether in the Roman Empire, the medieval papal monarchy, the Islamic Caliphate, or the modern nation-state. And the dictum that corrupt men deserve harsh rulers is good Pauline and Augustinian doctrine. Although he was uncommonly blunt about it, Machiavelli had made no new discovery, nor did he propose a new solution to the problem.

Machiavelli exalted power—even naked, brutal power, uninhibited by religious dictates or moral scruples—because this was the one reality that seemed to him effective. He recommended the use of power to whatever extent necessary—by the prince, by the aristocracy, by whoever could hold a balance between aristocracy and populace—to provide stability and security and to drive the "barbarians" out of Italy. Perhaps this was a counsel of despair ("how we live is so far removed from how we ought to live"). But Machiavelli did not adore the person or the trappings of monarchy; still less did he worship the state. He formulated no clear conception of the nature of the state, nor did he foresee its future role and evolution. He had no intimation either of Leviathan or of the Welfare State. His greatest service—and the source of his unceasing fascination—is that he called attention, more sharply than any of his contemporaries and most of his successors, to the consequences of alternate lines of action, emphatically including the

---

[16] *Discourses, op. cit.,* Bk. I, Chap. 2.

consequences of the separation of politics from morality. He did not view the wave of the future with indifference, nor did he fail to sound an alarm.

THE RISE AND DECLINE OF CIVIC HUMANISM

Renaissance political ideals were reflected in, and to some extent shaped by, the scholars and intellectuals known generally as humanists, whose influence is evident in every aspect of the culture of the age. Broadly speaking, Machiavelli belongs to this group, in spite of his individuality, his paradoxes, and his running quarrel with the times. Nurtured in youth on ancient Latin authors, he retained a lifelong devotion to them, and he shared the humanists' faith in the efficacy of classical models. Where he differed from most humanists was in his approach to politics. Enamored of the belief that the restoration of elegant letters and manners would inaugurate a new age of refinement, they tended to idealize contemporary institutions. And if the state disappointed them, they had other resources —aesthetic, philosophical, and religious—to fall back on. Not so Machiavelli, for whom politics was an abiding passion and commitment. If the state betrayed its members or perverted the natural ends of society, then, in his judgment, man had failed abysmally in his quest for the good life. But in spite of significant differences, the course of humanist political thought parallels the experience of Machiavelli. The humanists' disillusionment, while not marked with the same acid bitterness, was equally profound.

Early Italian humanists, repelled by the arid dialectics of scholasticism and absorbed in the neglected treasures of antiquity, had felt somewhat isolated from the society in which they lived. While not intentionally withdrawing from the world or hiding their light under a bushel, they cultivated a scholarly detachment and extolled the virtues of a life of contemplation. However, even Petrarch, the "father of humanism," felt the pull of competing subjective and objective loyalties, and from the later fourteenth century onward, humanists became increasingly involved in civic affairs, not only as observers but as active participants. They held office in the Italian republics and served as secretaries, advisers, or prestigious ornaments in the despotisms. And aside from their interest in government as a gateway to personal advancement, they valued the state as a natural form of human association. Man, they affirmed, is a social animal, who can fully develop his capacities and attain happiness only in cooperation with his fellows. Throughout the Renaissance, debate persisted in humanist circles over the respective merits of a life of active engagement and a life of withdrawal and meditation; and the desirability of striking a balance between these two complementary ideals was frequently acknowledged.

Humanists generally looked upon the state as only one of many legitimate forms of association, and not necessarily the highest. The incredibly versatile Leon Battista Alberti (1404–72), influential architect and author, wrote *Della famiglia*, a famous book in praise of the family, which was still a strongly knit and multifunctional unit. While Alberti also stressed the importance of a civic community and the necessity of devoting oneself energetically to civic service, his approach to the state was aesthetic and idealistic. He perceived it as a harmoniously organized body within a network of perfect relationships extending throughout God's great universe. And when the brutal realities of the Medicean dictatorship intruded upon his vision, he found solace in the reflection that the family, founded upon love, is nobler than the state.

Politically volatile Florence witnessed the fullest outpouring of speculation on the nature and ends of government. Here a group of humanists, entrenched in affairs of the community, called upon the discipline of history, to illuminate the city's destiny and to assist in its fulfillment. Beginning with the last quarter of the fourteenth century, a succession of humanist historians held the important post of chancellor (first secretary) of the republic and from this vantage point promoted the rise of what Hans Baron has termed "civic humanism." This phenomenon, which reached its climax in Florence in the early 1400s, represents a notable attempt to bring scholarship to bear upon practical affairs, uniting intellectual and political resources to defend the state and enable its citizens to enjoy true freedom. Although laudable, the movement proved ultimately sterile, because it remained the project of a small privileged group —and, even among them, highly theoretical—and because with the drift toward despotism the realities of politics became less and less amenable to the ideals of the humanists.

Florence's courageous and successful opposition to the attempt of the Visconti of Milan to dominate all of northern Italy awakened a burst of confidence among her inhabitants. The fact that Florence had assumed the foremost role in a struggle against tyranny encouraged intellectuals to concern themselves directly in civic affairs. They also voiced the conviction that an atmosphere of freedom was essential not only for the welfare of the citizen but for the fullest development of literature and the arts. In a vein reminiscent of Periclean Athens, writers idealized the polis and its government, hailing it as the true educator of citizens and the means of establishing fruitful concord between private interests and public good. The robust, civic-centered spirit of this period is reflected also in the works of such leading contemporary Florentine artists as Donatello, Masaccio, Ghiberti, and Brunelleschi, who glorified a public world calculated to arouse heroic instincts and enlist unreserved allegiance.

Leonardo Bruni's *History of the Florentine People*—written about 1440 during his term in office as chancellor—delivered a ringing tribute to the ideal of a free republic as exemplified by Florence. No worshiper of Caesar, Bruni attributed the decline of ancient Rome to the despotism of her imperial period, hailed the collapse of the Empire because it freed subject peoples, and credited the factional struggles in Italian city-states with inaugurating the first era of Italian liberty since the early Roman republic. In 1428 Bruni had composed a eulogy to one of the Florentine heroes of the conflict with Milan. Like the famous Funeral Oration of Pericles on which it was modeled, the eulogy sang the praises of democracy. Florence's laws "aim, above all, at the liberty and equality of all citizens," Bruni asserted. "We do not tremble before one man as a lord, nor are we servants to the power of a few." [17] Ten years later, in the midst of the struggle against the last Visconti duke, another humanist historian penned an equally strong manifesto. Poggio Bracciolini (chancellor, 1453–58), in a letter to a Milanese propagandist, boldly claimed Florentine liberty to be of a special quality, "more solid and truer" than any found elsewhere:

For not one or another single man governs here, nor does the arrogance of optimates or noblemen command, but the people are called on the basis of equal right to perform public functions in the commonwealth. As a consequence, highly placed and humble persons, members of noble families and

---

[17] Hans Baron, *The Crisis of the Early Italian Renaissance*, Vol. I, (Princeton: Princeton University Press, 1955), pp. 364, 372.

commoners, rich and poor work together with a common zeal for the cause of liberty.[18]

These were noble sentiments, more inspiring than the usual sober memoranda of historians. Unfortunately, they did not correspond to the political or economic facts of life in fifteenth-century Florence. The humanist patriots were spokesmen for the successful class of "new citizens" who had worked their way into the ranks of the prosperous elite and raised themselves far above the multitude. After being admitted to Florentine citizenship, Leonardo Bruni, enterprising son of a small grain dealer from Arezzo, had received a generous tax exemption, and as he rose to political prominence he became one of the wealthiest members of the community. A self-made man, he could look down with disdain on those he had left so far behind. In his *History of the Florentine People*, apropos the *Ciompi* revolt of 1378, he admonished the ruling oligarchy never to allow the masses "to take political initiative or to have weapons" because there is "no end or measure to the unbridled desire of the lawless rabble." [19] Apparently there was no end to the avarice of the patriciate Bruno so eloquently represented. Both he and Poggio Bracciolini (also of lower middle-class origin) canonized bourgeois propensities as virtues, arguing that the acquisitive instinct is natural and is a positive advantage to the state. They described wealth as "blood to the city," and Poggio flatly declared, "For the commonwealth, money is the nerve of life and those who lust for money are its foundation." As a rationalization of the financial interests of a dominant minority, civic humanism tended to degenerate into crass materialism.

The political liberty lauded by civic humanists existed chiefly in their imaginations. The government of Florence had long been democratic only in theory and outward form, and in 1434 it came under the grip of Cosimo de' Medici. Bruni, appointed chancellor seven years earlier, remained in office as a colleague rather than a creature of Cosimo; but he was careful not to antagonize the new establishment, and his successors in the chancellorship were more

---

18 *Ibid.*, p. 354.

19 Lauro Martines, *The Social World of the Florentine Humanists 1390–1460* (Princeton: Princeton University Press, 1963), p. 42.

directly indebted to Medici patronage. Partly from timidity and partly from self-interest, humanist intellectuals accommodated to the currents of political change and, even before the accession of the Medici, lent their talents to serve an aggressive oligarchy. Consequently, "in large part, the force of humanism in the Florentine community was the disguised force of the ruling class itself." [20] Political regimes of whatever coloration find ready employment for rhetoricians. But as the Medici tightened their reins over the public life of the city, it became difficult, even in formal rhetorical discourse, to nourish the illusion of an association of free citizens directing their own affairs. Critics brave enough to speak out were exiled by Cosimo and Lorenzo. Other humanists who sincerely valued freedom took refuge in the safer fields of literature and philosophy or returned to the ideal of quiet contemplation and the inner world of mystic experience. Political crises of the fifteenth century and the solidification of despotism did not destroy humanism nor entirely extinguish its influence on political thought, but they tended to deflect it from contemporary issues and to alienate it from the society in which it had taken root.

NORTHERN CHRISTIAN HUMANISTS— MORE AND ERASMUS

The humanist movement spread from Italy into northern Europe, and there too it had political impact. The pursuit of classical literary studies, while refining Latin diction and remolding educational curricula, stimulated inquiry into contemporary society and institutions. Northern humanists began to examine the historical foundations of the Church and in doing so provoked acrimonious disputes that helped prepare the way for the Reformation of the sixteenth century. An unprecedented expansion of governmental power and intensified international conflict made them acutely aware of political problems; and an opportunity to help solve the problems seemed to be presented, particularly in the early decades of the sixteenth century, when "barbarian" monarchs beyond the Alps, no less than Italian despots, manifested a desire to cultivate the society of humanists.

The political atmosphere of northern and western Europe, where a similar power struggle operated over a wider area, was no cleaner

---

[20] *Ibid.*, p. 270.

than that of Italy. Perhaps because of the greater magnitude of the conflict among the rising national states of the north, a few hardy individuals raised dissenting voices on behalf of moral values that seemed in danger of being swept away. Like Machiavelli, they were concerned with the impact of politics upon society and, like him, disturbed by the drift of events. But in opposing the thesis that the ends of statecraft justify the means and that the state is bound by no higher law, they naturally drew upon the European religious heritage to support their arguments and accordingly are associated with what is called the "Christian Renaissance." They are usually regarded as idealists, in contrast to Machiavelli the realist; but the distinction has only limited validity. Among those who were not mere bystanders but, like the Italian civic humanists, active participants in government, the most striking example is the English statesman Sir Thomas More (1478–1535).

More's political teachings convey a tone and emphasis the opposite of Machiavelli's. The two men differed radically in personality, and they occupy radically different niches in the historical hall of fame: Machiavelli's name—"Old Nick"—became a euphemism for the devil, while the martyred More was canonized by the Roman Catholic Church. Nevertheless, there are striking points of similarity between the diabolical Florentine and the sainted Englishman. Their careers ran roughly parallel. Both were theorists only incidentally; they were primarily interested in the practical aspects of government. Both had the advantage of firsthand experience in government service. Machiavelli ended his days in involuntary political retirement; More was executed by the king he had loyally served up to the point where his conscience could stretch no farther. Each produced a small but unforgettable book which applies value judgments to the study of politics. *The Prince*, written in 1513, had a very small circulation during Machiavelli's lifetime. *Utopia*, composed during 1515 and 1516, was first published at Louvain, and no English translation of the Latin original appeared until sixteen years after the author's death (1551). Both *The Prince* and *Utopia* are unorthodox and provocative; and while More's book is commonly regarded as a fantasy, it is as pointed and pertinent as Machiavelli's.

Book One of *Utopia*, which is in the form of a dialogue and contains a biting attack on the injustices of English society, is partly autobiographical. Weighing the advisability of accepting a royal appointment, More put into the mouth of his interlocutor his own misgivings about a career in the king's service. Sir Thomas possessed the very qualities of wisdom and modesty that Machiavelli advised a prince to look for in choosing his counselors, and evidently More concurred in Machiavelli's estimate of the prince in relation to his ministers, especially when the prince in question was the willful Tudor, Henry VIII. This portion of the *Utopia*, reflecting More's anxiety as he was pressed to become one of the king's ministers, is prophetic of the tragic conclusion of the author's career. Book Two, most of which was actually written first, illuminates from a different vantage point More's deep dissatisfaction with contemporary political norms. It describes the imaginary commonwealth of Utopia ("Nowhere"), vaguely located on some transoceanic island far removed from the evils corrupting European states. The inhabitants of Utopia, in contrast to Europeans, live under a benign, semi-communistic paternalism, which, however unexciting, is dedicated to the welfare of all. They have eradicated crime, not by increasing the stringency of penal laws but by abolishing both poverty and wealth. In Utopia there are no wastrels and idlers, no swaggering nobles, no begging monks, and—the author's profession notwithstanding—few laws and no lawyers. Lawyers are hardly needed in a community whose members, instead of scrambling for private profit, pursue the common good. And where everyone is required to share in necessary labor, everyone is rewarded with a share of leisure, which is devoted not to frivolity and vain display but to the lifelong cultivation of the mind. The Utopians enjoy freedom of opinion and of religion, although those who deny the immortality of the soul are barred from office. Equally remarkable, their foreign policy aims primarily at avoiding war, which means—in the context of the times as interpreted by More—that they have as little as possible to do with any other state.

In depicting an ideal harmonious commonwealth founded on mutual aid rather than on fraud and plunder, More brings into sharp relief the stupidities of European power politics and the injustices of contemporary society. He excoriates the evils of the enclosure movement that is driving poor English tenants from their lands and turning them into beggars and thieves: "Your sheep, that were wont to be so meek and tame . . . become so great devourers and so wild, that they eat up and swallow down the very men themselves." Within the whole roster of European states he "can perceive nothing but a certain conspiracy of rich men procuring their own commodities under the name and title of the commonwealth." Institutions so perverse would seemingly require the most drastic remedies, even the remolding of human behavior in order to expunge the sins of greed and pride. More's narrator reports that the Utopians have eradicated the root of all evil not only by establishing a community of property but also by the novel and unlikely device of restricting use of gold and silver to such things as children's toys and chamber pots. Wedded to an opposite set of values, how could European society ever be emancipated from its fatal obsessions? More confesses grave doubts as to whether it is possible for a man of integrity and conviction to accept government employment without being ruined, and he intimates that the only alternative to treacherous diplomacy, war, and international anarchy is isolationism. The likelihood of genuine reform is therefore extremely remote.

Though the conclusion is pessimistic, *Utopia*, like Machiavelli's very different but equally astringent essay, carries a message of hope and promise. More was neither a cynic nor an inveterate pessimist. A deep religious faith sustained him throughout a lifetime of full and purposeful participation in the affairs of the secular world. Although he esteemed the monastic life of renunciation and was by temperament drawn toward it, he deliberately rejected it. Anchored in religious conviction, he was stimulated by the physical and intellectual currents swirling around him. Even *Utopia*, a moral and political tract, reflects a multiplicity of interests. The excitement of geographical discovery—specifically the published account of Amerigo Vespucci's voyages—suggested the scheme of using the wondrous New World as a setting for an idyllic but still human community. Homage to the new learning is illustrated by an account of how the Utopians succeeded in mastering the Greek language in the space of less than three years and of how, being "marvelous quick in invention," they could build a printing press and manufacture paper after simply hearing the process described. The Utopians also quickly and gladly embraced Christianity, while rejecting its bigotry and intolerance—an even more amazing feat.

Thomas More—ascetic, saint, spinner of fantasy—brought the medieval religious vision of humanity into focus upon his own distraught society. Fully aware of the imperfections in human nature, he was equally convinced that improvement was possible. If he was an idealist, he was also a realist—far more so than most of the humanists. For the specific wrongs he saw he proposed remedies that were specific enough, though so radical as to confound the conventional wisdom of our day as well as his own. While recognizing that the Utopian model must remain something he "may rather wish for than hope after," he nevertheless convinced himself that an intelligent monarch whose court was, in Erasmus' words, "the seat and citadel of the best studies and of the highest characters," could be induced to use his enormous powers for the public weal. Two years after completing *Utopia*, in which he had explored his misgivings so unreservedly, he accepted appointment to the royal council of Henry VIII.

More the Christian humanist shared with Machiavelli a conviction that great possibilities beckoned and that the resources of European civilization were adequate to cope with them. Both men believed that government could be an agency for good; but while Machiavelli sought to give it the necessary force, More saw with deeper vision the need for a fundamental shift in priorities and goals. Like Machiavelli, he was saddened to discover that those who could have led their fellows to satisfying achievements refused to do so or led them in the wrong direction. In More's case the discovery cost him his life.

Erasmus of Rotterdam (1466?–1536), close friend and admirer of Sir Thomas More, exerted a wider influence upon the thought of his contemporaries. Greatest of the northern humanists—perhaps of all the Renaissance humanists—Erasmus surveyed the society, morals, and ideals of his age with a keen eye and dissected them with one of the sharpest pens in the history of Western letters. He was only incidentally interested in government and not at all in politics in the narrow sense. But he was nevertheless deeply concerned with the human condition, and he offered some trenchant comments upon the practices of contemporary rulers. Like More's, his precepts stood in antithesis to those of Machiavelli. Having accepted an honorary position as counselor to the young Prince Charles of Hapsburg (later Emperor Charles v), Erasmus composed for him a little manual entitled *The Education of a Christian Prince* (1516). Though nearly contemporary with *The Prince* (1513), its tone, spirit, and argument are so different that it is hard to recognize the two books as products of the same age. Almost item for item in their delineation of the proper policy for a ruler they point in opposite directions. Erasmus admonishes the sovereign to strive above everything else for peace; Machiavelli says his first duty is to study and prepare for war. One pleads for honesty and integrity, the other for consummate duplicity masked by an appearance of virtue. Erasmus' ideal ruler will work energetically to improve the condition of his people, by promoting education, by avoiding war, by economizing so that he can reduce taxes; Machiavelli's hero seeks to strengthen the state by maintaining and bolstering his own power. For Erasmus, religion is the guide to conduct; his prince is first a Christian and then a ruler. In Machiavelli's judgment, /religion is a kind of opiate of the people/ and he finds the corrupt Christianity of his day less useful for promoting the ends of statecraft than were the cults of pagan Rome.

Erasmus' antipathy to tyranny, duplicity, and strife animates most of his writings. In his greatest popular success, *Praise of Folly*, it ripples through the light irony and occasionally thunders forth with unexpected vehemence. Abuses in high places, whether ecclesiastic, academic, or monarchic, are unsparingly attacked in a hard hitting parody that pricks at the foibles and failures of the whole human race. The burden of the fable is that all men, from the simplest peasant to the most exalted potentate, have taken Folly for their teacher, guide, and mainstay. All, in one form or another, are Folly's disciples and would find life unbearable without her. Such is the assertion, although Erasmus very subtly distinguishes between various levels of "folly," some of which are to be abhorred, others gently indulged, and still others cherished and emulated because they carry a man beyond the bounds of prudent self-regard (the folly of the Cross is the supreme example).

In spite of the barbs and the ridicule, no one who reads the *Praise of Folly* carefully could call Erasmus a misanthrope. Along with chastisement he offers encouragement and, underneath the sarcasm, compassion. It is clear that Erasmus loved his fellow creatures deeply enough to care about their fate. He respected human nature and held high hopes for it.

In his political ideals Erasmus was a son of the High Middle Ages, although, with his aversion for the monastic life and Scholastic metaphysics, he would not have cared to admit it. To him the separation of statesmanship from the plane of ethics was unthinkable, just as he could conceive of no dichotomy between the enthusiasm of a classical scholar and the loyalties of a Christian. Particularly in his overall view of European society, Erasmus retained the vantage point of the late medieval centuries, which made him something less than an accurate interpreter of current events. He was largely unaffected by any sentiment of nationalism. Born in Rotterdam, educated in Deventer and Paris, equally at home in England, Italy, Germany, or Switzerland, he became a cosmopolite, a citizen of the Western world. Warfare among the rising European states he regarded with anguish and abhorrence. He pleaded with princes to sheath their swords, look after their peoples' welfare, and settle their disputes by arbitration. Peace and the advancement of education and scholarship—the progress of "good letters"—he saw as the means to universal happiness. His political ideal was not the nation-state but a Christian commonwealth that transcended and resolved regional animosities. Mistrustful of absolute power, he endorsed the principle of elective monarchy—sound medieval doctrine—and even expressed a preference for republics, although these bold suggestions were by no means intended to incite revolution. He was no proponent of democracy and, in spite of his belief in the fundamental goodness of human nature, could not bring himself to rely on the political judgment of the common man. Like his opposite number Machiavelli, he was so disturbed by the tumult of the times that he came to regard stability as a pearl of great price, for which other values might have to be forsaken. As a safeguard against anarchy he upheld the authority of the ruler, while exhorting him to be merciful.

Erasmus' idealism and his latent optimism eventually led him to view the future with a confidence that can at best be called naive. In February 1517, with storms brewing on the horizon, he could write to a friend in such an incredibly hopeful vein as this:

I anticipate the approach of a golden age: so clearly do we see the minds of princes, as if changed by inspiration, devoting all their energies to the pursuit of peace. In this effort Pope Leo x and Francis the King of the French have been the principal leaders. . . . Therefore when I see that the highest sovereigns of Europe, Francis of France, Charles, the Catholic King, Henry of England and the Emperor Maximilian have set all their warlike preparations aside and established peace upon solid and as I hope adamantine foundations, I am led to a confident hope that not only morality and Christian piety but also a genuine and purer literature may come to renewed life or greater splendor; especially as this object is pursued with equal zeal in various parts of the world.[21]

---

[21] Letter to Wolfgang Capito, quoted in Myron Gilmore, *The World of Humanism, 1453–1517* (New York: Harper & Row, 1962), pp. 260–61.

This glowing prophecy was written only a year after Pope Leo x had despoiled one of the papal territories to bestow it upon his nephew Lorenzo; two years after the French king Francis I had invaded Italy and seized the duchy of Milan; six months after the same king had wrung from the pope permission to reduce the French church to a subservient branch of the monarchy (by the Concordat of Bologna, August 1516); and eight months before Martin Luther published his *Ninety-five Theses* in Wittenberg. Erasmus was not the only one who read the signs too optimistically. Harder heads than his—Machiavelli's among them—dared believe the hour was near when the tangled affairs of Europe might be brought through crisis to a state of order and stability. The next year his sagacious and prudent friend Thomas More thrust lingering doubts aside to enter the service of one of the "highest sovereigns" in whom Erasmus placed his hopes. Also in extenuation it should be added that this was the period when Erasmus, after many frustrations and disappointments, was approaching the summit of his own career and reputation. Naturally, the prospects before him appeared particularly bright.

Erasmus' naiveté does not diminish his stature as a humanist and a thinker any more than Machiavelli's indignant recrimination destroys his value as a political commentator. Each of these men strove sincerely to come to grips with the problems of their age, and not of their age only. Both failed to a considerable degree, but both, in their very different ways and even in their failures, provided insights extending beyond the confines of their immediate era. It is not easy, or necessary, to determine which of these two contrasting Renaissance figures was more nearly right in his judgments. The political history of the post-Renaissance centuries—marked by the ascendancy of militarized secular states and by insensate conflict among them—seemed to vindicate all too amply the themes of Machiavelli. More recently, with the dawning realization that human survival may depend upon acceptance of some form of world community that would render the untrammeled nation-state an anachronism, Erasmus' impractical vision has begun to take on greater relevance. It is an irony of history, and one of its sources of encouragement, that the hopeless ideals of yesterday become the prosaic realities of today—or tomorrow.

Together with other thinkers of the age, Erasmus, More, and Machiavelli shared a conviction that, without any change in human nature or any drastic altering of institutions, the political order could be made to serve desirable human ends. The most remarkable quality, even in Machiavelli, is not pessimism but a persistent feeling —sometimes enthusiastic, sometimes petulant—that splendid opportunities lie at hand, waiting to be seized upon. Erasmus' great anticipations, though unfulfilled, were not sheer self-delusion. It is too easy to say that optimism, or a restless expectancy, supplied the underlying motif of the Renaissance, which was, after all, the "rebirth" of human confidence and self-assertion. What inspired such an attitude? Was it a sense of release from the decaying medieval order? Was it the perfection of Latin and Greek studies? Was it the emancipation of the intellect from the shackles of religion? The last dictum would certainly not apply to the Christian humanist Erasmus, nor would it apply very fully to most leaders of opinion. Doubtless a whole constellation of factors was responsible. Beyond the visible material changes—at this stage only slight—elusive but significant psychological factors can be detected.

A world of the imagination was opening. Fundamentally it was not so much a new world as a richer and ampler setting for a world that had never been realized or fully explored but had been sketched in the minds of Europeans for centuries. Now, it seemed, the time had come for its actualization. The revival of elements of classical culture—content and spirit as well as forms—provided a stimulus, but not a sufficient one: the classical world was long since dead. Machiavelli implored his countrymen to adopt the old Roman virtues while avoiding the old Roman mistakes; but he could make such a plea in good faith only because he knew that viable and vigorous civic communities had recently developed. Erasmus saw a bright future for his generation if classical intellectual discipline joined forces with Christian piety and compassion. If the wit and wisdom of the ancients—"Saint Socrates" and the rest—could be refined and amplified through the "philosophy of Christ," then human nature might attain its full stature. The thinkers of the Renaissance, visionaries as they may have been, were not repudiating medieval ideals. For their inspiration they drew deeply on the entire European heritage, Christian no less than pagan.

They were disappointed in their high hopes. Italians failed to unite, either under a Borgia or under a Medici, to drive out the barbarians. The instrumentality of power, more and more intensely employed, did not bring stability to Italy or to the rest of Europe.

Erasmus' ideal suffered a ruder shattering than Machiavelli's. Even in the intellectual community he found not peace but a bundle of swords. Instead of uniting in defense of reason and tolerance, men of letters enlisted in the theological conflict that eventually split Western Christendom into hostile warring fragments. Erasmus experienced the fate of all neutralists in an ideological war: he was damned by Catholics and Protestants alike. Needless to say, his maxims for the conduct of the princely office did not become the guidelines by which contemporary sovereigns set their course. The rulers he appealed to were by no means incompetent. The sixteenth century spawned "magnificent monarchs"—from Suleiman the Magnificent, "Commander of the Faithful," in Istanbul to Henry the Hangman, "Defender of the Faith," in Windsor. But insofar as any of these monarchs succeeded, it was by catering to and profiting from the material interests and ambitions of his own subjects. Political tides were not favorable to the ideals of the humanists. These ideals nonetheless were germane to the cultural heritage that nurtured them and relevant to the needs of the time. They are still relevant, though still opposed to the tides of national and international politics.

REFERENCES AND SUGGESTIONS
FOR FURTHER READING

MACHIAVELLI

History of Florence and of the Affairs of Italy (New York: Harper & Row, 1960), with Introduction by Felix Gilbert.

The Letters of Machiavelli, trans. and ed. Allan Gilbert (New York: Capricorn Books, 1961). A selection of letters written between 1498 and 1527, with Introduction by the editor.

The Prince, trans. Luigi Ricci. Also *Discourses on the First Ten Books of Livy,* trans. Christian E. Detmold (New York: Modern Library, 1940), with Introduction by Max Lerner.

INTERPRETATIONS OF MACHIAVELLI

Butterfield, Herbert, *The Statecraft of Machiavelli* (New York: Collier, 1962). An unfavorable judgment.

Chabod, Federico, *Machiavelli and the Renaissance,* trans. David Moore (Cambridge, Mass.: Harvard University Press, 1960). Highly illuminating commentary on critical issues of the Renaissance, extending beyond the confines of politics.

Gilbert, Allan H., *Machiavelli's Prince and Its Forerunners* (New York: Barnes and Noble, 1968).

Gilbert, Felix, *Machiavelli and Guicciardini* (Princeton: Princeton University Press, 1965). Admirable discussion of Florentine conception of politics, humanist influence, and the careers and theories of these two prominent figures.

Hale, John R., *Machiavelli and Renaissance Italy* (New York: Collier, 1960), Teach Yourself History Library. Excellent brief account of Machiavelli's life and his political and literary careers.

Harbison, E. Harris, "Machiavelli's *Prince* and More's *Utopia,*" in William H. Werkmeister, ed., *Facets of the Renaissance* (New York: Harper & Row, 1963).

Mattingly, Garrett, "Machiavelli," in J. H. Plumb, ed., *Renaissance Profiles* (New York: Harper & Row, 1965).

Ridolfi, Roberto, *The Life of Niccolò Machiavelli,* trans. Cecil Grayson (Chicago: University of Chicago Press, 1963). The best biography, not an analysis of Machiavelli's thought.

Whitfield, John H., *Machiavelli* (New York: Russell & Russell, 1965). Erudite, probing, vigorously reasoned; sees Machiavelli as a moralist and as enthusiastic rather than ironic.

Changing interpretations of Machiavelli are summarized by Eric W. Cochrane, "Machiavelli: 1940–1960," in *Journal of Modern History,* 33 (1961), 113–36.

For Guicciardini, see References for Chapter V.

CIVIC HUMANISM

Baron, Hans, *The Crisis of the Early Italian Renaissance,* 2 vols. (Princeton: Princeton University Press, 1955). A highly influential work. Its enthusiastic portrayal of Florentine humanism needs to be balanced by Lauro Martines, *The Social World of the Florentine Humanists, 1390–1460* (Princeton: Princeton University Press, 1963). Also the works of Brucker, Gilbert, Becker, and Martines cited in References for Chapter II.

Garin, Eugenio, *Italian Humanism: Philosophy and Civic Life in the Renaissance,* trans. Peter Munz (New York: Harper & Row, 1965), Chap. II.

NORTHERN CHRISTIAN HUMANISTS

See also References for Chapter V.

More, Thomas, *Utopia,* is available in many editions and several English translations, although the earliest, by Ralph Robinson in 1551, is still a favorite. The Everyman's Library revised edition (New York, 1951) uses modernized spelling, as does Mildred Campbell, *The Utopia . . . , including Roper's Life of More, and Letters of More and His Daughter Margaret* (New York: Van Nostrand, 1947). The latest and presumably definitive edition of *Utopia* is by Edward L. Surtz and J. H. Hexter, Vol. IV of the Yale edition of More's works (New Haven: Yale University Press, 1965), with Latin and English texts (the latter a revision of G. C. Richards' 1923 translation) and extensive notes and commentary. Other translations from the Latin are by H. V. S. Ogden (New York: Crofts Classics, 1949), and Paul Turner (Baltimore: Penguin Classics, 1965).

BIOGRAPHIES AND INTERPRETATIONS OF MORE

Chambers, Raymond W., *Thomas More* (Ann Arbor, Mich.: Ann Arbor Paperbacks, 1958).

Hexter, J. H., *More's Utopia: The Biography of an Idea* (Princeton: Princeton University Press, 1952). A brilliant piece of scholarly detective work and a penetrating analysis of More's ideas and objectives; indispensable.

Roper, William, "The Life of Sir Thomas More," in Richard S. Sylvester and Davis P. Harding, eds., *Two Early Tudor Lives* (New Haven: Yale University Press, 1962). A tribute by More's son-in-law.

Also suggestive are Russell Ames, *Citizen Thomas More and His Utopia* (New York: Russell & Russell, 1969), and Edward L. Surtz's twin studies: *The Praise of Pleasure; Philosophy, Education and Communism in More's Utopia* (Cambridge, Mass.: Harvard University Press, 1957), and *The Praise of Wisdom; a Commentary on the Religious and Moral Problems and Backgrounds of St. Thomas More's Utopia* (Chicago: Loyola University Press, 1957).

ERASMUS

The Education of a Christian Prince, trans. L. K. Born (New York: Octagon Books, 1965).
The Praise of Folly, trans. Hoyt Hudson (New York: Modern Library, 1962). An attractive modern English version with essay and commentary. The Ann Arbor Paperbacks edition (1958) uses the John Wilson translation of 1668.

BIOGRAPHIES AND INTERPRETATIONS OF ERASMUS

Allen, Percy S., *The Age of Erasmus* (New York: Russell & Russell, 1963).
Huizinga, Johan, *Erasmus and the Age of the Reformation,* trans. F. Hopman (New York: Harper & Row, 1957). Includes a selection of Erasmus' letters.
Phillips, Margaret M., *Erasmus and the Northern Renaissance* (New York: Collier, 1965). Interesting and informative.
Smith, Preserved, *Erasmus, A Study of His Life, Ideals, and Place in History* (New York: Frederick Ungar, 1960). An admiring study, gracefully written.

IV

THE CONDITION
OF SOCIETY

Strip us naked, and we shall all be found alike. Dress us
in their clothing, and they in ours, we shall appear
noble, they ignoble—for poverty and riches make all the
difference.
—Speech attributed to a seditious plebeian,
Machiavelli, HISTORY OF FLORENCE, Bk. III, Chap. 3

Whoever is favored little by fortune will not find it easy
to acquire honor and fame by means of his virtues.
—Leon Battista Alberti, DELLA FAMIGLIA, Bk. IV

THE PATTERN OF ECONOMIC CHANGE

Until recently it was assumed that the splendor and magnificent cultural achievements of the Renaissance were accompanied by, and a reflection of, an upsurge of material prosperity. Economic historians during the last few decades have pretty thoroughly demolished this assumption. They find that the Renaissance period in Italy —and apparently in western Europe quite generally—was one not of economic growth but of contraction, stagnation, even depression. Robert Lopez, a proponent of the depression thesis, reports general agreement as to three phases of economic activity between the late Middle Ages and the end of the Renaissance: a crest that reached its apex in the late thirteenth and early fourteenth centuries, a decline or "trough" in the late fourteenth and early fifteenth centuries, another crest in the late fifteenth; and he claims majority support for the contention that the second crest fell short of the first. His claim seems modest enough in view of the fact that Raymond de Roover, in a solid and well-documented study of Renaissance economy, denies the reality of a crest in the late fifteenth century and sees, instead, a deepening depression, citing as evidence reduction in the number of banks and an accompanying shrinkage of international trade.[1] If de Roover's conclusions are correct, an intellectual and artistic climax—the High Renaissance—coincided with severe economic dislocation.

While the causes of decline are not fully understood, its onset was signaled dramatically by the Black Death, which swept Europe in 1347–49. This calamity wiped out at least 30 percent of the total population—in some districts as much as one-half—and it struck again, with lessening severity, throughout the period of the Renaissance and Reformation. The epidemic not only depleted the ranks of society but for a time seemed to impair fertility. Drastically checked after several centuries of continuous growth, Europe's population long remained at a reduced level. Florence, for example, whose population had quadrupled during the thirteenth century, fell from 90,000 inhabitants to 50,000, and did not regain her former numbers until the eighteenth century. Michelangelo's Florence of the High Renaissance was appreciably smaller than Dante's of the early fourteenth century. Florence's experience was typical rather than unique. Not before the sixteenth century did demographic expansion resume in Europe. The slowing down cannot be accounted for by the Black Death, by recurring epidemics, or by the constant warfare of the era. The unprecedented and excessive swelling of population before the mid-fourteenth century has been suggested as a possible underlying cause of the precipitate decline, with the plague, in spite of its horrors, serving as a corrective for an intolerable situation. Whether or not one accepts this Malthusian explanation, there are indications of economic disruption during the earlier years of the fourteenth century. Florence's three leading banking firms failed shortly before the Black Death.

Disputed but impressive evidence points to a definite link between the demographic slump and a reduction in the scale of business operations, possibly of agriculture as well. Though the Medici bank (1397–1494) was an international institution and profitable enough to make its owners' political fortune, it never attained the size of its fourteenth-century predecessors. The Florentine woolen cloth industry, which had been the mainstay of the city's prosperity, fell off heavily during the fifteenth century. Fluctuations between

---

[1] Raymond de Roover, *The Rise and Decline of the Medici Bank, 1397–1494* (New York: Norton, 1966), pp. 3, 16, 372–374.

adversity and prosperity undoubtedly occurred in cities, and there were regional contrasts also. In the case of the woolen cloth industry, Florence's loss was to some extent England's gain, as raw wool began to be processed within the "domestic system" of the producing country. Europe as a whole, in spite of serious reverses, was not becoming poorer. In the northern countries a period of renewed economic growth seems to have begun about the middle of the fifteenth century and accelerated when the voyages of discovery gave direct access to Far Eastern products and to the New World. Nevertheless, the striking fact remains that Italy—cradle and center of the Renaissance—was losing its economic momentum at the very time it rose to the highest cultural eminence it has ever experienced.

Information on economic conditions and trends is sufficient to warrant several general conclusions. First, the direct debt of the Renaissance—and of the whole modern era—to the Middle Ages is larger than has commonly been recognized. The High Middle Ages, culminating in the late thirteenth century, supplied the material foundations on which Renaissance society and culture were erected. The traditional conception of a Commercial Revolution coinciding with the Renaissance has had to be radically revised. It is more in accord with the facts to postulate two commercial revolutions. The first extended from the late tenth to the early fourteenth century. The second, occurring in the sixteenth and seventeenth centuries, inaugurated a new era of expansion that led ultimately to the Industrial Revolution. The earlier revolution, the "medieval" one, was the more fundamental. It contributed a money economy, capital, techniques essential for international trade, and an urban middle class to employ these instruments; it also promoted the rise of autonomous cities which were to serve as focal points of Renaissance civilization. The relative stability and high level of productivity of the late Middle Ages bequeathed a legacy on which men of the Renaissance could draw to advantage, even while failing to replenish it.

Second, a critical comparison of medieval society and culture with the society and culture of the fourteenth, fifteenth, and early sixteenth centuries illustrates the danger of projecting a narrowly economic interpretation of history. The civilization of the High Middle Ages, resting on a sounder material base than any Europe had known since the Augustan age, placed a premium on spiritual goals, delineated in the works of the Scholastic theologian Thomas

Aquinas and the poet Dante. The Renaissance, beset with economic depression and social upheaval, has struck many observers as addicted to tangible, this-worldly, sensuous and sensual satisfactions. The popular impression does less than justice to the Renaissance, for its spokesmen valued the spiritual quest as deeply as their medieval forebears; but it is true that the Renaissance dared exhibit more fully and frankly a delight in material objects and sensations. Actually, there is evidence neither of a conscious shift in defined goals nor of anxiety over the appearance of clouds on the economic horizon. The material base of Renaissance society, though vulnerable, was still adequate not only to meet minimal human needs but to provide leisure for creativity, for reflection on the human condition and the requisites of a good society: it yielded a higher level of prosperity than had ever been enjoyed in the Middle Ages with the important exception of the phenomenal last half of the thirteenth century. Economic adversity did not arrest cultural evolution, nor noticeably retard it; certainly it did not predestine its form or its spirit.

The mood of the early Renaissance—illogical as it may seem— was predominantly optimistic. The Black Death, one of the most devastating calamities in the whole of Western history, failed to dispel the mood or to destroy initiative. Boccaccio's *Decameron* tales, which celebrated the delights of human wit and appetite, were composed while Florence was suffering an epidemic of the plague. The most notable progress toward a democratic state in Florence was accomplished by the generation following the Black Death; at the end of the century Florence emerged as champion of free republics against the tyrants of Milan, and her citizens, though still few in numbers, engaged in an ambitious program of territorial expansion. Italian publicists of the fourteenth and early fifteenth centuries expressed confidence rather than defeatism. The humanist chancellors Salutati and Bruni proudly cited Florence's wealth, her "flourishing" population, and the magnitude of her affairs—at a time when, judging from statistical records, population had dropped by at least one-third and the output of woolen cloth by two-thirds since their early fourteenth-century peak, and when the number of banks and the volume of their business were diminishing. The current of optimism was especially strong in Florence between about 1380 and 1420, reflecting both an economic upturn in the second decade of the fifteenth century and the satisfaction of the closely knit oligarchy that had gained control of the government of the republic. This favored and highly prosperous group could afford to be optimistic and could afford to express its gratitude by patronizing "civic humanism" and engaging in "an activism perhaps unparalleled in the annals of a city-state bourgeoisie since the halcyon days of the Roman Republic." [2] The optimistic outlook of Florentines was matched by inhabitants of other Italian centers. Contemporary chroniclers boasted of the size, wealth, and grandeur of their cities with such fervor that even modern historians, until recently, were inclined to accept their inflated testimonials.

In the long run Italy could not escape the effects of economic changes working to its disadvantage—the growth of the clothing industry in northern Europe, the supplanting of private family banking houses by state banks, the Turks' ousting of Venice from supremacy in the Levant trade, and finally the shifting of world trade routes to the great oceans, made possible by the second Commercial Revolution. Italian cities had long served as middlemen between northern Europe and the Mediterranean lands and had monopolized Europe's trade with the Far East. It is conceivable that they could have seized the initiative in the new era of commercial expansion. They were well equipped technically, they had experienced navigators, and they commanded capital resources greater than those at the disposal of most sixteenth-century monarchs. Italian seamen did contribute to the spectacular exploits of the age of discovery— Columbus was a Genoese, John Cabot a Venetian, Amerigo Vespucci a Florentine. If the leading Italian cities had been willing to combine forces, they might have won an overseas empire in advance of the Portuguese, Spanish, and French; but they were unable to combine even to save their own peninsula from being overrun. As Atlantic seaboard nations developed the great oceanic routes and established colonies in America and the Far East, the Italian trading states, including mighty Venice, lost their position of supremacy.

Renaissance civilization drew upon its inherited medieval capital, both material and spiritual. The fate of this civilization suggests a conclusion that no generation has been willing to accept—that things of the spirit are a more durable investment than consumable goods of this world. The Medici bank, the Venetian galleys, the

---

[2] Marvin B. Becker, *Florence in Transition*, Vol. II (Baltimore: Johns Hopkins Press, 1968), p. 164.

pomp of ducal courts have long since become only historical memories; the rotundas, the chapels, and the canvases and frescoes adorning them—works of dedicated artists paid for by wealthy patrons —remain not only as monuments to the past but as a source of delight and inspiration to the present. While squandering its material substance, the Renaissance did not exhaust its spiritual legacy. It revalued this legacy, enhanced it, and strove to convert it into the experience of living men and women. Unfortunately, it neglected to apply it to redressing the inequities of court, street, and market place.

The mood of optimism did not persist indefinitely. The High Renaissance of the late fifteenth and early sixteenth centuries, while producing the ripest works of genius, was colored by shades of doubt, resignation, and disillusionment, partly attributable to dwindling economic prospects and the collapse of political hopes. But if time had run out for the Italian cities, it was because they had not made the wisest use of the time allotted them. The distortions and injustices within their own societies—far more than the eclipse of the Levant trade or the vicissitudes of banking and industrial establishments—may be blamed for a deepening despondency and the slackening of civic and cultural vigor.

SOCIETY IN TURMOIL

The process of social change that characterized the later Middle Ages became so pronounced during the Renaissance that it makes the medieval order appear stable by comparison The dissolution of old bonds of allegiance led to conflict, confusion, and uncertainty as to the location and extent of authority. The notorious violence of the age has given it a certain lurid fascination. Some shocked observers have interpreted the violence as a sign of moral degeneracy, but it is better understood as a symptom of stress and strain within the social fabric. The changes taking place held the possibility of a freer and more productive society, with a wider range of opportunities, though their more immediate effect was to disrupt traditional restraints and to leave the weak at the mercy of the strong.

Whatever uncertainties attended the upper reaches of society, there is no doubt as to the abject state of the people at the bottom. Increasing social mobility did not bring equality or an improvement in living standards for the majority. Serfdom was disappearing in the more progressive agrarian regions, such as England, France, and the Netherlands, largely because it had ceased to be profitable, but the lowest class of rural labor—unorganized, undefended before the law—sank to the condition of a commodity. In the industrially advanced sections of Europe, merchant entrepreneurs who handled the exporting and importing of valuable wares forced local craft guilds into a subsidiary role or displaced them altogether. Surviving guilds tended to become closed corporations of masters. Journeymen were kept perpetually as wage earners. Even more unfortunate were the unskilled workers outside the guild system or absorbed into newly developing industries which had no guild tradition. Although not yet equipped with factories and heavy machinery, the fifteenth and sixteenth centuries evidenced somber aspects of modern industrial society, including strikes, blacklisting, and exploitation of the labor of women and children.

The numerous towns of northern Italy in the thirteenth and fourteenth centuries successfully extended their rule over adjacent country districts, forced the rural inhabitants to pay heavy taxes while denying them the privilege of communal citizenship, and, in spite of their essentially mercantile character, assumed the position of a feudal lord in relation to the body of country folk who supplied them with food, timber, and other raw materials. Although serfdom was a negligible factor in northern Italy, the institution of slavery revived when the Black Death of the mid-fourteenth century created a labor shortage. Florence, Genoa, Venice, and Siena imported slaves from Near Eastern markets, employing them chiefly as domestic servants.

A scramble for wealth, power, and personal distinction generated emotional excess that readily found an outlet in violence. In the hands of talented desperadoes murder became a fine art, practiced with ingenuity and a variety of methods. The lurid tales of the Borgia family, though largely fabricated, could gain currency because they did not greatly exceed authenticated instances of mayhem and treachery. Benvenuto Cellini's *Autobiography* casually relates his success in dispatching his personal enemies and quotes a pope as excusing him on the ground that "men like Benvenuto, unique in their profession, stand above the law." Although Cellini was an exceptional case and prone to exaggeration, the age showed a remarkable tolerance for outrageous acts that were performed with skill or daring or that contributed to some supposedly laudable end: successful assassins were frequently converted into heroes. "Blessed be the Lord, blessed be the Duke, blessed be this murder"—expressed the popular approval when one rapacious cardinal and papal administrator was dispatched.[3] The sordid accounts of Renaissance feuds suggest that no respect for sex, age, or sacred place could deter infuriated antagonists. The Pazzi conspiracy of 1478 against the Medici brothers called for the murder to be committed in the cathedral during high mass when the victims would be least prepared to resist. In the Romagna twenty people were butchered during one Sunday mass and their slayers absolved, for a consideration, by Pope Alexander vi.

While the most hideous crimes often went unpunished—or were privately avenged at compound interest—the judicial machinery of governments meted out senseless and cruel penalties for minor offences, especially when committed by the poor. The criminal codes of all the civilized states of Europe were barbarous, and remained so until affected by the humanitarian reform movements of the late eighteenth and nineteenth centuries. Counterfeiting, cattle-stealing, jail-breaking, and pocket-picking were only a few of a long list of capital offences. A condemned criminal might be hanged if he was fortunate; he might also be burned at the stake or boiled to death. Beating, branding, and mutilation were lesser forms of punishment, and torture was regularly employed to extract confessions. With the state, the law, and the judges setting such an example, it is no wonder that human sensibilities became blunted.

If there had been no other disasters during the fifteenth and sixteenth centuries, the interminable conflicts raging up and down the continent of Europe were almost sufficient in themselves to prevent the growth of a healthy society. Armed strife has been a feature of practically every epoch of civilization, and the wars of the Renaissance era are not the most important in military history. But while the destructive capacity of Renaissance armies seems infinitesimal by today's standards, it was far greater than could be inflicted by a press of armored knights. Artillery was coming into use, and infantry—cheaper and more expendable than mounted warriors—had begun to play a major role in combat.

The real victims of the wars of the despots were not soldiers or

---

[3] Ralph Roeder, *The Man of the Renaissance* (New York: Viking, 1933), p. 263.

the governments that hired them but civilian populations. Armies customarily lived off the land, robbing, pillaging, laying waste the fields, and raping and murdering the inhabitants. Troops that adhered to a disciplined restraint were a rare exception. It was cheaper for their employer to let them plunder than to pay wages, and *condottieri* found it necessary to offer the incentive of loot to hold the allegiance of their fighting men. Fortified towns might be starved into surrender by a long siege and then delivered to the lust and avarice of the captors. The famous sack of Rome in 1527 stands out as one of the most horrifying incidents of the wars of this epoch. The invading imperial forces, before which Pope Clement VII took refuge in the Castle of Sant' Angelo, included Spaniards and German Lutherans—all of them near the point of mutiny over arrears in pay. The sack, one of the most thorough on record, lasted a month. For days and nights the screams of victims—men, women, and children—rent the air; palaces were gutted, churches, hospitals, and tombs pillaged and smashed; corpses were left to rot in the streets. Almost half of the city's population is believed to have perished during this bestial visitation. The sack of Rome and its accompanying orgy of blood attracted wide attention because of the fame of the Eternal City, but the atrocities were only an extreme example of the common incidents of contemporary warfare.

The mores of the period looked upon war as a normal and necessary human activity. Baldassare Castiglione's idealistic treatise, *The Book of the Courtier,* starts with the assumption that "the principal and true profession of the courtier must be that of arms," and "the more our courtier excels in this art, the more he will merit praise." [4] One of the speakers in the *Courtier,* who criticizes contemporary rulers for neglecting the tasks of peace, stipulates:

princes ought not to make their people warlike out of a desire to dominate, but in order to defend themselves and their people . . . or in order to drive out tyrants and govern well those people who are badly treated; or in order to subject those who by nature deserve to become slaves, with the aim of giving them good government, ease, repose, and peace.[5]

---

[4] Baldassare Castiglione, *The Book of the Courtier,* trans. C. S. Singleton (New York: Anchor, 1959), Bk. I, par. 17.

[5] *Ibid.,* Bk. IV, par. 27.

The escape clauses seem sufficient to cover every alleged *casus belli,* ancient or modern.

Influential writers supported the high priority given to military pursuits as a function of the body politic. Machiavelli taught that the prince's first duty was to master the art of war and to wage it successfully. Religious leaders, including the Protestant Reformers, regarded armed conflict as inevitable if not desirable. To the Reformers the scourge of war could be an instrument of divine judgment, and they taught that subjects must submit to the violence of their rulers, whether directed against themselves or against the people of a neighboring state. Erasmus stood almost alone among intellectual leaders in advocating pacifism. Not surprisingly, those who profited directly from the bloody business showed little interest in halting it. A group of *condottieri,* fearing that Peace might raise her timid head in Italy, exclaimed, "Where shall we go then? We shall have to return to the hoe. Peace is death to us. War is our life." [6]

If man's position was imperiled by the roughness of the times, woman's remained far worse. The alleged emancipation of women during the Renaissance is a myth. Among all classes of society, women were typically regarded as sex objects, of possible commercial value. Legislation relating to female workers was designed to make them available on the labor market rather than to protect them from exploitation. The degradation of women is evidenced by the large number of professional prostitutes (some seven thousand in Rome and upwards of eleven thousand in Venice during the High Renaissance). Both social convention and the law upheld a double standard of sexual morality. Adultery was an acceptable pastime for a husband; a wife's unfaithfulness could be—although rarely was—punished by death. Marriage among members of the middle and upper classes retained the character of a property transaction arranged by parents of the two parties with the girl's dowry serving as inducement to an advantageous contract. The prospective bride might be betrothed at the age of three and married before she entered her teens. Supposedly, women of the aristocracy, reared in luxury and often well educated, enjoyed a greater degree of inde-

---

[6] Leona C. Gabel, ed., *Memoirs of a Renaissance Pope* (New York: Capricorn, 1962), p. 339.

pendence. If marriageable, however, they served as pawns in the game of alliance-building that became an obsession with both large and petty principalities. Many an attractive and high-spirited young woman, sacrificed on the altar of political expediency, was sent off as consort to a total stranger in an uncongenial environment. Surprisingly, some of these bartered brides developed a genuine love for their husbands, overlooked their infidelities, and assisted in the governance of the state or enhanced its luster by holding court for artists and writers.

Amid the pressures and intrigues of a power-oriented society, only a rare woman could carve out a career and win recognition in her own right. To succeed in the arena of politics she had to be of uncommonly tough fiber, able to play a man's game while employing her feminine wiles to take advantage of the weaknesses of the opposite sex. Such a woman was Caterina Sforza, niece of Duke Lodovico of Milan and mother—by her second husband, Giovanni de' Medici—of the heroic captain Giovanni "of the Black Band." Inured to violence (her first husband and two of her lovers were murdered), she repaid her injuries in like coin and with interest, while also giving free rein to her prodigious sensuality. Determined to maintain her rule over two petty states in the Romagna, she pitted herself against Cesare Borgia and paid a high price for her audacity. When she became his prisoner, Cesare took his revenge on Caterina's handsome body and then incarcerated her in a Roman dungeon.

ARISTOCRACY OLD AND NEW

The brutal aspects of Renaissance life are not proof of wholesale corruption or decadence. An age that displayed such exuberance and left such enduring works cannot fairly be called decadent. The seamy incidents, however, do reflect serious flaws in society and institutions. Whatever threat they posed to the general welfare was almost totally overlooked by those in a position of influence and authority, including hereditary sovereigns, the Church establishment, and the nobility. The same lack of comprehension characterized the leaders of capitalist enterprise, the class most responsible for upsetting the old order and the chief beneficiaries of change.

In confronting social and economic issues, little help came

from governments, not, however, from lack of power to act or from any commitment to *laissez faire.* This was an age of despots, when rulers did not scruple to interfere with the private lives of their subjects by prescribing wearing apparel, diet, and style of dwelling for different ranks of society, prohibiting or commanding emigration, suppressing publications, and punishing slight deviations from religious orthodoxy. But national monarchs and territorial princes were unlikely to take the initiative in curing social ills, since they were themselves the source of many of them. In fairness, it should be said that some contemporary rulers displayed intelligence and statesmanship. The best examples of enlightened despotism are to be found among the smaller Italian city-states, but even in the large northern countries the kings performed a valuable service in suppressing internal feuds and establishing common currencies and judicial systems. If they could have bridled their appetite for military conquest, they could have conferred more substantial benefits.

An important aspect of the transformation taking place in the social structure during the Renaissance is the changing role of the nobility. Political and economic trends alike were working to efface the usefulness of a hereditary noble class and reduce it ultimately to a decorative anachronism. In northern and western Europe the rise of centralized monarchies, beginning as early as the twelfth century, undermined feudalism and the power of the feudal barons. The nobles lost their monopoly of military affairs as infantry, artillery, and mercenary commanders replaced the old feudal levy. As an instrument of government, monarchs preferred a professional bureaucracy to a hierarchy of vassals, and tended to pick their servants and ministers from the more docile middle class. In the economic sphere the wealth of landed aristocrats had to compete with the accumulating capital of merchants, bankers, and manufacturers. In Italy, the early growth of an urban society had seriously weakened the position of feudal suzerains before the close of the thirteenth century, ousting them from government of the communes or forcing them to coalesce with a merchant class of humble origin but corporate strength.

Although the ingredients of aristocracy were changing and its essential functions diminishing, the nobles retained much of their former prominence. Still basking in the lingering medieval tradition that had assigned them the place of "Second Estate," outranked only by the clergy, they also possessed great wealth, derived mainly from land but including the profits of forest and mineral exploitation as well as agriculture. In Italy especially, many of them, recognizing that capital no less than land could command the road to power, engaged in trade. Conversely, family fortunes built on business enterprise might elevate their owners to the rank of nobility after a generation or so; but birth was still the easiest mode of access to privilege.

The Church, while fighting savage battles with princely rivals, retained its ancient alliance with the nobility of blood. Its higher officials, normally recruited from their ranks, looked with jaundiced eyes upon the presumptuous aspirations of the common people. Pope Pius II (1458–64) could never forgive the Sienese for having expelled the nobles from their city—his own family among them—and he heaped contempt upon merchants and traders, though he grudgingly conceded that Cosimo de' Medici "was more cultured than merchants usually are." "Traders care nothing for religion," he hissed when angry with Venice, and he explained the alleged rudeness of Venetian ambassadors as "inherited from their fishermen ancestors." Pope Pius was perhaps exceptional in his antipathy toward not only the bourgeois but all the lower classes, whose whole duty as he saw it was to be meek and obedient. He abhorred democracy, and he was so undiscriminating that he applied the term—invidiously—to the oligarchy of Venice.

The prejudice in favor of aristocratic lineage ran deep and found support among eminent critics of contemporary mores. The great Erasmus—himself the illegitimate son of a priest and a physician's daughter—despised those "born from the very dregs of society." In his *Education of a Christian Prince,* while stressing the duty of the ruler to promote the public welfare, he admonished him above all else never to embrace the opinions of the common people. While it is true that many individuals of lowly origin rose to positions of importance through their own talents, it was difficult to dispel the aura surrounding inherited gentility. The great artist Michelangelo retained intense pride in his noble ancestry and assured his father, who had objected to the descendant of a count becoming a mere artisan, that his aim in life was to restore the family to its former status.

While economic forces were disrupting the traditional hierarchy, class consciousness grew even more intense. The combined influence of ingrained prejudice and heated rivalries fostered the belief that if classes did not exist they would have to be invented. The city-states of Renaissance Italy, social and political laboratories, attempted to develop criteria for determining rank and prestige— a difficult task, in view of the mixed origins and changing composition of the dominant factions. In fifteenth-century Florence, requisites for an elevated social position included, first and foremost, wealth—honorably, that is, not too *recently* acquired; second, a record of service in public office; third, descent from a Florentine family of long-standing reputation; and, ideally, marriage connections with another family of economic and political consequence.[7] A ranking of orders in terms of occupation or profession also reveals the close connection between economic and political leverage. International merchants acquired a place at the top, above local businessmen, druggists, or goldsmiths, and far above artisans and small shopkeepers; while at the same time lawyers in Florence rose to a dignified station, above that of physicians and school-teachers, because of their indispensable services to the communal government.[8] Power and social eminence joined together were jealously prized and, in the later stages of the Renaissance, tightly restricted. By the mid-fifteenth century some four hundred families or less controlled the Florentine republic, which they tended to view as their private possession; and a comparable situation obtained in other leading Italian cities, whether republics or principalities.

Whether the ruling elite of Renaissance Italy constituted a nobility is debatable. It has been aptly called a patriciate, a convenient term that avoids the pitfalls of precise definition. It was not identical with the old medieval nobility—not even in Venice, although here the aristocracy had a distinct legal status. In Genoa a feudal aristocracy continued a separate existence beside the urban mercantile oligarchy. Generally the elite community or patriciate was compounded of various elements, including descendants of feudal houses, great merchants and financiers whose wealth had

---

[7] Lauro Martines, *The Social World of the Florentine Humanists, 1390–1460* (Princeton: Princeton University Press, 1963), p. 18.

[8] Gene A. Brucker, *Renaissance Florence* (New York: Wiley, 1969), pp. 102–103; see also Lauro Martines, *Lawyers and Statecraft in Renaissance Florence* (Princeton: Princeton University Press, 1968), p. 476.

accumulated over the span of several generations, and also nouveaux riches, some of obscure antecedents, who managed to brazen their way into social acceptance.

But even when a capitalist economy permeated the power structure of Italian communities, it failed to broaden its base. The patriciate hardened into an aristocracy and closed its ranks as firmly as possible against outsiders. The social mobility characteristic of Italian towns during the thirteenth and early fourteenth centuries virtually ceased by the opening of the fifteenth, with the consolidation of oligarchic regimes. Particularly striking is the example of Florence, where aggressive bourgeois leaders won an early victory over the nobles but were gradually transformed into their likeness. During the fifteenth century a fondness for the affectations of gentility pervaded the upper classes, evidenced in coats of arms, elaborately staged tournaments, and lavish expenditure on dress, building, and entertainment. At the same time the patriciate became less productive economically, dissipating inherited capital instead of augmenting it, or investing in property and deserting the risky world of business for the quiet security of country estates. The trend was by no means universal, nor did it represent a return to feudalism; but the fifteenth and sixteenth centuries witnessed a closer conformity to aristocratic tastes and manners among the upper social strata than had the two centuries preceding, at least in Italy. While the French and Spanish influence that accompanied the invasions of Italy contributed to this development, an equally important factor was erosion of the base of prosperity that had sustained the dominant group. As Italy's economic opportunities narrowed, her ruling classes became less confident and more arrogant. But in attempting to relieve their insecurities by imitating the nobility, they were seeking help from a dubious quarter. The nobles were experiencing an identity crisis of their own.

Hereditary principalities—some insignificant in size—flaunted more openly than republics the doctrine that honors and authority are a birthright of the few. Even petty Italian despots maintained courts and tried to surround them not only with lackeys and retainers but also with writers and artists who could legitimate and add glory to their reign. Among this special order of aristocratic servitors, the one who made the most memorable attempt to formulate a code for the noble class was Baldassare Castiglione in his *Book of the Courtier,* completed about 1518, although not published until 1528, a year before the author's death.

Castiglione was a nobleman's nobleman. Born to the rank of count, educated in the humanist circles of Milan and Mantua, he spent his whole adult life in the service of ecclesiastical and secular princes. He traveled to England and to Spain, where he represented Pope Clement VII at the court of Emperor Charles V; but his fondest memories were of his ten years' association with the small but highly cultivated Italian court of the Montefeltro family, dukes of Urbino. *The Book of the Courtier* is purportedly based on a series of informal but serious discussions centering around the theme of the ideal courtier and his counterpart, the perfect court lady. The participants in the dialogue are real people, some of them distinguished, who were residents or visitors in the ducal household at Urbino in the early sixteenth century. Castiglione represents himself simply as recorder of these remarkable nocturnal conversations, but he admits that he was in England at the time they took place and that he obtained them second hand, through "a faithful report." Whether or not the picture presented truly reflects the ideas of Castiglione's circle, it undoubtedly reflects his own.

The hypothetical figure that emerges from Castiglione's pages is a synthesis of gracious manners and solid virtues. The discussants agree that the courtier—preferably of noble birth—should receive a thorough and well-rounded education, to make him proficient not only in arms and manly sports but also in the gentler arts of music and poetry, dancing, and conversation. The perfect courtier turns out to be nothing less than a humanist scholar (at home in Latin, Greek, and the vernacular) as well as an articulate, knowledgeable, and unaffected gentleman—in short, a man for all places and all seasons and endowed with a winning personality. In spite of meticulous concern for such trivialities as dress, gesture, and the propriety of jokes, the burden of the argument is the overriding importance of sincerity, character, and fidelity to moral principles.

There is something paradoxical about Castiglione's prescription. The creature fashioned with such loving care is designed for a single purpose—to serve a prince. He must apply his knowledge and talents to satisfy the whims of his master. The qualities of integrity and sensitivity demanded by Castiglione seem hardly appropriate for the docile servant of a despot; they might rather be an impediment, leading to hopeless frustration or even schizo-phrenia. This possibility is not overlooked by Castiglione's protag-onists, who approach it with arguments reminiscent of Thomas More's in his *Utopia*. One speaker bluntly asks whether the courtier is bound to commit a dishonorable act at the command of his prince. He is told that in such a case it is the courtier's duty to disobey, but he is reminded that many evil things appear at first sight to be good while others that appear evil are actually good. The logical next question—how one can distinguish what is really good from what appears to be good—is left unanswered.[9]

Perhaps the most provocative aspect of *The Book of the Courtier* is its concern with the moral deficiencies of governments and with the possibility of correcting them.[10] A ruler who has power without knowing how to govern "may be said to be the deadliest plague that exists on earth." Castiglione, who had plenty of opportunity to observe the conduct of rulers, berates them for their abuses, incompetence, and ignorance. Yet the courtier must convert the prince into an instrument of his people's salvation. His task will be no easy one. In the words of the interlocutor:

I say, then, that, since the princes of today are so corrupted by evil customs and by ignorance and a false esteem of themselves . . . the Courtier . . . must seek to gain the good will and captivate the mind of his prince . . . and also, little by little, to inform his prince's mind with goodness, and teach him continence, fortitude, justice, and temperance.

Combining the skills of tutor, entertainer, and psychiatrist, and "using the veil of pleasure," the courtier "will be able to lead his prince by the austere path of virtue." Temperance, the supreme virtue, is not an innate gift of the gods but a quality that can be acquired by all men—even by one so sunk in his vices as a Renais-sance prince.

It was as a book of manners that the *Courtier* retained its popularity for several centuries. But it is far more than that. It touches on a wide range of serious topics, including the role of women and the nature of love. It concerns itself with the good society and offers a critique of politics. In this last respect it may

---

[9] Castiglione, *op. cit.*, Bk. II, par. 23.
[10] *Ibid.*, Bk. IV, pars. 8, 9, 10.

be compared with Machiavelli's *Prince,* though it must suffer by the comparison. The lofty precepts of Castiglione, while inherently worthy, seem far more remote from reality than the steely maxims and barbs of Machiavelli. But just as Machiavelli's writings reflect the bruised idealism of a defeated republican, so does the *Courtier* reflect the malaise of a nobility proud of its attainments but sensing its own obsolescence and frustrated by lack of opportunity for employing its talents purposefully.

Despite its gaiety and sparkle, its wit and optimism, Castiglione's book has something of pathos in it. So does his career. Like Erasmus, he looked hopefully to the young princes emerging upon the European stage—Francis I of France, Henry VIII of England, reared "in all kind of virtue," and Charles of Spain, of such breeding and talents that he might one day "eclipse the name of many ancient emperors." Ingenuous and trusting by nature, Castiglione deceived himself even about the personages of his dialogue; they were not the shining examples of virtue and magnanimity he makes them out to be. Giuliano de' Medici (son of *Il Magnifico* and brother of Pope Leo x), who in the *Courtier* delivers an eloquent tribute to the sanctity of the marriage contract, was a notorious philanderer. After the court of Urbino was scattered in 1516, Castiglione passed his life in faithful service to frivolous or ungrateful employers, bearing the brunt of their wrangles, exhausting his energies and his hopes. This modestly endowed but great-hearted man deserved better of fortune. One of his few rewards was the blessing of a happy marriage—to a girl of fifteen when he was thirty-eight—but this was snatched from him when his young wife died of fever. The final blow was a slanderous attack on his character during his service as papal nuncio in Spain at the time of the sack of Rome in 1527. The man of unimpeachable honor, "one of the best gentlemen in the world," was accused of treachery.

THE CHURCH—A MISSED OPPORTUNITY

The traditional antidote to the iniquities of society and of its secular rulers was the ministration of the clergy. Throughout the Dark Ages and the feudal age the Church had presented a challenge to Caesar and to the heirs of Caesar; it had set the sights by which society might find its course. Although deeply dyed with the sordidness of its surroundings, the medieval Church—or significant elements within it—had retained something of its disinterested character even in the most hopeless periods. It fought to preserve its independent organization and competed successfully with emperors and lords for jurisdiction in both spiritual and temporal affairs. During the High Middle Ages, together with cultural and intellectual leadership, it contributed to economic progress—to improvements in agriculture, to urban growth, to the stability essential to an expansion of commerce. The Church had been injured materially and spiritually by the "Babylonian captivity" of the fourteenth century and by the Great Schism which followed, but its resources were still tremendous, and during the fifteenth century it recovered much of its strength and prestige. Crises in the social, economic, and political spheres during the Renaissance offered the Church a rare opportunity to exert itself anew—at the very least to cushion the shock of change and, at best, to lead in the recovery or redefining of values. Its failure to rise to this challenge could hardly have been more abysmal. Not that the Church was timid or passive. Its officers, by no means reticent, moved in the forefront of contemporary affairs and rose to a pinnacle of influence in matters of taste and aesthetics, but they offered little moral leadership or spiritual sustenance.

The Renaissance Church suffered from the same limitations that hampered the other powerful orders of society. It moved with and conformed to currents of the time, refusing to oppose them unless they threatened its own direct interests. The medieval Church, in spite of its hierarchical structure, had cut across the caste system in important ways and embodied some democratic elements. Men of humble birth could enter its service and, in very exceptional cases, rise to the highest posts. And while striving to retain their own temporal jurisdiction, medieval popes had assisted the eleventh- and twelfth-century communes in their struggle for independence against nobles and emperors. By contrast, the Renaissance Church abhorred democratic movements of any kind and sided with the despots. Its own hierarchy showed an increasingly aristocratic complexion: after the mid-fifteenth century it selected bishops and other high officials almost exclusively from the patriciate —the nobles and the wealthiest of the bourgeoisie. Bought and sold by, and inevitably allied with, great plutocratic houses, the Church could hardly adopt a program unfriendly to their interests.

The deficiencies of the Church cannot be attributed solely

to clerical immorality, the extent and significance of which may easily be overemphasized. All ranks of the clergy, secular and regular, had their share of charlatans, cheats, thieves, and lechers; all ranks were guilty of ignorance, indifference, and sheer incapacity. At the same time, churchmen as a whole were probably somewhat above the average moral level of society, and numbered in their ranks individuals of the staunchest character and dedication to their calling. Chaucer, in his Prologue to *The Canterbury Tales*, presents sharp and amusing sketches of the sleek, hard-riding monk who scorned St. Augustine's austerities and "followed the new world's more spacious way"; of the festive friar who

> knew the taverns well in every town
> And every innkeeper and barmaid too
> Better than lepers, beggars and that crew;

and of the Summoner "as hot and lecherous as a sparrow." But Chaucer pays honest tribute to the humble Parson, poor in goods but "rich in holy thought and work":

> Christ and His Twelve Apostles and their lore
> He taught, but followed it himself before.[11]

For the pornographer in search of ecclesiastical scandal, all roads led to Rome. Conditions in the papal entourage during the High Renaissance, even allowing for exaggeration, were lurid enough. Pope Alexander vi (Rodrigo Borgia) achieved distinction by the variety and intensity of his reputed orgies. Guicciardini, hardly a puritan, called him "a serpent" who, "giving every example of horrible cruelty, monstrous lust, and unheard of avarice . . . had poisoned the whole world," and cited Alexander's continual good fortune as proof that God does not punish the wicked in this life.[12] Whether better or worse than he was painted, Rodrigo Borgia was not the only sinner to occupy the papal chair; prostitution, blackmail, and felonious assault flourished under other pontificates

---

[11] *The Canterbury Tales*, trans. Nevill Coghill (New York: Penguin Books, 1951).

[12] William S. Bouwsma, *Venice and the Defense of Republican Liberty* (Berkeley: University of California Press, 1968), p. 25.

as well. One of Boccaccio's *Decameron* stories tells of a Jew who converted to the Christian faith after a visit to Rome convinced him that any religion able to withstand such depredations as were being inflicted upon it by its own chief ministers must be supported by a supernatural Power. The anecdote illustrates a fairly widespread attitude toward the Roman curia. Contempt for the clergy was often openly expressed, although seldom with the venom of the petty Italian tyrant who declared, "I should be happy if I could see every priest in the world hanged. . . . It would be well for the human race if this scourge of mankind did not exist." [13] The excessive numbers of clergy, both secular and regular, made them particularly burdensome in Italy, which contained almost as many episcopal sees as all other countries of western Europe combined. At the same time, Italians were jealous of the fame of their Eternal City and of its preeminence in Western Christendom. Humanists and artists, while embarrassed by the scandals of the curia, felt obliged to keep the horn of plenty flowing. The historian Guicciardini confided:

I know of no one who loathes the ambition, the avarice, and the sensuality of the clergy more than I. . . . In spite of all this, the positions I have held under several popes have forced me, for my own good, to further their interests. Were it not for that, I should have loved Martin Luther as much as myself.[14]

Machiavelli hated the papacy, not only for its corruption but for its pursuit of policies that divided and ruined Italy. In *The Prince* he reserved his bitterest sarcasm for the chapter on ecclesiastical principalities, whose rulers "alone have states without defending them, have subjects without governing them." In the *Discourses* he subscribed to the prevalent judgment that "the nearer people are to the Church of Rome, which is the head of our religion, the less religious are they." [15] But Machiavelli gave no more support to the Lutheran revolt than did his younger friend Guicciardini, and he angled hopefully for a papal appointment.

---

[13] *Memoirs of a Renaissance Pope, op. cit.*, pp. 334–335.

[14] *Maxims and Reflections of a Renaissance Statesman,* trans. Mario Domandi (New York: Harper & Row, 1965), p. 48.

[15] Machiavelli, *Discourses on the First Ten Books of Livy,* trans. Christian E. Detmold (New York: Modern Library, 1940), Bk. I, Chap. 12.

On the whole the Renaissance popes, not all of whom were vicious or debauched, reflected the vigorous spirit of the age and contributed to its record of accomplishment. They tightened authority over the Papal States, augmented their revenues both by taxation and by selling offices and dispensations, and if they failed to make life safe in the city of Rome they transformed the capital into a deservedly famous center of beauty, wit, and learning. They embraced lustily all the principal pursuits of the Renaissance, emphatically including the race for power, employing their extensive resources, their not inconsiderable personal talents, and whatever they could muster of waning spiritual prestige to bolster their position as local monarchs and dominate the savage game of Italian politics. Such a preoccupation, disastrous both for Italy and for the Church, blinded them to other responsibilities. A vague sense of the hollowness of their achievements haunts the frivolity and meretricious excess of the papal court under Pope Leo x, the Medici who followed that master builder Julius ii. The Leonine age was a golden one for the swarm of venal functionaries trafficking in indulgences, no less than for the artists and writers who were patronized so lavishly. In view of his wanton dispersal of his family's wealth and of the Church's, the statement attributed to Leo—"Let us enjoy the papacy, since God has given it to us"— should have been coupled with Louis xv's "After us the deluge."

The corruption and worldliness of the Church does not prove that religion was dying or that the Renaissance was "pagan" at heart. Christianity remained a vital and potent influence, illuminating the works of the greatest artists and philosophers and also stirring a ferment in society at large. Impatience with conventional forms, and discontent with the meager spiritual fare being offered, provoked anticlericalism among laymen and anticurialism among enlightened clergy, but not an abandonment of faith. People sought new interpretations of religion, new modes of expression relevant to their own experience and needs. Some men of wealth and piety showed their dissatisfaction with traditional religious practices by making charitable donations not to endow monasteries and convents, which now seemed of doubtful usefulness, but to found hospitals or schools.

Proof of a deep attachment to religious values are the efforts on behalf of Church reform, in which many educated persons shared. A reform movement agitated within the Church long before the celebrated Catholic Reformation of the sixteenth century. It sought to raise moral standards through personal example and also to reactivate reform proposals which the great Councils of the early fifteenth century had entertained but never put into effect. Emphasizing piety and sincerity as opposed to dogma, it was evangelistic in spirit, linked to the devotional mysticism of the late Middle Ages. Although the movement originated independently, it anticipated several of the doctrines that Protestants eventually embraced. With objectives similar to those of the northern Christian humanists, the evangelical reformers called for purification of the Church, the revival of general councils, decentralization of Church government, and greater participation by laymen. They went beyond exhortations to righteous living to emphasize the role of faith; a few even advanced the position that salvation depends on faith alone, coming as a free gift of God to sinful man—essentially Luther's doctrine of justification by faith.

The evangelical movement, active before and during the Renaissance, arose from various quarters—from the Netherlands, Germany, Spain, and Italy itself, where the influence of Savonarola continued long after his death. Italian reform took concrete shape in the "Oratory of Divine Love," a society of clergy and laymen founded at Rome in 1517, and gathered momentum during the early sixteenth century in Venice, where it attracted sympathetic response among both upper and lower classes. In 1513 a group of Venetian clergy, led by the learned humanist theologian and ecclesiastical statesman Gasparo Contarini, petitioned Pope Leo x to effect reforms in the Church. Renaissance popes, however, chose to ignore or rebuff those who advised them to put their own house in order, until the Protestant rebellion, by threatening the loss of all northern Europe, finally stirred them to action. Contarini headed a commission of cardinals that presented a sweeping set of proposals to Pope Paul iii in 1537. His plea for reconciliation with defecting Protestants fell on deaf ears. The Reformation popes of the middle and later sixteenth century weeded out long-standing abuses, tightened ecclesiastical discipline, and infused the Church with a new and militant vigor; but the success of the Catholic Reformation—requiring conformity in ritual and belief and undeviating allegiance to a monarchical institution—entailed the defeat and suppression of liberal Catholic reform.

The peculiar nature of the Renaissance papacy and its relationship to currents of the age can perhaps be seen most clearly neither in the period of decadence nor in the Reformation that followed, but in its adolescent stage, particularly through the career of a remarkable pope of the fifteenth century. Pius II (1458-64) has sometimes been chosen to illustrate the "typical man" of the Renaissance, though he lived before the High Renaissance and though he brought an atypical degree of dedication to the papal office. Trained in the law and in humanist scholarship, a facile and prodigious author, he was one of the most avid observers of his century, and he performed the invaluable service of preserving his reflections for posterity in a verbose but startlingly frank autobiography known as the *Commentaries of Pius II*.[16]

Born of an impoverished noble family from Siena, Aeneas Sylvius Piccolomini made his way from penury to riches and power by the ladder of Church preferment. Beginning as a bishop's secretary, he was picked by the Emperor Frederick III as secretary and Privy Councilor, and appointed Apostolic Secretary by Pope Eugenius IV. In 1447, at the age of forty-two, he formally entered the priesthood and within the space of three years became successively Bishop of Trieste and Bishop of Siena. He obtained the cardinal's hat in 1456 and only two years later, at the death of Calixtus III, was elected pope and assumed the name of Pius. The six years of his pontificate testify to his resolution and toughness of character. Unfortunately they also constitute a brilliant exercise in futility.

As Pius conceived it, the main tasks of the papacy—and sufficiently demanding ones—were to maintain a compelling public image and to exercise adroit political leadership. The entire ecclesiastical apparatus was enmeshed in politics, indistinguishable from the kind practiced in secular states except that it took on a bizarre quality from an interlarding of conventional piety and from the fact that churchmen were adept at imputing the loftiest motives to the most calculated maneuvers. Pius's own *Commentaries* sufficiently reveal both the ecclesiastical political atmosphere and his complete acceptance of it. With unblinking candor he recounts the proceedings of the conclave of cardinals which elected him pope. To outwit his chief rival for the Holy Office, Guillaume, Bishop of Ostia and Cardinal of Rouen, Aeneas approached his colleagues individually,

---

[16] *Memoirs of a Renaissance Pope, op. cit.*

warning or encouraging, and probing the sensitive spots of each. With a blast of worldly wisdom he jarred the Spaniard Rodrigo Borgia (the future Alexander vi), who was anxious for his post of Vice-Chancellor: "You young fool! Will you then put an enemy of your nation in the Apostle's chair? . . . you will find yourself among the hindmost, if a Frenchman is pope." Skillfully he blended the claims of honor, propriety, and personal ambition: "Where is your conscience: your zeal for justice? your common sense?" The twelve votes needed for an election were eked out as the waverers "acceded" to the Bishop of Siena, in spite of Rouen's attempt to forestall the final decision by dragging one of the members out of the room.

For Pius ii, as for secular territorial lords, war was a major instrument of policy. He fondly describes his three huge artillery pieces capable of hurling stones that could smash a wall twenty feet thick, and tells how he named this unholy trinity—one after his mother and two after himself. Shortly after dictating a bull of canonization for the peace-loving Catherine of Siena, he set forth to review his cavalry and delighted in the sparkle of harness and armor: "For what fairer sight than troops in battle array?" And if the troops "devastated the country far and wide, ruining the ripening grain everywhere," it was only a just punishment for the "mad presumption" of opposing the pope and "the righteous vengeance of God."

In the vicissitudes of war and politics the popes could use their spiritual prerogatives to terrorize, to cajole, to sanctify their side of every dispute. Their extravagant claims—too naive to be hypocritical—indicate a large and perhaps fatal blind spot in their vision. Pius ii, as revealed by his own account, was a practicing Machiavellian, without Machiavelli's qualms and doubts. He could vary his tactics, trim and tack, stand on the rock of the Divine Will or bow to the dictates of prudence. He could even accept defeat; but it never occurred to him that he was fighting the wrong campaign. Frequently he found himself compelled to compromise a principle or to sacrifice the best interests of the Church.

In its late medieval twilight the papacy could still thunder, although the earth no longer trembled. Once, in castigating the Venetian republic, Pius struck a note of eloquence both apt and prophetic: "The state is your God." And he warned the Venetians, "This god of yours will perish, I say will perish! Do not think it is immortal. . . . No power was ever greater than the Roman Empire and yet God overthrew it." Pius failed to see that his prophecy applied with equal force to the sacerdotal empire over which he proudly presided. When the citizens of Rome were recovering from a murderous epidemic of hooliganism that had raged unchecked for weeks, Pius reminded them of their singular good fortune in having as ruler no mere duke, king, or emperor, but one who "truly is called King of Kings and Lord of Lords."

To most contemporary Italians the benefits bestowed by the Church seemed great enough to outweigh its faults. Possession of the papacy established Italy's primacy over all other European nations. As Pius ii phrased it, "We still have the Apostleship though we have lost the Imperium." If this was an empty boast, the Church purveyed more tangible favors. The physical presence of the pope and his retinue excited the people. They might fight his armies in the field, but crowds thronged to welcome or even drag him into their cities and sometimes struggled so roughly over the privilege of carrying his chair that his cavalry had to drive them back with arrows and lances. The pope traveled with a bodyguard.

Ancient Roman emperors had provided bread and circuses for the populace. If the popes gave little bread they at least offered circuses on a prodigious scale. The pope was ex officio grand master of ceremonies, keeper of the revels, supreme showman of Renaissance Italy. The age was fond of pageantry, and most Italian towns staged a variety of spectacles—tournaments, processions, races, festivals, and carnivals. But none could equal the carnival of Rome. It presented all the splendors of pagan mythology sanctified by the hallowed traditions of Christianity. Gods and goddesses, nymphs, dragons and giants mingled with the glorious company of saints and martyrs. Pius relates in detail the celebration of the Feast of Corpus Christi at Viterbo in June 1462. He had the entire street leading from the citadel to the cathedral widened and remodeled. Each cardinal was assigned his own section to decorate and each tried to outdo the others. Crowds thronged into Viterbo from neighboring areas "for the sake of indulgences or to see the show." In one exhibit a youth, impersonating the Savior, sweat blood and filled a cup from the wound in his side. A tableau of the Last Supper, with Christ and the disciples, included the figure of St. Thomas Aquinas administering the sacrament. St. Michael beheaded a huge dragon, while out of the monster, "demons fell headlong baying like hounds."

There were flowers, triumphal arches, lavish tapestries, altars of gold and silver, fountains of wine, choirs and orchestras, handsome boys representing angels perched on pillars or swinging from ropes. As the pope approached Borgia's area—a seventy-four-foot span with a purple curtain enclosing a sumptuous bed chamber—two singing urchins chanted, "Lift up your gates, O princes, and King Pius, lord of the world, will come in." Around a model of Christ's tomb erected in the town square, a group of figures enacted the drama of the Resurrection, complete with soldiers, angels, and light and sound effects. Even this tour de force was perhaps surpassed by a spectacle in front of the cathedral—the Assumption of the Blessed Virgin Mary—in which a "most lovely girl" was borne aloft on the hands of angels and, while ascending heavenward, "dropped her girdle into the outstretched hands of an apostle." Before the excitement of this mammoth celebration had subsided, a sudden epidemic of the plague struck the city. While the terrified cardinals fled to safer quarters, Pius reflected: "O flesh! O life of men! how fragile and how fleeting ye are!"

The most colossal fete arranged by Pius was intended to further his ultimate ambition as head of Western Christendom—a crusade against the Turks. Ever since the capture of Constantinople in 1453, he had cherished the scheme of a great crusade, and he clung to it with stubborn tenacity in the face of repeated discouragements. At last the advance of Turkish arms into Greek territory gave him an instrument he hoped would be useful in his plan to roll back the infidel tide in the East. A tyrant of the Peloponnesus, driven out by the Ottomans, had carried off from its sanctuary in Patras a head reputed to be that of St. Andrew the Apostle. Outbidding other European courts, Pius persuaded the exiled despot to surrender the sacred prize to papal agents at Ancona on the Adriatic coast, while he made elaborate preparations for its reception. By Palm Sunday of 1462 all was in readiness. Three cardinals were commissioned to escort the relic to the outskirts of the Eternal City; proclamations sent throughout the land offered plenary remission of sins for all who came to Rome; and Pius noted with satisfaction that the influx from Italy and the Transalpine countries equalled the previous record set by Nicholas v's jubilee.

Through all the pomp and carnival atmosphere, Pius never lost sight of his ultimate objective. His public address, nominally directed to the severed head of St. Andrew, was intended to arouse the crowned heads of Europe. But the monarchs had their own domestic problems and were too bitterly embroiled with one another to join in such an expensive and dubious undertaking. Though Pius was the last to admit it, the age of crusading was past.

When all attempts to arouse the kings had failed, Pius fell back on the one remaining recourse. He called upon the clergy and curia to purge themselves of their vices and return to the example set by Christians of the Apostolic age: "It is not enough to be confessors and preach to the peoples. . . . We must draw near to those earlier saints who gave their bodies as witnesses of their Lord." He had never been more sincere. In proof, the tired old man, swollen with gout and suffering from a variety of ailments, prepared himself to sail against the Turks with whatever forces chose to accompany him. Aeneas the humanist, the sophisticate, the calculating politician, the pontiff who reveled in pageantry and craved to be hailed as "lord of the world"—Aeneas chose to end his days by taking the cross and seeking martyrdom. He bade farewell to the Rome he loved, waited at Ancona for the arrival of promised Venetian ships, and died without leaving the harbor, on August 14, 1464.

Like the charge of the Light Brigade, Pius's final gesture was magnificent, but it was neither war nor a return to the Church's historic mission nor a sacrifice destined to commit the Church to any of the critical issues confronting European society. Still, with all his superficiality, Pius did make an effort to inject high purpose into the churchly office, which is more than can be said for most of his successors during the next hundred years.

THE PATTERN OF SOCIAL CHANGE

European society during the Renaissance was in a state of commotion with little sense of direction, beset with problems that have continued to our own day. It is a moot question whether the movement of social forces was toward a condition of greater freedom for the individual. Burckhardt hailed the Renaissance for its "discovery of the world and of man," which he interpreted as the necessary step to the modern age of progress and liberty. Doubtless some aspects of Renaissance civilization did make for freedom. It was a time of splendid opportunities for gifted and resolute individuals. The man who surpassed his fellows in skill, knowledge, or power was certain to be looked up to, even when envied or feared. Although aristocratic prejudices remained deeply implanted, hereditary social barriers could be broken, and in exceptional cases the accident of birth might be overlooked—a number of famous Renaissance figures were born out of wedlock. The humanists' liberal estimate of man's potentialities encouraged self-assertiveness and allowed the individual to regard himself as the focal point of his universe and give high priority to the demands of his own personality.

The much acclaimed individualism of the Renaissance, however, needs to be carefully examined. Renaissance thinkers, while extremely interested in individual personality, were highly selective in their preferences. Their emphasis was upon the elements of difference, of distinction, not upon those of identity. They honored the "universal man." They were generally indifferent to the needs, condition, or even the existence of the majority of ordinary mortals. It is tempting to seize upon individualism as the hallmark of an age that inspires admiration, because this concept has played such a prominent part throughout the whole modern era. The history of the Western world during the last five hundred years can be written in terms of the increasing recognition and expanding role of the individual. But individualism is an abstraction; its validity can be analyzed only in context, as an operating principle in the institutions of a particular time and place. The more familiar and the more widely accepted the concept becomes, the more it tends to degenerate into an *ism* or to dissolve into its opposite, as our own age has so starkly demonstrated.

The repudiation of medieval corporate ties—no longer applicable in the light of national and regional differences and the growing complexity of cosmopolitan centers—did not establish a condition of freedom, but it necessitated a search for new principles of authority. The search was neither intensive nor very successful, partly because it demanded long and arduous effort and partly because it was easily perverted into a scramble for personal advantage. The problem of reconciling authority with freedom is a perpetual one, not yet resolved, and men of the Renaissance can hardly be condemned for failing. But neither can an era that witnessed the destruction of safeguards protecting the individual against abuses of power, and that left him exposed to the caprice of a dominant few, be viewed as the dawn of freedom. Absolutism triumphed in the western European monarchies, tyranny and oligarchy in the Italian city-states.

The tentative and halting, but still promising, steps toward democracy taken by the late medieval communes were almost completely obliterated in the republics of Renaissance Italy. Among Italian states, Venice probably came closest to achieving a society in which individual security and dignity were preserved under the restraint of effective government. This fabulously rich republic, endowed with a maritime empire and controlled by a closely-knit nobility, was not a democracy, nor a utopia. It was reputed to be overly materialistic, gaudy, and licentious. Nevertheless the Venetians, during their period of greatest splendor and prosperity, managed to keep a reasonable concord between the rights of the individual and the claims of the state. Their accomplishment explains the much envied stability of the Venetian constitution and the remarkably low incidence of revolutionary or class strife. The common people, although denied political initiative, were protected at Law and had the benefit of an extensive public welfare program, including medical facilities, subsidized food distribution, and old-age pensions. With a disciplined citizenry and—significantly—an equally disciplined ruling class, a relaxed atmosphere developed, tolerant of individual differences that did not endanger public order. Venice permitted a degree of freedom of speech that Petrarch in the fourteenth century regarded as excessive, offered asylum to political exiles from other states, and encouraged both a variety of religious opinion and participation by laymen in affairs of the Church.

Venice was an exceptional case and, even though exceptionally fortunate, not a perfect model for all time. By and large, the recognized leaders of Italian Renaissance society—the nobility, the Church, the richly endowed patriciate—showed little initiative and offered feeble guidance in the problem of adapting institutions to human needs. What of the middle class, that prosaic but indispensable remnant that is expected to come to the rescue in times of stress? The answer is that the middle class was in retreat, a dwindling force in Renaissance society. In a broad sense, its emergence in the late Middle Ages had made the Renaissance possible. The activity of merchants, manufacturers, and bankers had laid the groundwork for an advanced civilization and remained a potent influence throughout the Renaissance. Italian cities reached the peak of prosperity, and retained as much of it as they could, by exploiting the types of enterprise usually associated with bourgeois initiative. Nevertheless, what these communities lacked during their proudest years was the balance of a broad middle stratum within their societies.

The rise of the bourgeoisie had been a striking and revolutionary phenomenon of the late Middle Ages, beginning as early as the eleventh century. Though small, medieval towns developed sufficient solidarity among their inhabitants to enable them to unite effectively for common economic and political objectives. The splendid Renaissance cities, when not ruled by a tyrant, were in the hands of a patriciate which had fattened on the fruits of commerce and industry but which, monopolizing both economic and political benefits, assumed the prerogatives of a nobility. By the late fourteenth century, concentration of wealth at the top of the social pyramid had begun to divide and polarize urban society, and this disruptive trend continued during the next two hundred years or longer. Tax returns for Florence in the mid-fifteenth century (1457) reveal that 82 percent of the city's households were poor, one-third of them actual paupers, and eleven families—2 percent of the population— extremely rich. Such powerful families as the Medici and Strozzi, though of *popolani* origin, had risen to the level of high bourgeoisie and aspired to reach even higher. Obviously the middle class had shrunk to a small and ineffective minority. Not only in Florence but in other northern Italian cities the broad and vigorous middle class of the thirteenth century had grown small and weak by the fifteenth, with far more of its members sinking to proletarian status than ascending higher.

It is true that what might be called a bourgeois mentality had taken shape before the close of the Middle Ages, and during the Renaissance permeated the whole social structure, including its aristocratic top layer. The patriciate, as it eclipsed the middle class, still projected the profile of the hard-driving businessman, honoring possessors of wealth and exalting the profit motive. The Church's ancient prohibition against usury, if not openly repudiated, was deftly circumvented, especially under the impact of self-made capitalist entrepreneurs. Large-scale financiers had for long successfully contended that their peculiar transactions fell within the strictures of canon law. While lauding the operations of international bankers and wholesale merchants as productive and ennobling, prevailing opinion looked down upon petty moneylending as degrading and sinful, and made pawnbroking—tolerated as a necessity—technically illegal. Centuries before Calvin and the so-called Protestant ethic, the growth of a capitalist economy in Catholic Europe had engendered the doctrine that private profit is public good and that riches are the reward, if not the necessary prerequisite, of virtue. Even the ascetic reformer Savonarola promised the Florentines that moral regeneration would bring great material blessings to the chosen city of God. Most of the humanists, in spite of their genuine commitment to intellectual and spiritual values, did not oppose the materialistic tide. They were themselves among its beneficiaries, sprung from the upper classes or welcomed as loyal allies and apologists.

The bourgeoisie, though a significant segment of Renaissance society and active within it, played an ambiguous role, unsustained by any ideological program of its own. In the large European monarchies successful kings could bend all classes to their will—nobles and burghers, merchants and country gentlemen. The civic humanism of the northern Italian cities withered as it accommodated to despotism. An oligarchic patriciate, while skimming off the ablest middle-class talents, acquired not only the manners but the cautious conservatism of an aristocracy. The urban middle-class movement, temporarily blocked by the Renaissance, eventually resumed with accelerating force and with far-reaching effect upon the course of civilization. Yet, throughout the centuries the bourgeois protagonist—now hero, now villain—has preserved an ambivalent character. Resourceful, supple, but willing to sell himself to the highest bidder, he has been both the hope and the despair of modern society. Desire for profits led him to put a premium on efficient administration for the sake of order and stability; but the regimes developing in Europe were bound to produce disorder because they equated law with the interests of a sovereign responsible to no higher tribunal and reduced the European community to a condition of international anarchy. The bourgeoisie supported monarchs in their rise to absolutism; later they led the revolutions which overthrew royal absolutism. In the nineteenth century they created the machinery of democracy; in the twentieth century they helped dictators destroy democracy.

The petty bourgeois of Renaissance times, having refused to join forces with the wretched masses below him, and having been gradually excluded from the seats of the mighty, clung desperately to the precarious position he still retained. Caught in the press of competition, the small entrepreneur tended to keep his eyes on the main chance, while deferring to codes inherited from the past and to the custodians of right and truth in this world and the next. "In the name of God and of profit"—the heading adorning the double-entry ledgers of a Prato firm—is an invocation to personal ambition but hardly subversive of the status quo. A wealthy Florentine merchant who advised his fellows to distrust both the ignorant rabble and the nobles admonished them also to shun political office: "Remain in your shop. The merchant's hands should be ink-stained."[17]

REFERENCES AND SUGGESTIONS FOR FURTHER READING

ECONOMY OF THE LATE MIDDLE AGES AND RENAISSANCE

Cambridge Economic History of Europe, Vol. I (2nd ed. 1966), Chap. VIII; Vol. II (1952), Chaps. IV, V, VI, VII; Vol. III (1963).

de Roover, Raymond, *The Rise and Decline of the Medici Bank, 1397–1494* (New York: Norton, 1966). Definitive study of Medici finances and illuminating for economic trends in Italy and Europe as a whole; a landmark in economic Renaissance scholarship.

Lopez, Robert S., "Hard Times and Investment in Culture," in Wallace K. Ferguson *et al.*, eds., *The Renaissance* (New York: Harper & Row, 1962). *The Three Ages of the Italian Renaissance* (Charlottesville: University of Virginia Press, 1970). Lively essays.

Lucki, Emil, *History of the Renaissance*, Vol. I: *Economy and Society* (Salt Lake City: University of Utah Press, 1963).

Luzzatto, Gino, *An Economic History of Italy from the Fall of the Roman Empire to the Beginning of the Sixteenth Century*, trans. Philip Jones (New York: Barnes and Noble, 1961). A judicious work.

More recent full-length treatments include Robert S. Lopez, *The Commercial Revolution of the Middle Ages, 950–1350* (Englewood Cliffs, N. J.: Prentice-Hall, 1971), and Harry A. Mis-

---

[17] Jean Lucas-Dubreton, *Daily Life in Florence in the Time of the Medici*, trans. A. Lytton Sells (New York: Macmillan, 1961), p. 140.

kimin, *The Economy of Early Renaissance Europe, 1300–1460* (Englewood Cliffs, N. J.: Prentice-Hall, 1969).

A famous scholarly debate on Renaissance economic trends is Robert S. Lopez and H. A. Miskimin, "The Economic Depression of the Renaissance," *Economic History Review,* 2nd Series, XIV (1962), 408–426; opposed by C. M. Cipolla, *ibid.,* XVI (1964), 519–529 (with rebuttal by Lopez and Miskimin).

An able summary of changing interpretations of Renaissance economy is given by David Herlihy in the introductory chapter of his *Medieval and Renaissance Pistoia* (New Haven: Yale University Press, 1967).

SOCIETY AND SOCIAL CLASSES

Breisach, Ernst, *Caterina Sforza, a Renaissance Virago* (Chicago: University of Chicago Press, 1967).

Castiglione, Baldassare, *The Book of the Courtier,* trans. Charles S. Singleton (New York: Anchor, 1959). Everyman's Library edition (New York: 1928) uses Sir Thomas Hoby translation of 1561. An abridged edition is Friench Simpson, trans. (New York: Frederick Ungar, 1959).

Crane, Thomas F., *Italian Social Customs of the Sixteenth Century and Their Influence on the Literatures of Europe* (New Haven: Yale University Press, 1920). Deals chiefly with etiquette, style, and pastimes of courtly society.

Goldthwaite, Richard A., *Private Wealth in Renaissance Florence: A Study of Four Families* (Princeton: Princeton University Press, 1968). Denies any significant decline in business initiative among the Florentine patriciate before the sixteenth century.

Lucas-Dubreton, Jean, *Daily Life in Florence in the Time of the Medici,* trans. A. Lytton Sells (New York: Macmillan, 1961). Interesting anecdotes, thumbnail personality sketches, and unsubstantiated gossip.

Martines, Lauro, *The Social World of the Florentine Humanists, 1390–1460* (Princeton: Princeton University Press, 1963). Valuable material is also found in the works of Martines, Brucker, Becker, and Bouwsma cited in References for Chapter II.

Origo, Iris, "The Domestic Enemy: The Eastern Slaves in Tuscany in the Fourteenth and Fifteenth Centuries," *Speculum,* 30 (1955), 326–366.

Smith, Preserved, *The Age of the Reformation* (New York: Holt, Rinehart & Winston, 1920). Chapter X ("Social Conditions") of this classic is still rewarding reading although Smith, following the tradition of Max Weber, Werner Sombart, and R. H. Tawney, assigns too positive a role to the bourgeoisie.

von Martin, Alfred, *Sociology of the Renaissance*, trans. W. L. Luetkens (New York: Harper & Row, 1963), with Introduction by Wallace K. Ferguson. A brief treatise interpreting Italian Renaissance society as dominated by a high bourgeoisie who assimilated and monopolized humanist culture; stimulating argument but abstract and schematic.

THE CHURCH

Becker, Marvin B., "Church and State in Florence on the Eve of the Renaissance (1343–1382)," *Speculum,* 37 (1962), 509–527.

Gabel, Leona C., ed., *Memoirs of a Renaissance Pope* (New York: Capricorn, 1962). An exceedingly useful abridgement of the *Commentaries of Pius II,* trans. Florence A. Gragg and Leona C. Gabel, Smith College Studies in History, 5 vols. Fascinating and revealing.

Gilbert, Felix, "Religion and Politics in the Thought of Gasparo Contarini," in Theodore K. Rabb and Jerrold E. Seigel, eds., *Action and Conviction in Early Modern Europe: Essays in Memory of E. H. Harbison* (Princeton: Princeton University Press, 1969).

Gilchrist, J. T., *The Church and Economic Activity in the Middle Ages* (New York: St. Martin's, 1969). A thoughtful examination of changes in the Church and its position in society.

Grimm, Harold J., *The Reformation Era, 1500–1650* (New York: Macmillan, 1954).

Lucki, Emil, *History of the Renaissance*, Vol. II; *The Church and Religion* (Salt Lake City: University of Utah Press, 1964).

New Cambridge Modern History, Vol. II: *The Reformation, 1520–1559*, Chaps. VIII, IX.

Partner, Peter, "The 'Budget' of the Roman Church in the Renaissance Period," in Ernest F. Jacob, ed., *Italian Renaissance Studies* (New York: Barnes and Noble, 1960).

V

LETTERS
AND LEARNING

*Dante Alighieri, who dwelt in the house of Philosophy . . .
awakened those half-sleeping sisters, the Muses, and
drew Phoebus back to his lyre.
[Petrarch] revived in noble spirits the hope which had
almost died, and showed that contrary to the belief of
many, the way to Parnassus is open and its summit
accessible.*
—Giovanni Boccaccio, LETTER TO JACOPO PIZZINGHE

THE HUMANIST MOVEMENT AND ITS INFLUENCE

In the narrowest sense the Renaissance was a literary movement,
initiated by a classical revival and characterized throughout by a
consuming interest in both oral and written expression. Logically,
literature should have constituted the essence and crowning achievement of the era; yet this is not unequivocally the case. In view of
the high level of talent during the Renaissance, the quantity of
writing, and the adulation accorded the world of letters, it is remarkable that so much of the product has little permanent worth
as literature. Of the voluminous Latin works, relatively few are any
longer of interest except to specialists. The only two that have retained wide popularity are brief and atypical—*Utopia*, by an Englishman, and *Praise of Folly*, by a Dutchman who considered it
one of his lesser efforts. The most treasured items in the Renaissance
literary storehouse are, with few exceptions, written in the vernacular rather than in the Latin and Greek so highly touted by the
humanists. Furthermore, several of the greatest masterpieces are
identified with regions other than Italy. This certainly is not because Italians were less gifted than French, Spanish, or English

118

writers; nor should it suggest that the indebtedness of the rest of Europe to Italy for Renaissance culture has been exaggerated. The Renaissance was primarily an Italian manifestation, and Italian influence played an important part throughout. The phenomenon illustrates, rather, how difficult it is to predict or determine the course of literary development. Inevitably, local conditions and interests stamp their characteristics upon a writer and mold the channels of expression. National schools of literature were emerging, and Italians had no nationality. Italian humanists—inclined to scorn the rest of Europe as too barbarous to deserve much notice—thought of themselves as leaders in promoting a universal culture which, because its roots were in classical Rome, would always center around them. Actually, the bonds of unity among Europeans were becoming weaker, and the cultivation of scholarship and belles-lettres could readily be turned to the interests of particular groups, sects, or nationalities.

National literatures matured rather late, and it could be argued that those which boast of geniuses surpassing the Italian masters do not belong to the Renaissance at all. The argument cannot be settled because there is no clear dividing point between the Renaissance and more modern times and because some literary and artistic elements stemming from the Renaissance have been employed ever since. The Spanish Renaissance was certainly a very limited affair, completely overshadowed by the Catholic Reformation. Yet Cervantes—perhaps in spite of this "Renaissance" rather than because of it—produced one of the great novels of all time. The age of Elizabethan drama is usually regarded as the climax of the Renaissance in England. Shakespeare, who had no peer in Italy or elsewhere, knew "small Latin and less Greek" and did very well without them. No doubt the creative geniuses of the period and the evolving national schools of literature all exhibit certain Renaissance characteristics, but it is useless and misleading to attach to them the same common denominator.

One must search in vain for a single literary work encompassing the substance and ideals of the Renaissance in the same measure that the *Divine Comedy* epitomizes the age of Dante and Aquinas. Petrarch's beautiful Italian poems, models for his successors and prized down to our own day, sprang from the tradition of medieval courtly love poetry, and Petrarch did not regard them as his greatest contribution. Boccaccio's gusty tales illustrate the skill of a good story teller with a keen sense of timing and of the topical. The love lyrics and carnival songs of Lorenzo de' Medici are admirable for their spontaneity, grace, and youthful spirit of abandon, but they reflect only one small segment of Lorenzo's personality. Machiavelli wrote brilliant comedies, yet no one would think of him primarily as a dramatist; his fame lies in his serious essays on politics and warfare and in his history. Even the prince of humanists, Erasmus—so prolific that he almost seemed to swim in ink, and one of the most effective writers in the whole Western tradition—left no real literary masterpiece. He came closest to it in the *Praise of Folly*, which was intended partly as a diversion for his friends and partly as a tract for the times.

It is a striking fact that three of the greatest literary figures of the Italian Renaissance—Dante, Petrarch, and Boccaccio—appeared at the very beginning. Dante (1265–1321), whose genius overshadows the others, was primarily a man of the Middle Ages, whence he drew the religious faith that inspires the *Divine Comedy*. But in spite of shifting viewpoints and attitudes, he exerted a powerful influence over his successors. His most tangible contribution to the development of Italian literature was his defense of the vernacular and his choice of it for his most important work. By writing immortal poetry in the Tuscan tongue (pretending it was not a Florentine dialect but "Italian") he gave the people of the divided peninsula a common linguistic bond and a vehicle for artistic expression that would long outlast the Renaissance. Although Petrarch's life (1304–74) overlapped Dante's, he differed from Dante so markedly that he seems to herald a new era. Nevertheless, he was in many ways closer to Dante than to writers and thinkers of the later Renaissance. Giovanni Boccaccio (1313–75)—a somewhat wayward disciple of Petrarch and ardent admirer of both Petrarch and Dante—was intelligent enough to recognize his inferiority to both but gifted enough to make a significant contribution of his own.

Petrarch (Francesco Petrarca) cannot be considered merely as a figure in literary history, even though he was among the most talented, vigorous, and appealing of all writers. His poetry—sonnets, lyrics, and other forms—was praised by some Renaissance critics as superior to that of the ancients. But his chief function, as he conceived it, was to rehabilitate the literature of classical Rome, and his activity in this behalf earned him the posthumous title "father of humanism." He urged his friends to join him in the search for lost manuscripts; he pored over classical texts and extolled the diction and style of the Augustan age, even though his own Latin retained traces of the medieval vehicle that he disliked. He longed to communicate with the ancient authors he read and admired, and he composed letters addressed to many of them—"father" Cicero, "brother" Vergil, Livy, Seneca, Homer, and others. He was not a victim of hallucination nor was he trying desperately to escape from the present. He believed these ancient spirits could be made to speak again to the men of his own day and to those who would come after him. Petrarch himself composed one famous autobiographical essay addressed to posterity.

The "revival of learning" begun by Petrarch was an important achievement and a force that continuously influenced the interests, attitudes, and ideals of writers throughout the Renaissance and beyond. The scholars who devoted themselves to restoring ancient letters and to recovering the full dimension of the literary heritage of Greece and Rome came to be known as humanists, a term with varying connotations but one that invariably suggests a breadth of interests and sympathies. Petrarch, who pioneered in the rediscovery of long neglected texts, adopted as his motto a line from Terence: "I am a man, and nothing human do I consider alien to myself." From one standpoint the humanist movement appears as an esoteric enterprise of a small group of scholars, and a reactionary one, in that it looked back to a vanished past rather than to the future. Actually it was far more than this and, though it did have limitations, the charges of sterility and pedantry leveled against it are scarcely fair. It is true that the search for old manuscripts became an absorbing vocation, accompanied by a rather indiscriminate enthusiasm for ancient writers. And it is not surprising that some classicists in the excitement and pride of discovery allowed their admiration of ancient models to lead them into slavish imitation. The term "Ciceronianism" designated a kind of occupational disease to which devotees of the new literary activity were exposed and to which many succumbed, although Petrarch, initiator of the cult of classicism, had warned against it. At the very end of the Italian Renaissance Pietro Bembo, eminent humanist scholar and literary arbiter of the age of Leo x, refused to budge from an uncompromising Ciceronianism in Latin discourse, although he also recognized the merits of the Tuscan dialect employed by Dante. A cardinal of the Church, Bembo hesitated to read St. Paul's Epistles for fear they might corrupt his style. Other Latinists, however, opposed the craven imitation of any author living or dead, and Bembo's far greater contemporary, the Dutch Erasmus, wrote a book against the Ciceronians and demonstrated with his own pen that classical Latin, and classical Greek as well, could be used as a living language to express fresh and forceful ideas.

The dividing line between scholarship and pedantry is always a thin one, and this was as true during the Renaissance as in other times. Many instances could be cited of a narrow-minded attitude inhibiting spontaneity. Just as conservative champions of scholasticism resented every attack upon the inviolability of their traditions, so did the innovating humanists attempt to establish their own inflexible standards. The study of Greek was retarded for a time not only by the scarcity of good teachers but also by the indifference of the Latinists. Even in the fifteenth and sixteenth centuries when Greek studies were flourishing, there was still a tendency to look upon Roman civilization as the greatest of the pre-Christian era and to assume that the Romans had assimilated whatever of value the Greeks could teach and then had surpassed them. The veneration of Latin and Greek also incited an attitude of contempt for the "vulgar" dialect of ordinary speech, particularly in fifteenth-century Italy.

In spite of limitations and distortions, the humanist movement —in Italy or in the countries to which it spread—cannot be dismissed as reactionary. The goal of the humanists was not actually a return to an archaic past, even though their veneration of the literary giants of antiquity sometimes approached idolatry. The attempt to recover the body of ancient literature, the comparative study of manuscripts, the work of editing and annotating all served to sharpen the tools of critical analysis. Moreover, and equally important, the "new learning" stimulated the imagination of its disciples and opened to them new vistas for exploration in the present. While primarily devoted to grammar, rhetoric, poetry, and history, the humanists concerned themselves with a generous spectrum of experience. They took an active interest in community affairs, and they aspired to set the tone not only in literature and discourse but also in aesthetics, manners, and education—in all that relates to the good life, including the area of moral values.

Petrarch was honored by later humanists as the one who "opened the way" to the acquisition of learning. But although rightly regarded as having launched a movement that spread over much of Europe, he was too complex and many-sided to be easily classified or to be relegated to the position of a vague father figure. When he said "I look forward and backward," he meant that he stood between a distant ancient world of light and a present one of ignorant darkness, but to later generations he seems to stand between the obscure medieval world and the brighter modern one. In some respects he foreshadows the modern temper. Endowed with a lively intellect and a warm, vibrant personality, Petrarch was keenly sensitive to events and currents of his day but at the same time deeply introspective. He yielded to sensuality but yearned to sublimate his appetites, he deprecated his own talents but craved approval, and he pretended to despise the fame he so eagerly sought after and received in generous measure. In an age of ignorance and superstition he distrusted miracles, rejected astrology, and evinced a healthy skepticism. With his ambition, his passionate attachments, and his foibles, he stands out as a full-fleshed human being as well as a scholar and rare creative artist, and although he professed to be ill suited to the age in which he was born he would have made his mark in any age.

Yet Petrarch in his contrasting attitudes and inner conflicts suggests at the outset the contradictions that were to plague the entire Renaissance. Like those who came after him, he was excited by the prospect of restoring a golden age of letters. He believed his work would be of lasting benefit to mankind. The perfecting of grammar and philology, the editing and emending of texts, to which he contributed so much, he regarded as a necessary step in recovering the wisdom of the past, which in turn would ensure a more satisfying life in the present. But he was at the same time afflicted with doubts, not only about the degree of response to his message but about the adequacy of the message itself.

Although Petrarch recognized the great distance that separated the past from his own day, his imagination made the glories of antiquity live again. He developed a deep and lyrical devotion to the city of Rome—not as the capital of Christendom (which in his day it was not) nor as the seat of the Holy Roman Empire (as Dante regarded it) but as the Eternal City, center of civilization. In the Rienzo affair of 1347 he fell victim to his romantic dreams and forgot the distance separating the golden age of Rome from his own. Cola di Rienzo, an adventurer enamored of the legends and symbols of antiquity, seized control of the city of Rome for a brief period and proclaimed the restoration of the ancient republic. Calling himself "Tribune of Liberty" and "illustrious prefect," he defied the noble families that dominated the city during the pope's absence in Avignon, and he eventually conceived himself as member of a new trinity—with the pope and the emperor—which would make Rome once again the capital of the world. Although Cola di Rienzo's program was fantastic and hopeless from the start, Petrarch thrilled at its boldness and hailed the man as the reincarnation of Romulus, Brutus, and Camillus—"Author of Roman liberty, Roman peace and Roman tranquility." [1]

Not only did Petrarch's dream of a reborn Roman state collapse; even his dedicated faith in the nobility of the Latin language was ill rewarded. His own Latin was not sufficiently polished to escape the reproaches of pedantic classicists of the following century, and he himself, in composing a group of penitential psalms, resorted to the strong ringing cadence of the Vulgate Latin Bible. A long epic poem in imitation of Vergil (*Africa*), intended to be his supreme achievement, remained unfinished and is seldom read. Far happier is the fate of his sparkling shorter poems in the vernacular—even though while writing them he lamented the poor judgment of the public that denied him a sufficient audience of Latin readers.

Finally, Petrarch's classical armament proved least adequate in dealing with moral problems, an area he considered more important than scholarship or any intellectual attainment. Although enchanted by the cool and balanced temper of Cicero, he insisted he was a member of no philosophical sect—Aristotelian, Epicurean, or Stoic —but was first and last a Christian. He sought for a happy union of the Ciceronian and Christian dispensations, but he developed his humanism within the bosom of the Church—indeed, with its assistance, as ecclesiastical sinecures awarded him by the pope gave him leisure without onerous obligations. He accepted Christianity unquestioningly, including its commendation of asceticism. To his brother, a Carthusian monk, he wrote fervent letters deploring the shame of carnality, describing conception as a sin and the body as a "vile prison." In melancholy moments he turned for solace to St. Augustine, the great fountainhead of Christian pessimism and transcendent faith. Late in life he wrote: "I am a clumsy searcher . . .

---

[1] Quoted by Myron Gilmore in William H. Werkmeister, ed., *Facets of the Renaissance* (New York: Harper & Row, 1963), p. 82.

I flee error and fall into doubt. . . . Thus I have finally joined that humble band that knows nothing, holds nothing as certain, doubts everything—outside of the things that it is sacrilege to doubt." [2]

The inner struggle that tormented Petrarch is depicted strikingly in a little book which he called the *Secret* and which he kept to himself during his lifetime. It is in some ways the most remarkable of his writings. Apparently intended as a kind of spiritual purge for its author, it is so deeply perceptive psychologically that it has deservedly been called "the first great example of literary introspection." [3] In 1342–43, when he wrote the *Secret*, Petrarch was undergoing a period of crisis. He had just accepted a church benefice but was troubled by feelings of sin and unworthiness. While his brother prepared to take the vows of the austere Carthusian order, Francesco was having an illicit affair. Actually he worried less about the temporary carnel liaison with an unnamed woman—who bore him a daughter—than about his highly poeticized love for Laura, a married woman he had been worshipping from a distance, and chiefly with his pen, over a period of sixteen years. Seeking release for his inner tensions, he wrote his "secret book," casting it in the form of a dialogue between St. Augustine and himself, with Truth in the figure of a woman sitting in silent judgment. St. Augustine charges Petrarch with wasting his time and talents, in pursuit of false images of good: "What are you doing, poor little man? What are you dreaming?" He strikes at things dearest to the poet's heart—his craving for fame, his fascination with beauty. When Petrarch argues that his love for Laura is pure and ennobling, as shown by his verses to the lady, the stern saint replies that all earthly love is sinful because it diverts the soul to adoration of the creature rather than the Creator. Admitting his weakness in becoming infatuated with a woman, Petrarch also lays bare his vanity, confessing his persistent and calculating efforts to have the laurel crown awarded him in a ceremony at Rome. He even jibes at his own pedantry, explaining that he has been white-haired since youth, like Domitian, Pompilius, and Vergil—to which Augustine retorts: "If you had been bald you would have dragged in Julius Caesar!"

---

[2] Quoted by Morris Bishop in J. H. Plumb, ed., *Renaissance Profiles* (New York: Harper & Row, 1965), p. 8.

[3] Morris Bishop, *Petrarch and His World* (Bloomington: Indiana University Press, 1963), p. 213.

While it is clear that St. Augustine wins the debate, it is equally clear that Petrarch will not renounce his chosen path—at least not yet. "The care for mortal things must come first in mortal minds; eternal concerns will succeed in their turn to the transitory." Meanwhile he can only pray, "May the storms of my spirit subside, and the world be silent, and fortune molest me no more." Petrarch weathered the crisis in solitude and, fortunately for posterity, continued to dedicate his talents to study and writing. He never resolved the dilemma of opposing value systems but he strove, usually with good cheer, to advocate the cause of letters, not for its own sake but as an adjunct to the quest of morality and the good life.

The paths opened by Petrarch were broadened into highways by Italian humanists of the next two centuries. While perfecting their classical Latin and, during the early fifteenth century, adding to this a knowledge of Greek and translating Greek classics into Latin, they also acquired a position of leadership in various fields of culture. Encompassing a wide range of viewpoints and interests, they differed from one another and sometimes engaged in violent quarrels. But although the humanists formed no guild, fraternity, or philosophical school, they did hold certain tenets in common. Jealous guardians of refined discourse, they also believed themselves to be purveyors of truth. They aimed to unite rhetoric and philosophy, or, more grandly, eloquence and wisdom. Humane letters—rhetoric, poetry, oratory, and history—they upheld as the true basis of knowledge and ethics, in preference to the formal curricula in law, medicine, and theology which the universities had inherited from the Middle Ages and with which the humanist program competed.

There were inherent contradictions in the thought and teachings of the humanists which they never completely succeeded in reconciling—opposition between the art of persuasion and the discipline of reason, between intuition or sentiment and logic, between the truth derived from experience or custom and that attributed to revelation. Efforts to resolve these contradictions produced a mass of arguments and apologetics which necessitated examination of various philosophical traditions and extended beyond the confines of purely literary scholarship. The humanists did not view their intellectual problem as a conflict between reason and faith, between the secular wisdom of the pagans and the spiritual wisdom of Christian revelation. Practically all of them considered themselves Christians and acknowledged the validity of Christianity, however far removed their personal conduct may have been from the example of Christ and the saints (Christian humility was the least conspicuous of their virtues). They believed that familiarity with the sophisticated gentility of ancient Greek and Roman thinkers need not threaten the faith of a true Christian but could broaden and enrich it. However, their synthesis of Christian and pagan value systems was superficial and highly theoretical, a literary excursion rather than a basic rethinking in terms of the live issues of their own day.

Italian Renaissance humanists performed a valuable and lasting service in restoring a large body of neglected classics, raising the standards of scholarship, broadening and vitalizing educational curricula, and, beyond these specific contributions, directing attention to the great questions that eternally confront mankind. They entered the lists in behalf of beauty, goodness, and freedom. Nevertheless, the humanist movement suffered from deficiencies that prevented it from attaining its full objectives. With all their emphasis upon the central importance of man and the necessity of understanding him, the humanists almost entirely ignored the analytical approach to human nature, preferring to rely upon Greek and Roman aphorisms or their own preferential judgments—often noble but entirely subjective. A more serious limitation is that the humanists were part of, or closely identified with, a privileged elite and, consciously or unconsciously, shaped their ideas accordingly. They exalted Man but regarded most men as unworthy of notice; they hailed liberty but made their peace with and adorned the courts of tyrants. Another fundamental defect was their excessive devotion to the models of antiquity and their tendency to substitute eloquent discourse for original thought. In the long run the reliance upon rhetoric led to sterility, even in the area of literature.

THE ITALIAN LITERARY RENAISSANCE

Although the roots of Italian literature reach far back beyond the Renaissance, its development was necessarily greatly affected by the ascendance of the humanists. The most memorable authors were those who, while accepting humanist canons of form and taste, kept them from stifling an original talent. Giovanni Boccaccio, Petrarch's younger friend and disciple, merits a place among these rare few, even though much of his work is conventional and imitative. Boccaccio has often been cited as proof of the emergence of secular attitudes out of the mists of medieval religiosity that had shrouded the world of Dante and Petrarch. This is far from accurate. His literary works incorporate a number of contrasting elements—earthy sensuality and ascetic piety, shrewd common sense and erudition, realism and romantic fancy. While Petrarch addressed himself to a small circle of scholars, Boccaccio bestowed his talents freely to entertain —though his audience was still more aristocratic than bourgeois.

A prose composition of his early youth, entitled *Fiammetta* after a Neapolitan lady and which explores the tortures of unconsummated love, has been called the first psychological romance in literary history. *Decameron*, the masterpiece that earned Boccaccio the title of founder of Italian prose, is a loose collection of stories culled from diverse sources and illustrating pungently the varied facets of human nature. Many of the tales hinge upon such themes as a wife's infidelity, the rewards of craft and deceitfulness, and especially the stupidity, greed, and concupiscence of the clergy. One, for example, relates with delicious innocence how a young maiden seeking instruction in holiness is seduced by a hermit monk who gladly teaches her to "put the devil in hell."

In spite of the bawdy abandon and the racy, irreverent humor of the *Decameron*, Boccaccio cannot be considered a revolutionary breaking with the past or the apostle of a new secular temper. Like his mentor Petrarch, he was torn between conflicting loyalties, but his emotional and psychological tensions are not wholly explained in terms of the rival claims of literary ambition and a longing for salvation. They are related also to doubts as to the proper function of literature and the models it should strive to emulate. In some respects Boccaccio remained more medieval than Petrarch. This is illustrated even by the *Decameron*, his most original, uninhibited, and successful work, which has been called with some justification "the inarticulate side of the Middle Ages come to definite expression." [4] Not only are many of the tales derived from old fables and folklore—including moralizing anecdotes from medieval sermons— but also the characters, situations, and the exposure to ridicule of the frailties of clergy and laity alike follow a well marked medieval vernacular tradition. There is no brooding over the human condition in the *Decameron*, no vaunting of man's grandeur nor bewailing

---

[4] J. H. Whitfield, *Petrarch and the Renascence* (New York: Haskell House, 1969), p. 23.

of his depravity, but a cheerful acceptance of men and women as they are. And just as there is no blasphemy or serious impiety, neither is there "humanism" in the Renaissance sense.

Boccaccio did become a humanist, but one who was more diligent than enthusiastic. At Petrarch's urging he dutifully applied himself to Latin studies and, though handicapped by the lack of a competent teacher, attempted to learn Greek. During the last twenty years of his life he wrote mainly in Latin, industriously producing a series of learned and encyclopedic works which won the admiration of contemporaries but are of relatively little value for the history of European thought or letters. The most remarkable of these Latin efforts is the *Genealogy of the Pagan Gods,* a mythological encyclopedia divided into fifteen books—medieval in its legalistic formulas and extensive use of allegory but containing a spirited and eloquent defense of poetry.

Boccaccio deserves his place as a Renaissance literary figure because of his positive effect upon Italian prose and poetry. His mythological pastorals—reflecting the courtly life of Naples where he spent part of his youth, and contrasting markedly with the unaffected realism of the *Decameron*—were echoed by later poets, including Lorenzo de' Medici, and influenced the pastoral romances that became popular at the end of the fifteenth century. But he illustrates both in his life and his works what a powerful sway the Middle Ages retained over the inaugurators of the new era. One revealing trait in Boccaccio's makeup is his attitude toward Dante. Petrarch—who had to defend himself to Boccaccio against the charge of jealousy—could muster no enthusiasm for his renowned compatriot, whom he reproached for committing a major work to the vulgar tongue. Boccaccio, on the other hand, unceasingly admired Dante, wrote a life of the poet and a commentary on the first sixteen cantos of the *Inferno,* and at the very close of his life felt honored by an invitation to lecture on the *Divine Comedy* at the University of Florence. It is true that Boccaccio worshipped his hero from afar and that he was not able to penetrate very deeply into Dante's thought, but he was fully aware of his greatness. And although the sensuality that enlivens his early Italian works transgressed Petrarch's standards of decorum, his capitulation to the self-denying otherworldly ideal was more unconditional than Petrarch's. Notwithstanding his mocking jests at the knavery and silliness of ecclesiastics, Boccaccio revered the Church and her teachings and eventually entered the priesthood.

In his later life he repented of his youthful amorous follies with an abjectness that would have pleased a St. Bernard.

The directions marked out by Dante, Petrarch, and Boccaccio led ultimately to a distinctive Italian literature, but only after a long struggle to establish the respectability of the language these pioneers had employed so effectively. Many humanists viewed with scorn the dialects spoken by the people and upheld pure Latinity as the touchstone of literary excellence. With support in official circles, the classical obsession reached a climax in the late fifteenth and early sixteenth centuries. Fortunately, some talented writers of the fifteenth century, notably Lorenzo de' Medici, dared to use the "vulgar," and it found influential champions, including the prominent architect and man of all talents, Leon Battista Alberti. While the vernacular gradually won recognition, sectional rivalries provoked argument over which Italian dialect qualified as the true vulgar. Tuscan was bound to prevail because it was the most polished and had been adopted even by those who deprecated it and claimed to be writing in a purer Italian. Further debate ensued over the proper form of Tuscan. Pietro Bembo, most celebrated Latinist of the early 1500s who nevertheless lent his weight to the cause of the vernacular, argued for the fourteenth-century Tuscan of Petrarch, which had already become archaic. Machiavelli, with characteristic local patriotism and disdain for affectation, adopted and defended in his writings the living language of contemporary Florence. It was the living language that emerged victorious and vigorous enough to make the sixteenth century a great age of Italian poetry and prose.

The long controversy over language produced mixed results. Latin scholarship, and eventually Greek, matured and established itself firmly in school curricula; and the vernacular, far from being stunted by its competition with Latin, actually grew richer. On the other hand, the battle of the pedants wasted time and energy and left a heritage of artificiality and formalism.

The numerous types of fifteenth- and sixteenth-century Italian literature were derived chiefly from classical models, although short lyric forms—including the sonnet and *canzone* brought to perfection by Dante and Petrarch—were also utilized. In spite of abundant talent, literature did not evolve spontaneously. It was less an outpouring of popular experience and feeling than something imposed from above by craftsmen jealous of their function and prerogatives. As the body of writings increased, along with it grew a school of critics, who undertook to define authoritatively the style, character, and purport of the several genres, their formulas leaving little room for original statement or free play of imagination. Aristocratic though it was, Italian society appeared not aristocratic enough to satisfy the arbiters of literary taste, who would refine it by imposing their own canons of art. They created a literary hierarchy to delineate an ideal social hierarchy.

Sixteenth-century critics generally accorded the epic highest literary rank, not only because of adulation of Vergil and his Rome but also because the epic glorified the heroism of born aristocrats and illustrated their essential role as rulers of the people. In the field of drama they placed tragedy above comedy, as had the ancient Greeks, but not so much for its cathartic value as its aristocratic nature. Critics insisted that characters in a tragedy must be of noble birth, with commoners rigidly excluded, and that the ideal tragic hero is a king. Comedy, they held, should portray the life of middle-class people—again excluding laborers and paupers—and should show that their lot is happy so long as they shun vices and accept their humble role in the life of the state. Italian critics of the sixteenth century expounded a theory of literature as class conscious as that of a twentieth-century Marxist, although from an opposite point of view. They esteemed literature for its propaganda value, equating it with the interests of a privileged aristocracy or an inflexible monarchic political order, and they went so far as to assert that poetry is by its very nature aristocratic, can be practiced only by one of gentle birth, and serves to purge the citizen of emotions dangerous to the state.

The critics, dependent on the patronage of Renaissance princes, were more royalist than the king, more aristocratic than the nobility. They could not make society as hierarchical as they viewed it in their imagination, nor could they force every writer into their mold. Still, class prejudice and the exalting of form over content damaged the quality of Italian belles-lettres. The stilted tragedies of the period are of little merit, and by far the best comedies were contributed by Machiavelli, whose works antedate the rules formulated in the later 1500s. His justly famous *Mandragola* was hardly calculated "to chastise vices and make the audience shun evil ways." What this cleverly constructed and wittily wicked piece seems to demonstrate is that virtue is a vulnerable and impractical commodity. The play's theme is the betrayal and seduction of a resolutely faithful wife by means of a stratagem in which her father confessor—a venal friar —plays a key role; and the plot's success is celebrated in church and in the presence of the duped husband.

The epic or "heroic poem" dominated sixteenth-century Italian literature and, in spite of its derivative origin and artificiality, was handled with skill and depth of feeling by a few gifted poets. In choosing the epic as vehicle, poets made their task doubly difficult. Vergil's great *Aeneid,* though not indigenous, was well suited to the age of Augustus, a period when the Roman Empire had been brought under the rule of one man who epitomized the political traditions of an entire nation. Italians had no Augustus, were not a nation, and were not being drawn together into a single state. The true epic is born of a heroic, semibarbarous age like the Homeric, or like the feudal age that produced the *Song of Roland.* Lacking both the proper milieu and a native epic hero, Italian poets imported Roland (Orlando) from the medieval French *chanson de geste* and, around his legendary deeds of prowess against the Saracens, wove their fanciful tales. But while choosing their protagonist from the early European feudal age, they enveloped him in the atmosphere of late medieval chivalry with its elaborate and ritualized cult of love. Hence, the Italian epics bore a distinctly romantic flavor. The greatest of them is the *Orlando Furioso* of Lodovico Ariosto (1474–1533).

Ariosto, a sensitive spirit with insight into human emotion and character, had also a fine ear for the music of words. His long poem —over which he labored for some twenty-five years—is a remarkable example of craftsmanship, deservedly admired for its delicate, haunting beauty. Its rare excellence, however, underlines the remoteness of the sophisticated literary tradition from the realities of contemporary life. In Ariosto's hands, the obsolete paraphernalia of chivalry become purely symbolic and decorative. He introduces magical devices and freely mingles the credible with the incredible—not to startle the reader nor because the plot demands it but to suggest that things appearing to be real may actually be only fantasy. What does come through as real, beneath the fascinating play of light and shadow, are not the escapades, the shifting landscapes, or the war of Christian against Saracen, but the devious and indelible traits of human nature, which Ariosto probes with sympathy, restrained irony, and sometimes cutting comment. A memorable passage, relating to the hero's temporary insanity brought on by the waywardness of his beloved (hence the *furioso* of the title), describes a visit to the moon by one of the knights to recover Orlando's missing wits. On the moon he finds everything that has been lost on earth, including the pomp of fallen kingdoms, broken vows, bellows for blowing up empty promises, much time and money squandered, but not a speck of folly: the earth still holds it all. And this aristocratic poet of "gentle disillusionment" confounds the aristocratic ethos in his treatment of the fair but fickle Angelica, an Indian princess who is the chief object of pursuit throughout the poem. Unable to love any of the knights who languish, fight, and go mad over her, she gives herself to a low-born page, a Saracen "of mean desserts."

With his sense of balance, decorum, and psychological acuity, Ariosto held up a mirror to urbane society; but in transforming the sprawling materials of his predecessors into a unified work of art he refined away its epic qualities. His message is not the glory of heroic deeds but the fragility of human hopes and strivings.

THE USES OF HISTORY

The Renaissance witnessed a growing awareness of the importance of history and brought forth a large body of historical literature. Devoting greater attention to the thread of secular events than had their medieval predecessors, humanist writers contributed substantially to the foundations of modern historical scholarship and historiography. Medieval ecclesiastical chroniclers—with some notable exceptions—had paid homage to the timeless while occupying themselves with the trivial. Renaissance historians were most interested in their own times, but they tried to relate them to what had gone before. Admiration and nostalgia for the grandeur that once was Rome stimulated archaeological studies. In the fifteenth century Flavio Biondo and Poggio Bracciolini prepared careful descriptions of ancient Rome, utilizing topographical and numismatic evidence as well as manuscript sources. The critical approach of the humanists, together with their demands for solid factual knowledge, helped to disperse masses of legendary material that had stood unchallenged for centuries. Historians began to disregard accounts of miracles and divine intervention in human affairs. They inquired into the ancestry of contemporary peoples, no longer content to credit their descent from a mythical hero-founder. They tried to reconstruct the history of individual cities and, gradually, of Italy as a whole. Some investigators attempted to penetrate beyond Roman records in search of origins and, even more significantly, abandoned the stock concept of the persisting unity of the European community under the Holy Roman Empire. As they became cognizant of the changes that had taken place since the decay of Rome, they began to view these changes as not entirely for the worse but as essential to the evolution of the Italian communes. Flavio Biondo, apparently first to use the term "middle ages," dated their beginning with Constantine's division of the Empire in the early fourth century, and he showed some grasp of their significance as a distinctive period rather than a barren interlude.

In northern and western Europe, where the traditions of chivalry were deeply imbedded, the new analytical attitude toward history encountered stronger resistance. Before the close of the fifteenth century, German scholars were discarding the legends that attributed the founding of German cities to fugitives from the Trojan wars, while in France, Burgundy, and the Low Countries, the knightly epic and romance still engaged the imagination of historians. In England the tales of King Arthur's Court and of the knights of Troy, Charlemagne, and Arthur dominated the literary scene through the early Tudor period. Polydore Vergil, an erudite Italian humanist residing in England in the reigns of Henry vii and Henry viii, startled the citizens of his adopted country by producing a history of England rejecting the fables of British origins found in Geoffrey of Monmouth's twelfth-century account, which had traced British descent from the Trojan Brut. Vergil's *English History,* rich in detail and remarkably objective, was an official history, commissioned by Henry vii to add luster to the Tudor dynasty, and it struck a note congenial to awakening nationalist sentiment. By the sixteenth century the influence of Italian historiographers had left its mark. In the northern countries as in Italy, the trend was toward factual, secularly oriented historical studies that utilized original materials but generally displayed a patriotic bias.

The fact that the humanists handled their materials with skill and discrimination does not mean they produced faultless or definitive histories. Italians in particular held the ancient Latin authorities in such reverence that they were loath to subject them to critical evaluation. While scorning the fables of medieval tradition and Christian mythology, they generally accepted the secular ones of Livy and Plutarch. And many Italians became so enamored of the art of rhetoric, resurrected from classical models, that they sacrificed both accuracy and depth to elegance of style. Flavio Biondo, the most perceptive if not the most entertaining of the fifteenth-century historians, suffered in popularity because he valued accurate scholarship above the arbitrary standards of formal rhetoric.

Lorenzo Valla shared in the worship of rhetoric: he saluted eloquence as "the queen of truth," placing it above philosophy and on a plane approaching divine wisdom. But although he wrote a book *On the Elegance of the Latin Language* and although he called oratory "the mother of history," his keen critical faculties made him one of the ablest of historians. He set a high standard in the critical examination of texts, recognizing clearly the need to take into account the historical period and setting of a document under scrutiny. His famous exposure of the so-called Donation of Constantine as a forgery, while skillfully employing the criteria now generally used by trained historians, was not in itself a prodigious achievement. The authenticity of the papal document had already been challenged by two churchmen, Reginald Peacock and Nicholas of Cusa. More remarkable was Valla's criticism of the Roman historian Livy, the idol of the humanists and accepted by most of them unreservedly.

Objectivity is an ideal always difficult to attain in historical studies, and few of the humanist historians could be credited with approaching it. They became willing propagandists—for eloquence, for morality, and for political programs. Leonardo Bruni and other Florentine historians of the early fifteenth century called upon history to stimulate in their fellow citizens a patriotic public spirit and devotion to the cause of freedom and republican institutions. Their preference for Livy as a model was based not only on admiration for his style and narrative skill but also on the fact that they identified him with the virtues of the Roman republic before it had been subverted into a despotism by the emperors. Stripped of its rhetoric, however, the "civic humanism" of Bruni and Poggio Bracciolini extolled the liberties of a privileged minority, and in any case it suffered eclipse with the ascendancy of the Medici.[5]

The greatest of the Florentine historians, and probably the greatest of Renaissance Italy, were Niccolò Machiavelli (1469–1527) and Francesco Guicciardini (1483–1540), whose careers co-

---

[5] Civic humanism and its relationship to history is discussed in Chapter III.

incided not with the early spring of republican hopes but with the hot summer of oppressive despotism. It is not strange that their works reflect a spirit of disenchantment. Both of these writers, although schooled in the classical tradition, avoided the stilted rhetoric, pomposity, and panegyrical tone so characteristic of earlier humanist historians, and both had keen powers of observation and the ability to detect the motives behind human actions. Their historical works convey a preoccupation with the politics and diplomacy of the day. The two men became close friends only in Machiavelli's late years when mutual antipathy to the Medici regime (restored after the collapse of the Florentine republic in 1512) drew them together. Though they differed decidedly in background, in temperament, and in their historical method, they shared an adverse judgment on the drift of Italian politics in the sixteenth century.

The humanist historians confined their narratives mainly to political and military affairs. Machiavelli was no exception, but he went farther than others in conforming the actual stream of events to the pattern of his own political ideals. He looked for examples—especially classical examples—to support these ideals, reviewing the past not with detachment or objectivity but in the hope of vindicating policies he believed in and hoped to see adopted. Struggling against the tide of events, he sought for a formula to deflect it in a happier direction. He clung to the conviction that men could learn valuable lessons from history but was equally sure that his contemporaries had learned nothing. In exasperation he abandoned the discipline that historical research imposes. He did not scruple to distort the record or even invent it. Observation of political behavior convinced him that it was not enough—as earlier humanists had believed—to persuade people to read history. The lessons of history would have to be extracted, systematized, and developed into a hard and fast formula. He cited examples of jurisprudence and medicine as proof that knowledge could be logically organized into a body of working principles, to be kept intact and ready for application whenever the need arose.

The school of jurisprudence Machiavelli held up to admiration was formalistic and purely deductive—a dismal example of the rigid type of scholasticism infuriating to humanists, and seemingly the least likely source of inspiration for improving the utility of historical studies. But Machiavelli longed for a program—one deriving its authority from the past but capable of being imposed inflexibly upon the present. In postulating an a priori historical-political science (based on random aphorisms rather than on a thorough analysis of any historical epoch past or present), he was seeking a short cut and renouncing the essential discipline of the historical approach to knowledge.

Guicciardini, unlike Machiavelli, belonged to a rich and influential Florentine family. He retained a lifelong aristocratic bias, although he believed that rule by an elite ("noble and intelligent men of experience") could be reconciled with republican institutions. He distrusted abstractions and theoretical programs, and he reproached Machiavelli both for his tendency to put things in absolute terms and for his addiction to the example of ancient Rome. Guicciardini was far more of a realist than Machiavelli. His principles were flexible, as doubtless they had to be during his long years of service to the Medici, but he was neither cynical, unscrupulous, nor immoral. His mind was completely unphilosophical, but it was extraordinarily keen and observant. Although, with Machiavelli, he hoped to uncover the laws or norms governing human behavior, he was more immediately concerned with establishing the facts. And while he respected the formal conventions of humanist historiography, he broke with his predecessors in adopting a pragmatic approach and in espousing relativism. Discarding idealized versions of events, he preferred to lay bare the motives behind individual behavior and to examine the actual working of institutions.

Guicciardini produced three histories, two of Florence (the second of which he never finished) and one—his last and greatest work—of Italy as a whole. The development of his thought over the thirty-year period covering the composition of these histories is illustrated by successive changes in his treatment of Lorenzo de' Medici. The *Florentine History* (1509), written against the background of the troubled regime that Machiavelli served, is marked by the current republican anti-Medicean sentiment and is critical of *Il Magnifico*, although Guicciardini conceded it would be hard to find "a better and more pleasant tyrant." Reviewing Florentine political institutions some twenty years later *(Del reggimento di Firenze)*, he found Lorenzo admirable in comparison with the rule of the ill-fated republic, and he concluded that, because the Medicean regime had been better than its successor, its reliance upon force was justified. In the *History of Italy*, executed in the last two years of the author's life when not only the Florentine republic but hopes of an independent Italy had collapsed, Lorenzo de' Medici appears not merely vindicated but transformed into a paragon, almost a superhuman figure, and his epoch is viewed nostalgically as a golden age. In his crowning historical masterpiece Guicciardini's realism overreached itself and constrained him to romanticize a segment of the not very distant past.

The character of the *History of Italy*—a long work of twenty books covering the period from 1492 to 1534—signalizes not only the final phase of Guicciardini's historical perspective but a fundamental change in Italian Renaissance attitudes. In this *History* Guicciardini, without curtailing his faculty for cool, relentless analysis, abandons the search for rational principles operating in human affairs. It is a work of disillusionment and pessimism, of despair for the fortunes of the Italian city-states and for the condition of mankind in general. It glorifies the age of Lorenzo so eloquently that modern historians have been reluctant to recognize the severity of the political and economic crises convulsing Italy in the late fifteenth century. Guicciardini's earlier writings, though often scathing, carried the assumption that man can learn from his mistakes and, within limits, fashion his destiny. At the end he could see man only as the victim of a struggle he is powerless to control. The splendid *History of Italy* is more than a history; it is a tragedy, delineating deepening crises and the onset of degeneracy—not only in politics but also in morals, even in art. Man appears to be at the mercy of cosmic forces; and while history can illuminate the darkness that surrounds him and help him to retain his pride, it cannot alter his fate.

Thus, the conception of the role of history and the character of historical writing in Italy followed a cycle. It began with the enthusiastic revival of ancient Roman texts, admired both as literary models and as proof of the virtues of the ancients, against which the deficiencies of contemporary society could be measured. Then the idea took root that this exemplary classical history, brought up to date, could offer guidance for the sensible conduct of human affairs and become the means of improving or perfecting contemporary institutions. But in spite of the widening interest in history and refinement of the techniques of scholarship, the practical results in social and political fields were disappointing. The texture of Renaissance politics proved to be stubbornly resistant to the ideal patterns described by the humanists, who gradually and reluctantly relinquished their didactic role.

The early humanists inclined to the belief that external forces —usually designated as Fortune or Necessity—could be opposed and perhaps turned to advantage by man's own reason, his innate capacity, his will. Against impersonal or God-directed *Fortuna* they balanced the power of human *virtù*. This belief gradually disintegrated with the multiplication of Italian regimes based apparently on sheer force rather than reason, especially after repeated invasions of armed barbarians from the north had demonstrated the helplessness of the land that acknowledged no peer in intellectual and artistic attainments. Sixteenth-century historians, in contrast to their predecessors, tended to accept Fortune as all-powerful and unalterable, and therefore gave up the attempt to seek out the causes of events or to determine the laws of politics. Not only were the "lessons of history" found difficult to apply, they were even more difficult to discover, and doubt arose as to whether any such lessons existed. The doubt led not to the abandonment of history as an intellectual pursuit but to the sloughing off of responsibility for defining ideal goals. History was cultivated to serve dynastic, national, or sectarian interests, or purely for the pleasure afforded by investigation of the past. Not until the age of the Enlightenment was history again seriously put forward as an instrument for the renovation or salvation of society.

EDUCATION OLD AND NEW

A transformation in the character of education paralleled the rise of Renaissance scholarship and literature. The number of schools increased, the curriculum was broadened, and the techniques and objectives of education came under scrutiny. The famous European universities did not to any appreciable degree initiate educational reform. For the most part they set a sorry example of resistance to change. Professors in the Arts and Theology faculties, content in the cultivation of their well-fenced scholastic gardens, did not wish to be disturbed by the new learning. Some humanists managed to make their way behind the academic walls and gradually won acceptance, but only after a severe struggle. The University of Paris, once the chief intellectual center of Europe, in the late fifteenth century was engaged in a forlorn battle between rival late-medieval metaphysical schools. Not until 1508 was Greek taught on a regular basis at Paris. The English universities long clung to the medieval Scholastic tradition in spite of the presence of several very able humanists. Conservative theologians abhorred Greek as the language of heresy. As late as 1518 a violent anti-Greek reaction broke out at Oxford, and only the intervention of Henry viii silenced the "Trojans," as the opponents of Greek studies were called. In Germany the adamant conservatism of the Schoolmen provoked the famous Reuchlin controversy. When Johann Reuchlin defended the study not only of Greek but of Hebrew as well, he was accused of heresy. To discredit his adversaries—reactionary theologians at the University of Cologne—some German humanists composed the *Letters of Obscure Men* (1516–17), a coarse but effective piece of satire and buffoonery. The Reuchlin affair, which illustrates the difficulties in the way of reforming higher education in Germany, drove some of the humanists into the ranks of Luther at the time of his breach with the Catholic Church.

Universities eventually responded to the new learning and embraced it, but too late to furnish much leadership in the difficult task of reshaping an outmoded educational system. Humanist studies, finally enshrined in the curriculum, became as sacrosanct as scholasticism had once been, and thereby sacrificed something of their early vitality.

The real impetus for educational reform evidenced itself at the lower level, especially in schools privately founded by humanists who were themselves inspired by the new learning and eager to impart it to the younger generation. The program of studies in the most famous humanist schools was ambitious and well rounded, although lacking many subjects that would now be considered essential. The most serious deficiency, by our standards, was the meagerness of scientific instruction. The omission of science, however, resulted not from a desire to make the curriculum easy, but largely from the fact that natural sciences were associated with the Aristotelian-scholastic tradition. Science seemed to be sterile, abstract, and also tainted with materialism in the eyes of humanist educators, who wished to concentrate on training personality and character. The humanist ideal of education was the cultivation of the mind, to provide satisfaction to the individual and to equip him for a worthy role in society.

The scope and aims of educational reforms are well exemplified by two distinguished and beloved Italian schoolmasters, Vittorino da Feltre and Guarino da Verona. Vittorino (1378–1446), finding the atmosphere of the University of Padua unsatisfying, taught privately at Venice for a while and then accepted the invitation of Marquis Gian Francesco Gonzaga to establish a school in a Gonzaga villa at Mantua. This school, appropriately named "The Happy House," deservedly attracted wide attention. In view of its aristocratic auspices and environment, the institution was remarkably democratic in operation. Vittorino set up scholarships for poor students and opened the doors to girls on an equal basis with boys. All students, whether of noble or humble birth, were subject to the same discipline and instruction. While emphasizing the classics, the course of studies also included Italian literature, mathematics, drawing, music, religion, and physical education (riding, swimming, fencing). Vittorino conceived his function as teacher to be the development of the whole personality, physical, mental, and moral. His establishment was a school for the building of character, and it left an indelible mark on several of the leading figures of the fifteenth century, including Lorenzo Valla.

Similar in his approach to education was Vittorino's friend Guarino da Verona (1374–1460), the leading Greek scholar of his generation. Like Vittorino, he entered the service of a princely household, the Este family of Ferrara, and he too attracted pupils from a wide area. The careers of such humanist educators as Vittorino and Guarino, and the high esteem in which they were held, indicate how inaccurate it is to brand Renaissance learning as a pagan movement. The new emphasis in education could properly be called secular in that it aimed to prepare young people for a satisfying role in the world, but it placed a premium upon moral and spiritual development. It sought to produce a worthy human product by exposing young minds to the best in classical pagan and medieval Christian traditions.

Among the most influential educational centers in northern Europe were the schools established in the Netherlands and western Germany by the Brethren of the Common Life, an organization which had been founded in the Dutch town of Deventer by Gerard Groote (d. 1384). Although the Brethren movement originated independently of Italian humanism and under the influence of late medieval mysticism, it absorbed and adapted aspects of the

Renaissance, especially its emphasis upon the value of Latin and Greek studies. This brotherhood of Christian laymen sought to combine a deep but practical piety—the "modern devotion"—with active social service, including teaching. Although dedicated to a spiritual life, the members were not bound by vows, and their approach to religion was unconventional enough to provoke attempts on the part of the regular religious orders to suppress the brotherhood. The Brethren were little attracted to scholasticism either in its theological or educational guise. The movement produced one of the great classics of Christian mysticism—Thomas à Kempis' *Imitation of Christ* (ca. 1415). It also fostered schools with curricula enriched by generous doses of Latin and Greek literature. The schools of the Brethren stimulated curricular reform elsewhere, even at the university level, and they trained some of the most distinguished northern humanists including, during its early years, Erasmus of Rotterdam.

In England a small circle of humanists who have come to be known as "the Oxford Reformers" challenged the educational establishment and the dominant scholasticism. The personalities and varied careers of these men, all active in the early decades of the sixteenth century, encompass a wide range and illustrate how the humanist temper could be combined with the responsibilities of ordinary life. A common bond among them was their interest in spreading the new learning. Although not all were professional teachers, they were educators in the broadest sense. Thomas Linacre (d. 1524)—who earned an M.D. degree at Padua, practiced medicine in England, served as personal physician to King Henry VIII, and founded the London College of Physicians—also taught Greek at Oxford, compiled a Latin grammar, and translated the works of Galen into Latin. Thomas More had the advantage neither of residence in Italy nor of a university degree. After two years at Oxford he removed to the Inns of Court to prepare for his career as lawyer, parliamentarian, and royal servant. However, he managed to acquire competence in both Latin and Greek, championed the study of ancient languages including Hebrew, and influenced Henry VIII to defend friends of the new learning against attacks of the Oxford "Trojans." Aside from Erasmus, probably the most influential member of the Oxford Reformers was John Colet (d. 1519), in spite of the fact that he was least qualified to rank as a humanist. Colet, who became Dean of St. Paul's in London, had only a limited knowledge of Greek and little interest in the pagan classics. Although he favored Church reform and opposed clerical celibacy, he was himself inclined to mysticism and asceticism and honored faith above reason. Nevertheless he illustrates forcefully the link between late medieval piety and the humanist educational program. Before obtaining a degree in theology he dared to lecture at Oxford on St. Paul's Epistles, and he astonished his listeners because he abandoned the tiresome search for hidden symbolism and allegory in favor of a straightforward exposition of the text in the light of its literal meaning and historical setting. His most direct contribution to education was the reestablishment of St. Paul's School for Boys, which offered instruction in Latin and Greek and which, in spite of a strongly religious orientation, was not a Church foundation but was under the control of a company of London merchants. Even more significant, however, was Colet's influence upon the young Erasmus, in whom he awakened an interest—destined to be lifelong—in a critical examination of the literary foundations of Christianity.

Finally Erasmus, bound by ties of friendship to the Oxford group but a truly international figure, was above everything else an educator. He founded no school and was attached to none except for a brief period at Cambridge (1511–14). Still, he was one of the greatest teachers of all time. Almost everything he wrote (and he hardly ever stopped writing) was intended to instruct, to clarify, to illuminate—also frequently to entertain, to reprove, or even to infuriate. What teacher could aim for more? The whole of Europe was his schoolroom, and the curriculum he offered was the complementary disciplines of classical literature and Christian ethics stripped of obscurantism—"good letters" and the "philosophy of Christ." He wrote for schoolboys as well as for the intellectual elite. He prepared treatises on how to study and on how to teach and on the proper pronunciation of Latin and Greek words. His *Familiar Colloquies,* a perennial best seller which kept expanding in successive editions, was originally conceived as a set of exercises in Latin composition but grew into a wide-ranging collection of homilies, moral and psychological essays, parables, and ironic commentaries. Erasmus undertook to instruct the aristocracy in proper conduct by providing a handbook of the Christian knight *(Enchiridion Militis Christiani).* He aspired to educate the Christian prince *(Institutio Principis Christiani).* He would even teach the clergy how to preach (*Ecclesiastes.*) And through the mouth of Folly, with mingled doses of gall and honey, he would coax men to view themselves with some sense of proportion.

Erasmus' most ambitious undertaking, his Greek edition of the New Testament accompanied by a new Latin translation and commentary, was not only a work of critical scholarship—in this respect, deficient—but also an affirmation of his belief that the Scriptures should be an open book, to be apprehended by all seekers after religious truth. Saddened to discover that he had alarmed conservative churchmen by daring to tamper with the revered Latin Vulgate, Erasmus was optimistic enough to believe that if people had access to correct texts of the sacred writings they could clear away misunderstanding and thus make an end of religious controversy. While his Greek Testament was necessarily directed to an educated minority, Erasmus voiced his conviction that learning, especially Biblical learning, should be brought within reach of the common man. In the remarkable preface to his *Novum Instrumentum* (the Greek Testament) he called for translation of the Scriptures into vulgar tongues so that they might be read by "all little women" and sung by the plowman at his plow and the weaver at his loom.

. Although Renaissance humanism at its height was characterized by a desire to inform, or even reform, it had not originated as an academic movement, and its impact on education extended beyond the confines of the classroom. Aggressive humanists sought to reach as large an audience as possible, partly no doubt from a craving for fame but also from a desire to help mold public opinion. The public was necessarily a limited one, but the numerous literary academies that sprang up in the Italian cities drew their membership from various professions and included men of affairs as well as scholars. Many fifteenth-century Italian humanists made careers as public lecturers, sometimes attached to a university but often travelling widely to deliver their discourses. Those with oratorical skill and a reputation for classical learning had little trouble finding patrons and listeners. Francesco Filelfo (1398–1481)—in spite of his lack of originality, his vanity, and his penchant for quarreling with everyone who crossed his path—in the early 1430s was delivering four lectures a day in Florence, and he claimed (doubtless with exaggeration) that his daily audience numbered four hundred persons. More extravagant still was the boast of Girolamo Aleander

(Aleandro), who reported that at the University of Paris on a hot July day in 1511 he had held a distinguished crowd of two thousand spellbound for two hours and a half.

A finer example of the scholar-lecturer was Angelo Ambrogini (1454–94), more generally known as Poliziano, who served as tutor to the children of Lorenzo de' Medici and as professor of Greek and Latin at Florence. Besides writing beautiful Italian lyrics, he introduced his public lectures on Homer, Vergil, Hesiod, and the Greek dramatists with a remarkable set of original Latin poems composed as preludes to the course topics. A public teacher with the resources and imagination of Poliziano was a rare phenomenon even in Renaissance Italy, but the popularity and admiration which he aroused indicates that the worthiest exponents of humanism could hardly be classified as mere antiquarians.

THE PRESS—RIVAL AND ALLY

The rise of publishing houses furnishes another example—and an impressive one—of the zeal which the humanists displayed in their efforts to disseminate the treasures they had fallen heir to. The printing press—or, more accurately, the invention of the art of printing from movable type—was definitely not a humanist contribution. On the contrary, it appeared first in Germany, beginning about the middle of the fifteenth century, and its early issue ran heavily to pious tracts, conventional Latin grammars, and encyclopedias. At the outset it appeared to be more an instrument of the old learning than of the new. Italian humanists, for their part, were at first hostile to printed books, regarding the press as a barbarous German contraption which, at best, would impair learning by lowering it to the level of the multitude. Nevertheless, as the techniques of printing and book manufacture spread throughout the various European countries, humanists learned to accept the printed word and even welcomed it as an ally to their own cause. During the Renaissance, the era which witnessed the beginning of this momentous revolution in bookmaking, the average quality of the product was no more than mediocre—as it has been ever since. But the standard of diligent workmanship and high purpose set by the greatest publishers was fully equal to the best of any succeeding age.

The Aldine press of Venice was perhaps the most noteworthy among a number of distinguished Renaissance publishing houses.

Founded in 1493 by Aldus Manutius (Aldo Manuzio), it continued in the same family for three generations and brought to completion meticulous editions of most of the extant Greek classics. Although the firm was a financial success, Aldus was not primarily interested in profits. He was first a humanist, by education and vocation, who dedicated his energies to raising standards of scholarship and to making the fruits of scholarship accessible to others. His books were scrupulously edited, beautifully printed, yet sold as cheaply as possible. While the Aldine press carried out the whole process of book manufacture (except paper-making), it was much more than a factory; it was an educational establishment animated by a sense of mission. Following the example of other Italian cities, Aldus organized his own academy in Venice, which conducted its meetings in the Greek language. The academy served as an editorial board for the Press, encouraged and assisted struggling authors, and offered honorary membership to distinguished foreign scholars, including Erasmus. Aldus' unflagging services to literature were impelled by the feeling, expressed in one of his prefaces, that he was delivering the classics from bondage and bringing to light their hidden treasures.

The humanist movement in literature, education, and scholarship, far from standing apart from the main currents of Renaissance life, threw itself into the midst of them. It undertook to humanize institutions, to mold opinion, and to broaden the cultural base so that the common man would receive at least a few of its benefits. While creating many enduring intellectual monuments, the humanists deserve perhaps even more credit for attempting to establish a community of letters that would serve not merely as an ornament but as a beacon and guide for the wider human community.

The humanists devoted much effort to getting their message heard and to winning their way into positions of influence. But as a program of action the results of humanism proved disappointing. The fault lay partly in inherent deficiencies in the movement—inadequate understanding of human nature and the natural environment, and a tendency to gross oversimplification of problems—and partly in the fact that the character of society was changing to an extent that could not be predicted and that rendered it less and less conformable to concepts derived from either classical or medieval experience.

Both the degree and the dubious nature of its triumph are

illustrated by the relationship between humanism and the Church. In Italy the remarkable feature is the absence of serious conflict between them. Beginning with the mid-fifteenth century the popes had encouraged and patronized humanism and employed scores of talented laymen (the iconoclastic Lorenzo Valla, for example). In the High Renaissance they went so far as to reward writers and artists with preferment to the highest holy offices. Three classical scholars—Pietro Bembo, Jacopo Sadoleto, and Girolamo Aleander—were appointed cardinals, and Raphael was considered for the same honor. But if Italian humanists succeeded in capturing the papacy, they ended by themselves becoming captive. By identifying their cause and their fortunes with that of the popes they alienated themselves from intellectual leaders of northern Europe, and they inevitably suffered a loss in stature as papal prestige declined. Before the gravest European crisis of the age, the Protestant upheaval, humanism floundered. Humanists could neither prevent the break between Catholics and Protestants nor gain a commanding position within either faction. The religious struggle which split Western Christendom was not a struggle between the old learning and the new. Both Catholics and Protestants adopted and made use of the new learning. But both movements—the Reformation and the Counter Reformation—were inimical to the spirit and the program of the humanists.

REFERENCES AND SUGGESTIONS
FOR FURTHER READING

HUMANISM

Artz, Frederick B., *From the Renaissance to Romanticism: Trends in Style in Art, Literature, and Music, 1300–1830* (Chicago: University of Chicago Press, 1962). *Renaissance Humanism, 1300–1550* (Kent, Ohio: Kent State University Press, 1966), a succinct account.

Baron, Hans, *From Petrarch to Leonardo Bruni: Studies in Humanistic and Political Literature* (Chicago: University of Chicago Press, 1968). *Humanistic and Political Literature in Florence and Venice at the Beginning of the Quattrocento* (Cambridge, Mass.: Harvard University Press, 1955).

Bush, Douglas, *The Renaissance and English Humanism* (Toronto: University of Toronto Press, 1939).

Garin, Eugenio, *Italian Humanism*, trans. Peter Munz (New York: Harper & Row, 1965).

Gilmore, Myron, *The World of Humanism, 1453–1517* (New York: Harper & Row, 1962).

Gray, Hanna, "Renaissance Humanism: The Pursuit of Eloquence," in Paul Oskar Kristeller and Philip P. Wiener, eds., *Renaissance Essays* (New York: Harper & Row, 1968).

Kristeller, Paul Oskar, *Renaissance Thought: The Classic, Scholastic, and Humanistic Strains* (New York: Harper & Row, 1961). Unsurpassed as an introduction to the subject. *Renaissance Thought II: Papers on Humanism and the Arts* (New York: Harper & Row, 1965). *Eight Philosophers of the Italian Renaissance* (Stanford: Stanford University Press, 1964), Chaps. I and II (Petrarch and Valla).

Schevill, Ferdinand, *The First Century of Italian Humanism* (New York: Crofts, 1928). Brief extracts from the works of Petrarch, Valla, and others.

Seigel, Jerrold E., *Rhetoric and Philosophy in Renaissance Humanism: The Union of Eloquence and Wisdom, Petrarch to Valla* (Princeton: Princeton University Press, 1968). An illuminating study.

Weiss, Roberto, *The Dawn of Humanism in Italy* (London: H. K. Lewis, 1947). An inaugural university lecture.

FOR PETRARCH

Bishop, Morris, *Petrarch and His World* (Bloomington: Indiana University Press, 1963). Scholarly and beautifully written; probably the best full-length study of Petrarch in English. It includes a masterly condensation of the *Secret* (from which passages are quoted in this chapter). "Petrarch," in J. H. Plumb, ed., *Renaissance Profiles* (New York: Harper & Row, 1956).

Cassirer, Ernst, *et al.*, eds., *The Renaissance Philosophy of Man* (Chicago: University of Chicago Press, 1948), Chap. I. A generous selection of Petrarch's works translated with introduction by Hans Nachod.

Whitfield, John H., *Petrarch and the Renascence* (New York: Haskell House, 1969). Excellent discussion of Petrarch and his influence on later humanists; slightly distorted by an extreme prejudice against the Middle Ages.

ITALIAN RENAISSANCE LITERATURE

de Sanctis, Francesco, *History of Italian Literature,* trans. Joan Redfern, 2 vols. (New York: Harcourt Brace Jovanovich, 1931). (Original Italian edition was first published 1870–71.) A classic which reflects the romantic idealism of the nineteenth century and interprets the Renaissance as a period of decadence and spiritual emptiness.

Grayson, Cecil, "Lorenzo, Machiavelli, and the Italian Language," in Ernest F. Jacob, ed., *Italian Renaissance Studies* (New York: Barnes and Noble, 1960).

Convenient collections of Renaissance literature in translation are James B. Ross and Mary M. McLaughlin, eds., *The Portable Renaissance Reader* (New York: Viking, 1953); and Hiram C. Haydn and John C. Nelson, eds., *A Renaissance Treasury* (Garden City, N. Y.: Doubleday, 1953).

Hall, Vernon, Jr., *Renaissance Literary Criticism, a Study of Its Social Content* (New York: Columbia University Press, 1945).

Lucki, Emil, *History of the Renaissance,* Vol. IV: *Literature and Art* (Salt Lake City: University of Utah Press, 1965).

Olschki, Leonardo, *The Genius of Italy* (Ithaca, N.Y.: Cornell University Press, 1949). A sympathetic and stimulating survey.

Whitfield, John H., *A Short History of Italian Literature* (Baltimore: Penguin Books, 1960). Perceptive but compressed and sometimes cryptic.

Wilkins, Ernest H., *A History of Italian Literature* (Cambridge, Mass.: Harvard University Press, 1954). A solid, well-rounded study with illustrative quotations.

HISTORY

Baker, Herschel, *The Race of Time: Three Lectures on Renaissance Historiography* (Toronto: University of Toronto Press, 1967).

Bouwsma, William J., *Venice and the Defense of Republican Liberty* (Berkeley: University of California Press, 1968), for Venetian humanists and historians.

Burke, Peter, *The Renaissance Sense of the Past* (London: Edward Arnold, 1969). Brief extracts from sources, with commentary.

Gilbert, Felix, *Machiavelli and Guicciardini: Politics and History in Sixteenth-Century Florence* (Princeton: Princeton University Press, 1965). A searching analysis of humanist conceptions of politics and history, especially valuable for Guicciardini.

Gilmore, Myron, "The Renaissance Conception of the Lessons of History," in William H. Werkmeister, ed., *Facets of the Renaissance* (New York: Harper & Row, 1963).

Mazzeo, Joseph A., *Renaissance and Revolution: The Remaking of European Thought* (New York: Random House, 1965).

FOR GUICCIARDINI

The *History of Italy* has been recently translated and edited by Sidney Alexander (New York: Macmillan, 1969). An abridged English version of the *History of Italy* and the *History of Florence* is translated by Cecil Grayson and edited by John R. Hale (New York: Twayne, 1964).

Domandi, Mario, trans., *Maxims and Reflections of a Renaissance Statesman.* Introduction by Nicolai Rubinstein (New York: Harper & Row, 1965). A selection from Guicciardini's *Ricordi,* a wide ranging series of observations and aphorisms compiled during his mature years.

Ridolfi, Roberto, *The Life of Francesco Guicciardini,* trans. Cecil Grayson (New York: Knopf, 1968).

For Machiavelli, see also References for Chapter III.

EDUCATION

Harbison, E. Harris, *The Christian Scholar in the Age of the Reformation* (New York: Scribner's, 1956). Interpretive lectures on Italian and northern humanists and leaders of the Reformation.

Hexter, J. H., "Education of the Aristocracy in the Renaissance," *Journal of Modern History,* XXII (1950). Shows that the nobility of England, France, and the Netherlands were not the unlettered boors they have sometimes been pictured.

Hyma, Albert, *The Christian Renaissance: A History of the "Devotio Moderna"* (Grand Rapids, Mich.: William B. Eerdmans, 1924). *The Brethren of the Common Life* (Grand Rapids, Mich.: William B. Eerdmans, 1950). Definitive and sympathetic.

Lucki, Emil, *History of the Renaissance*, Vol. III: *Education, Learning, and Thought* (Salt Lake City: University of Utah Press, 1963).

Olin, John C., ed., *Christian Humanism and the Reformation: Desiderius Erasmus* (New York: Harper & Row, 1965). Selected writings of Erasmus, including the preface to his Greek edition of the New Testament.

Seebohm, Frederick, *The Oxford Reformers: John Colet, Erasmus and Thomas More*, 2nd rev. ed. (London: Longmans, 1869). A pioneer work of lasting value.

Ten Colloquies of Erasmus, trans. Craig R. Thompson (New York: Liberal Arts Press, 1957), with Introduction by the translator.

Weiss, Roberto, "Learning and Education in Western Europe from 1470 to 1520," in *New Cambridge Modern History*, Vol. I.

For Erasmus, see also References for Chapter III.

VI
THE FINE ARTS

All visible things derive their existence from nature, and from these same things is born painting. So therefore we may justly speak of it as the grandchild of nature and as related to God Himself.

—Leonardo da Vinci, NOTEBOOKS

THE HERITAGE FROM THE PAST

Whatever exaggeration the notion of a renaissance may entail, it comes closest to being justified in the domain of the arts. During this era the fine arts attained the recognition and freedom necessary to their full development. They emerged from the lowly status of crafts and successfully forced their way into the ancient and honorable society of Liberal Arts. The artist won acceptance as a man of professional standing, an individual worthy of admiration, able to hold his own among those born of privilege. It is true that even in Italy the artist was still heavily dependent upon the patronage of the rich and powerful—merchant princes, despots, and lords of the church—and even such a formidable genius as Michelangelo never let it be forgotten that he was of noble descent and no simple stonecutter. However, a person of genuine talent could win acclaim and substantial material rewards, and he could address himself to a fairly wide public. The several arts developed along distinctive lines and yet remained interdependent and mutually stimulating. Virtuosity was a hallmark of the age. Many of the most famous figures were equally competent in the three fields of sculpture, architecture, and painting—sometimes also in poetry and music. Music during the Renaissance underwent a development comparable to that in the other fine arts, but its position is somewhat exceptional. To a fuller extent than any of the others it represents both the culmination of a continuous tradition and a fresh creation. Apparently it was in music that the concept of a new departure was first articulated. As early as 1320 Philippe de Vitry, a French musician and poet and a friend of Petrarch, entitled his treatise on music *Ars Nova*—the New Art. During succeeding centuries, especially between 1450 and 1600, developments in music effected a break with medieval theory and practice that was nothing less than revolutionary. They included such changes as emancipation from rigidly fixed rhythmical patterns, tremendous expansion of the range of voices, abandonment of the old Pythagorean tonal system in favor of more flexible and expressive major and minor modes, the introduction of modulation and chromatics, and even experimentation with quarter tones. The Renaissance era witnessed both the ultimate refinement of polyphony and the clear definition and exploitation of harmony. And although vocal forms—including secular madrigals and motets as well as magnificent settings of religious texts for highly professional church choirs—reached a perfection which has never been surpassed, instrumental music also began to assume an independent role. More important than technical innovation was the attainment of an intimate and dramatic relationship between verbal text and musical setting—essential for the later genesis of the oratorio and the opera—and, through a rare union of skillful craftsmanship and spontaneity, the creation of a medium fully capable of expressing the whole range of human emotions.

No less than painting and sculpture, music epitomizes the genius of the Renaissance, and it also constitutes one of its most enduring and satisfying contributions. Nevertheless, the splendid musical edifice erected during the fifteenth and sixteenth centuries rested upon medieval foundations. The classical revival had little relevance to the deeply implanted Western musical heritage, although Renaissance musicians, like the humanists, became inspired by their admiration for antiquity. They studied the writings on music of Plato and other Greek authors, analyzed the meters of ancient poets, revived and adapted the Aeolian and Ionian modes, and even tried to rediscover the putative wonderworking principles of ancient Greek music. But the musical flowering of the Renaissance was not a graft from antiquity, it was the unpredictably rich bloom from seeds and plants that had slowly matured during the long medieval centuries. Although stimulated by the atmosphere of the Renaissance, music as an art form was only indirectly indebted to it, and it continued to evolve along its own course after the Renaissance had come to an end.

The superb quality of Renaissance art has been almost universally acknowledged, but there has long been disagreement as to its meaning—its relationship to the modern temper, and even to the age in which it flourished. One attractive but questionable interpretation, reflecting the thesis of Burckhardt and not yet entirely dispelled, views Renaissance art as the product of a mounting secularism encouraged and abetted by renewed contact with the world of antiquity. The revival of classical art, which paralleled the "revival of learning," provided the inspiration and the means for artists to emancipate themselves from the stifling traditions of their immediate past. As they recovered and improved upon ancient skills and gained confidence in their own powers, they threw off the shackles of medieval otherworldliness. Eschewing the supernatural, they rediscovered and rehabilitated the natural man and hailed him as self-sufficient. The extreme exponents of this theory regard Renaissance art as signifying a repudiation of Christianity and a revival of paganism. Not in the least deterred by the fact that the overwhelming majority of works dealt with religious subjects, they disregard such evidence or explain it as a purely formal concession to conventional mores. Religious trappings, they allege, were superficial, a face-saving device whereby the artist could avoid the suspicion of impiety and give free reign to his wayward inclinations under a veneer of Christian respectability.

The allegation is not without supporting evidence. The Church, increasingly wealthy and worldly, furnished much of the employment for artisans and artists, but many churchmen cared little for the religion they outwardly professed. Some openly preferred the pagan poets to the Bible and were quite willing to accept a Mercury or an Apollo depicted in the guise of an Apostle or martyr. Ultimately the papacy became the most munificent patron in all Italy, and during the High Renaissance several notoriously unchristian characters appeared in the garb of St. Peter. No wonder then that painters and sculptors, in the pay and under the eye of custodians of the faith, could indulge their worldly or voluptuous fantasies to the full.

In spite of its plausibility, this interpretation—which assumes that the religious elements in Renaissance art were extraneous and essentially false—cannot be accepted. It asks us to believe that the artist was sincere (if ever) only when portraying a classical or secular subject and that when he made a religious statement he didn't really mean what he was saying, no matter how eloquently he said it. It implies that he was like the modern commercial artist employed by an advertising agency, adept at improving the public image of his employer and extolling the virtues of a product to which he is personally indifferent or which he secretly despises. It is hard to see how anyone who has looked with open eyes at the sculpture, frescoes, and canvasses of the great Renaissance masters could accept such an explanation of how they came about. And it is impossible to square it with the impact of Renaissance art upon the public of that day or of later days, including representatives of the hard-bitten twentieth century who make their pilgrimage to the shrines of Florence, Rome, Venice, Padua, Verona, and the rest. If the Renaissance artists were lying, they were the most convincing and magnificent liars of all time, and modern hucksters should sit at the feet of Leonardo, Raphael, and Michelangelo.

Apart from a too facile dismissal of religious motivation, the interpretation of Renaissance art as a pagan reincarnation tends to obscure elements of continuity between the Middle Ages and the Renaissance. It does not detract from the achievements of Renaissance genius to recognize that they rested upon foundations already laid. In the case of music the continuity was most obvious and absolute. The representational arts also were linked to the Middle Ages, in different degrees. The debt was greatest in the case of sculpture, which, in spite of its subordination to architecture, had attained during the Gothic age a forceful and dignified naturalism. Medieval Europeans were by no means indifferent to or incapable of portraying human beauty. Abundant evidence to the contrary is provided by wood carvings—frequently painted—and statues of saints, apostles, Christ and the Virgin that adorn the doorways and recesses of Chartres, Orleans, Reims, and other great cathedrals. While the figures are typically rigid—partly from an imperfect understanding of anatomy and partly to prevent any interruption in the flow of vertical lines—the faces are lifelike and expressive, testifying to artistry of a high order. There is no sharp break between late Gothic and early Renaissance sculpture. The chief innovation of the Renaissance was to free statues from the cramping niches of pillars and door frames and let them stand in the open as independent entities.

In Italy, the prime center of the Renaissance, architecture shows a more decided break with the medieval past; but in northern Europe the Gothic tradition continued to reign supreme. The Gothic had never been fully developed in Italy and Italian architects had little to lose by repudiating it, as they did emphatically. However, as a distinctive Italian style developed, it incorporated early medieval Romanesque elements along with motifs derived from classical Rome. Italian Renaissance architecture was neither entirely Roman nor entirely new; in any case it was indebted to the Middle Ages, most directly for a craftsmanship refined by more than 500 years of experimentation. The accumulated knowledge of medieval architects, engineers, and stonemasons—presented as an offering *ad maiorem gloriam Dei*—could be drawn upon by an age devoted to the glorification of man and made to celebrate the personality of a prince, a pope, or the artist himself.

The most original and revolutionary developments occurred in painting, for the simple reason that here there was little to imitate and build upon, either from the Middle Ages or from antiquity. Painting had been the least developed of the ancient arts, and the surviving examples were cherished curiosities rather than impressive models. During the Middle Ages painting had played a minor role although not a negligible one. The colored miniatures of medieval illuminated manuscripts are highly decorative and at the same time surprisingly clear in their fine detail. The Trecento [1] Florentine painter Giotto di Bondone, a contemporary and friend of Dante, is usually credited with initiating the Renaissance movement in painting. His large wall frescoes are not mere decorative devices but vivid narratives, peopled with human beings who live and move and communicate directly to the beholder. Giotto was a rare innovating genius; the contrast between his work and that of his imme-

---

[1] The Italian terms *trecento* (1300s), *quattrocento* (1400s), and *cinquecento* (1500s) are commonly used to designate the Renaissance centuries, particularly when referring to the fine arts.

diate predecessors is so marked as to suggest a mutation. However, even in Renaissance Italy, when a new upsurge in the arts was arousing admiration and wonder, those who witnessed the phenomenon could not agree as to how and with whom it began. Boccaccio, Giotto's younger contemporary, marveling at the artist's ability to depict natural obects, hailed him as the genius who had restored the art of painting after an age of darkness. Later critics were not so sure where the credit belonged. Giotto's teacher, Cimabue, had been reared in the Byzantine school, characterized by sumptuous but highly formalized and rigid figures, and contemptuously dismissed by Florentines of the Cinquecento as "the Greek manner." But Cimabue's originality was such that it is debatable whether he should be considered the last Byzantine painter in Florence or the first of the realists. Giorgio Vasari in his celebrated *Lives*, written toward the end of the High Renaissance, expressed the contemporary consensus when he attributed the first stage of the rebirth of painting to Giotto and Cimabue jointly. Apparently Giotto profited from Cimabue's tutelage, although the pupil far outran his master. Giotto's naturalism, in spite of his flat backgrounds, is direct and appealing, his colors warm and clear, his scenes alive with human drama. But if he emancipated himself from medieval formalism, he clung devoutly to medieval ideals—his favorite subjects were episodes from the life of Christ and the life of St. Francis of Assisi.

Undeniably, a renewed interest in the monuments of ancient Rome contributed an essential ingredient to the artistic renaissance in Italy. Filippo Brunelleschi's visit to Rome, accompanied by his young friend the sculptor Donatello, at the dawn of the fifteenth century, conveniently marks the introduction of influence from this quarter, although of course many factors were responsible. Brunelleschi introduced Roman elements in his buildings in Florence, including the marvelous dome of the cathedral of Santa Maria del Fiore. Here, however, by retaining the upsweep of Gothic lines he transformed the concept of the dome into a novel structure, perfectly complementing the bell tower and the horizontal lines of the church itself. Italian architects not only studied and copied Roman models but also sought to reformulate the theoretical principles on which they were based. They imagined they had found them in a work by Vitruvius, a relatively minor architect and engineer of the first century B.C., whose treatise *On Architecture* had been rediscovered in the fifteenth century and was now elevated to a pinnacle of fame totally unwarranted by its intrinsic merit. Believing that Vitruvius held the key to the rules of proportion and harmony, Renaissance artists avidly pored over his turgid prose. Fortunately, in practice they allowed considerable latitude to their own imagination and Vitruvius, whose name became a byword for the genius of architecture, was actually only a catalyst, stimulating the efforts of Renaissance men to recover those elements of the Greco-Roman past which could best serve their present interests. The highly influential architect Leon Battista Alberti, although he accepted Vitruvius' conception of the harmony of parts, insisted that the architect must equip himself not only with draftsmanship and mathematics but with a broad liberal education and should regard his work as an important aspect of civic life.

The classical heritage, viewed in a new light by the Renaissance, had exerted a continuous influence all through the Middle Ages. It is visible in medieval art, where Christian subjects were often in outward form copies of pagan prototypes; and, conversely, where classical figures were anachronistically presented in the costumes and attitudes of medieval folk. The medieval treatment of classical elements was indiscriminate and haphazard; nevertheless, the surviving remnants of antique culture were more real and intimate to medieval Europeans than to their sophisticated descendants of the Renaissance. The past was nearer to them, not only in the chronological sense. The medieval mind was fascinated, awed, even terrified by the ghosts of a mysterious pagan culture that had gone underground but never entirely vanished. Christianity had triumphed over Hellas and Rome, but the pagan gods lived on in popular demonology, and even scholars attributed magical powers to such ancients as Vergil. Men of the Renaissance achieved a clearer perspective. Although they revered or idolized the world of antiquity and sometimes dreamed of recovering it, they recognized its distance from themselves. The counterpart of the revival of antiquity was an emancipation from its thrall. The ghosts were laid at last, or, rather, they were found to be harmless creatures—appealing, beautiful, but no more substantial than figments of fancy. As Erwin Panofsky so aptly expresses it:

The "distance" created by the Renaissance deprived antiquity of its realness. The classical world ceased to be both a possession and a menace. It became instead the object of a passionate nostalgia. . . . The Renaissance came to realize that Pan was dead—that the world of ancient Greece and Rome . . . was lost like Milton's Paradise and capable of being regained only in the spirit. . . . The Middle Ages had left antiquity unburied and alternately galvanized and exorcised its corpse. The Renaissance stood weeping at its grave and tried to resurrect its soul.[2]

The weeping was not excessive, however. There was also rejoicing in the discovery that ancient materials could readily be adapted to contemporary tastes.

Renaissance spokesmen tended to overlook their debt to the Middle Ages and to exaggerate the influence of antiquity. Their bias is understandable because they were departing in fundamental ways from the medieval pattern and because, as they began to see the Greco-Roman world in a new light, they were excited by a sense of discovery. Confident that they were reviving arts that had lain dormant too long, they blamed the barbarian invaders of the Roman Empire for degrading architecture and Christian fanaticism for destroying painting and sculpture. Vasari identified barbarian outrages and the "perfervid zeal of the new Christian religion" as twin causes of decline. The testimony of such eminent critics as Ghiberti and Vasari would seem to confirm the still popular notion that Renaissance artists resurrected the spirit of paganism. But the statements of a few enthusiasts are insufficient evidence, and the leaders of a movement are not always the best judges of its character. At any rate, the ecstatic tone in which they announced the dawn of a new artistic era suggests a closer affinity with the "perfervid zeal" of Christianity than with the cool restraint of the classical temper. They acclaimed a "rebirth," a "new life," an "awakening" from "slumber," the recovery of sight after an age of "blindness," and the conquest of "darkness" by "light."

Renaissance art was far more than a revival or reincarnation of an archaic past. The classical tradition, restudied and assimilated, provided incentive and, more particularly, a vocabulary of forms and symbols which could be modified or disregarded at will. But if aspiring artists went to school with the ancients, they graduated themselves *cum laude* and struck out on their own. The sculpture

---

[2] Erwin Panofsky, *Renaissance and Renascences in Western Art*, Vol. I (Stockholm: Almquist and Wiksell, 1960), pp. 112–113.

and painting of the High Renaissance is comparable to but independent of Greco-Roman art, and in many respects superior. Departures from antique models were not accidental or capricious but were determined by the interests of the artist and of the public he served. The artistic impulse attached itself to contemporary ideals, which were still rooted in religion. The most enduring and impressive works of Renaissance art are religious in intent and impact, although their content ranges all the way from a scrupulous adherence to Christian iconography to bold visions that overstep credal boundaries.

Renaissance historiographers attributed the felicitous progress of the fine arts to two equally important principles: first, fidelity to nature, acknowledged to be most prominent in painting; and second, a return to classical forms, most prominent in architecture. In striving for fidelity to nature, artists abandoned the traditional conception of a painting as an impenetrable barrier on which figures could be displayed, and began to think of it as an imaginary windowpane. Working with color and line, they undertook to impart a three-dimensional quality to a two-dimensional surface. Italian painters experimented with foreshortening and attempted to reduce the principles of perspective to scientific laws. They also studied anatomy, practiced dissection, and made careful drawings of organs, bones, and tissues. In his eagerness to see and faithfully reproduce the natural world, the artist turned botanist and physiologist, and through diligent observation advanced beyond the professional biological knowledge of his day. Leonardo da Vinci, who dissected more than thirty corpses and was the first to delineate accurately the human foetus, surpassed even Vesalius in brain anatomy and exemplified in his drawings the technique of graphic representation essential to anatomical studies. Leonardo was exceptional: while most of his fellow artists appropriated science for the service of art, he placed art at the service of science and probably deserves credit as the true founder of the science of anatomy. But Leonardo was no less a consummate artist, and his work epitomizes the happy union of science and art that sprang from a devotion to reality beginning with the early Renaissance. The researches of "painter-anatomists" substantially advanced the empirical method and compensate to some extent for the relative sterility of theoretical science during the fifteenth century. The majority of artists, however, were interested in factual observation and analysis only as a necessary preparation for their vocation. As they attained mastery over their materials they turned from the matter-of-fact data of science to the world of human action and aspiration.

CONTRASTS BETWEEN THE EARLY AND THE HIGH RENAISSANCE

The artistic Renaissance in Italy falls into two main periods, the first extending into the late Quattrocento and the second reaching its climax in the early Cinquecento. Although there is no sudden break, there are significant contrasts between the works of the earlier period and those of the High, or Classical Renaissance. Both periods reflect the influence of classical antiquity and both are related to the Middle Ages, in somewhat different ways. The Quattrocento was intensely preoccupied with technical problems—the perfecting of draftsmanship, the mastery of perspective and anatomical proportion, the selection of suitable media for the application of color. Theme and subject matter were equally important, however, and these reflect the buoyant confidence of the early Renaissance. While striving to imitate nature, painters delighted in human scenes, sometimes quite homely and unpretentious, showing ordinary people surrounded by everyday objects. Religious and secular themes were not rigidly separated. Frescoes designed for churches served both to commemorate sacred legends and to celebrate the color and pageantry of contemporary life. Patrons were fond of having their own likenesses and those of their family or friends immortalized on church walls or altarpieces. A fine example is Benozzo Gozzoli's fresco of the Journey of the Magi in the chapel of the Medici-Riccardi Palace in Florence. Instead of three lonely royal pilgrims it presents a gaily bedecked cavalcade, descending with jaunty assurance into the crowded foreground. The retinue includes a likeness of the artist himself, and the three kings are Cosimo, Piero, and Lorenzo de' Medici. There is often a note of playfulness in Florentine painting of the mid-Quattrocento. Fra Filippo Lippi in representing sacred figures made no attempt to spiritualize his models; the Virgin is a blooming Italian maiden, the Christ Child a lusty squirming infant, an angel a mischievous urchin.

The secular or jocose element in early Quattrocento art is not iconoclastic. Painting and sculpture—with some notable exceptions—

reflect no war of opposites, no struggle between flesh and spirit or between the claims of the Church and the attractions of the world. They reveal an ingenuous delight in the varied facets of human experience, including the solace of religion; and the religion was essentially that of the late Middle Ages. The serenity of the age that witnessed the perfection of Gothic architecture in France and the intellectual and poetic synthesis of two great Italians—Aquinas and Dante—still rested upon artists of the Renaissance, although they were less inhibited than their forebears, more articulate and self-assured. The cheerful family groups and festive scenes, the casual intermingling of sacred and profane, bespeak a sense of security in a well-regulated universe. These accents have their counterpart in late medieval art. The medieval craftsman, more restricted in his mode of expression than his successors who could command the full resources of painting, was somewhat more inclined to indulge in the fantastic. In Renaissance art, devils, monsters, and death figures tend to be replaced by servants and domestic animals—creatures subject to man's dominion. Under the influence not of a pagan revolt but of a religion grown increasingly humanistic, the artist and his public moved away from the shadows and into the sunlight.

The Florentine painter Sandro Botticelli (1444–1510) represents a transitional stage between the early and the High Renaissance. Although like his predecessors he reveled in beautiful objects, as shown in his delicate treatment of flowers, hair, and garments, he was not content to capture the passing scene, nor was he satisfied with beauty as an end in itself. His willowy nudes are fragile, rather than voluptuous, mournful, even troubled. Botticelli was a splendid craftsman with a rich and sensitive imagination, but his paintings are filled with allegory and symbolism that is not easy to fathom. If he can be called a "psychological" painter, it is not because of kinship to modern schools of psychology but because he attempted to probe deeply into the inner recesses of man's being.

The art of the High Renaissance, although indebted to the Trecento and Quattrocento, is marked by fundamental changes in mood and emphasis. Even in the matter of technical proficiency and subtlety, the advances are so remarkable as to compel admiration. While grappling with vaster subjects painters learned to keep their pictures from appearing crowded. They eliminated distracting details, enticed the utmost expression from bodily contour and gesture, and subjected complex and twisting forms to a continuous flow of line. Their figures seem capable of movement, even when they are at rest. They enhanced dramatic effect by a symmetry of design that directs the viewer's attention to a central figure or focal point of action. The effective use of geometrical patterns can be seen by comparing successive representations of the Last Supper of Christ and his disciples. In Ghirlandajo's *Last Supper* (1480), eleven of the disciples are seated on the far side of a long table with Christ just left of center and with Judas, on the near side of the table, slightly to the right. Leonardo da Vinci's famous treatment of the same subject, painted about fifteen years later, follows the same general scheme. But while Ghirlandajo's work is "an assemblage without a center," [3] Leonardo's is perfectly and dramatically unified. The disciples are grouped together in threes and these separate groups form a larger pyramid of which the apex is Christ, who has just announced his forthcoming betrayal by one of the twelve. The impact of the entire work is direct and overwhelming. Leonardo deliberately made the table too small, but this departure from literal reality strengthens the design and enhances the importance of the human characters. Leonardo, Andrea del Sarto, Raphael and other masters of the High Renaissance repeatedly used a triangular arrangement of figures, especially in representing the Holy Family, without, however, letting it become a trite formula. Leonardo's handling of perspective was daring and extremely original. In his *Mona Lisa* the foreground and central figure appear to be on an elevation high above the dreamlike landscape which winds and twists into the distance. Leonardo's compulsive interest in probing the secrets of nature is evident in his treatment of plants, rocks and other terrestrial phenomena. His *Virgin of the Rocks,* without sacrificing anything of its eloquence of expression, is both a study in geology and an exercise in geometrical proportions. Michelangelo, on the other hand, not only in his sculpture but also in his paintings, minimized or dispensed with background, lavishing his full resources upon human forms.

In addition to formal changes, sculpture and painting of the High Renaissance are characterized by a heightened seriousness of

[3] Heinrich Wölfflin, *The Art of the Italian Renaissance* (New York: Schocken, 1963), p. 30.

purpose and dignified splendor. The relaxed gaiety, the open-eyed delight in the world of nature so prominent in the works of the earlier period, gave way to a preoccupation with heroic forms and opulent grandeur. In a sense the art of the High, or Classical, stage, appealing to elevated tastes and to the intellect, is aristocratic, but it would be false to say it reflects the artificial standards of an introverted minority. The greatest artists dealt with universal themes and attempted to take the measure of man as a moral and spiritual being. While attaining formal perfection and outward magnificence, art became speculative and philosophical. It wove together many strands, some of them contradictory—classical, historical, secular, and religious. Raphael devoted one wall of the Sistine Chapel's Camera della Segnatura to a fresco celebrating pagan science and philosophy (*The School of Athens*), and another to Apollo and the Muses (*Parnassus*). Leonardo competed with Michelangelo for a commission from the Florentine government to commemorate a military victory. The prolific Michelangelo's creations include an Apollo, a Brutus, Leda and her swan lover, a tipsy Bacchus, battling centaurs. Benvenuto Cellini executed busts of his patrons and of pagan gods. Venetian painters of the High Renaissance were addicted to luxurious color, ornate architectural backgrounds, and exhibition of the undraped female form. Examples of such apparent departures from Christian sobriety could be multiplied. Nevertheless, the artists who were preeminent in their own day, and whose fame has endured, devoted themselves time and again to problems which Christian thinkers had wrestled with for centuries.

The art of the High Renaissance almost entirely excluded the element of playfulness, the lighthearted and the trivial. This is only partly explained by the fact that much of it was commissioned to satisfy the grandiose ambitions of popes and princes. In spite of examples of ornate extravagance and pomposity, the art of the High Renaissance is more profoundly religious than that of the early Renaissance. It drew upon a deeper stratum of the medieval heritage and hence adopted a more somber tone. If the religious art of the Quattrocento in its unaffected naturalism seemed to break away from medieval solemnity and mystery, the Cinquecento reversed the course and emphasized the miraculous and the supernatural. Angels were no longer permitted to walk but must hover in the air; the Madonna made her appearance on a cloud. Some of the most famous Italian artists of the High Renaissance were religious in the full and literal sense. Raphael's radiant Madonnas can hardly be explained as perfunctory tributes to conventional piety. Fra Bartolommeo, a major painter who commands the respect of modern connoisseurs for his "robust sensuality" and the "buoyant beauty" of his virile figures, was a pupil of Savonarola, remained a Dominican monk, and consecrated his talents to the golden legend of Christ and the Apostles. Botticelli, who painted ethereal madonnas as well as mythological allegories, succumbed so deeply to the spell of Savonarola that he never fully recovered.

To regard the art of the High Renaissance as paganism triumphant is to misunderstand it completely. At the same time, its religious aspects represent not a reactionary tide, nor a failure of nerve, but the fulfillment, or attempted fulfillment, of earlier promise. The religious significance of Cinquecento art lies not in externals, and certainly not in its having been produced for churches or papal chambers, but in the fact that it revived the theme of an inevitable struggle in which man is both the issue and the protagonist—a struggle between lower and higher impulses, a struggle for redemption and perfection. Like Dante and Aquinas—although employing a different idiom—artists of the High Renaissance were engaged with man's destiny, which they conceived in terms of a quest for salvation.

Renaissance art may truly be called humanist, but artists of the High Renaissance were less interested in the pictorial and fleeting aspects of the human panorama than in interpreting the essential nature of man. Like the dramatists of the golden age of Athens, they sought to delineate man's place in the universe, to assess his role as a moral being. The image that emerges from their work is not that of modern man—dwarfed or bemused by his own gigantic constructions—nor is it that of the ancient Greek or Roman. In contrast to the classical ideal they emphasize tension and struggle; when they show calm repose, it is not the harmony of "a sound mind in a healthy body" but a beatific state beyond the confines of ordinary experience. Their art both glorifies man and exposes his limitations. The power and beauty of the human creature are viewed against the background of cosmic forces and under the aspect of eternity. Renaissance art at its climax thus brings into the foreground concepts which had been nurtured, but only dimly articulated throughout the Christian Middle Ages, and carries them to the outer bounds of artistic imagination, beyond which they can only disintegrate.

Late Renaissance artists, in their soaring ambition, philosophical probing, and relentless quest for meaning, eventually stretched aesthetic sensibilities to the breaking point. Painters of the Cinquecento projected scenes of conflict and suffering—battles, the martyrdom of saints, the agony of Christ. They indulged in apocalyptic visions of Christ's ascent into Heaven, the Transfiguration, the conversion of St. Paul, the Last Judgment. Italian artists of this late period, consummate masters of all the artifices of their craft, seemed to remain unsatisfied with the act of creation even when flawlessly executed. The ultimate result was a straining for effect, an overreaching of technical virtuosity which impaired the noble serenity that crowns the works of the greatest masters. Michelangelo burst the bonds of realism and made a heroic effort to push beyond the frontiers of the visible world. He introduced more and more distortion, and in the final phase of his sculpture his figures became not only distorted but indistinct, half submerged in the primordial stone. With Michelangelo's successors in the age of "mannerism" and the baroque, distortion degenerated into contortion, offering a display of acrobatics with little meaning—"an anatomical museum." [4]

THE INFLUENCE OF NEOPLATONISM

Renaissance art, like that of the Middle Ages, is weighted with symbolism. Painters and sculptors drew freely upon both Christian and pagan sources; they did not hesitate to combine elements from these divergent traditions because they regarded them not as antithetical but as complementary aspects of truth. A recurrent motif in Renaissance art was the effort to reconcile the Greco-Roman view of life with the dogmas of Christianity, an effort that proved to be impossible, but which aroused creative faculties to the highest pitch. If it was impossible to achieve a complete accommodation between Greco-Roman mythology and Judaic-Christian scriptures, between pagan egoism and Christian renunciation, between Platonic reverie and Apostolic revelation, nevertheless a remarkable fusion did take place "in the brief burst of flame and light that was the High Renaissance." [5]

A strong current affecting Italian art of the later Renaissance

---

[4] *Ibid.*, p. 196.

[5] Panofsky, *op. cit.*, p. 203.

and contributing heavily to its symbolism was the cult of Neo-platonism, a mélange of religious and philosophical thought which derived, with modifications, from the mystical idealism of Plato. Although of pre-Christian origin and once an esoteric rival of Christianity, Neoplatonism had influenced Christian belief from St. Augustine onward. Its enthusiastic revival in the fifteenth century by Marsilio Ficino and his associates at the Florentine Academy was conceived not as a break with the established faith but as a means of strengthening religious insight and of bridging the gap between the classical philosophical heritage and Christianity.

The Neoplatonism of Plotinus (third century A.D.), which St. Augustine had embraced before his conversion to Christianity, was ascetic and pessimistic. It affirmed the inferiority of the physical world, regarding it as only a feeble reflection of the world of spirit emanating from God, the ultimate reality and source of all being. It taught that the human soul—although truly spirit and therefore indestructible—was imprisoned in the body, miserably entangled in vile matter. Man's only hope of release lay in a reunion of his soul with God—permanently after death, or temporarily through an ecstatic trance vouchsafed only to a few. All earthly hopes and triumphs were rejected as vain and illusory. This negative attitude toward the natural world, however, had been outgrown long before the end of the Middle Ages, and the Neoplatonic revival of the fifteenth century was infused with the optimistic spirit of the early Renaissance. Humanist Neoplatonists retained the belief in higher and lower degrees of reality and in the superiority of spirit over matter. They too defined the body as the prison of the soul, but they insisted that man could free his soul from bondage, that he could consciously direct it upward to a plane of experience far removed from the claims of the senses and animal appetites. Furthermore, they exalted reason, defining it as a uniquely human faculty—inferior to the divine intelligence, but like that intelligence, a motive force enabling man to direct his own destiny. Although set in the frame-work of a mystical and hierarchical world view which would reduce the individual to a mere peripheral object, Renaissance Neoplatonism actually magnified man's importance. It assigned him to the middle rung of the cosmic ladder, endowed him with the ability to move upward or downward according to his own volition, and hailed him as the connecting link between God and the world.

Renaissance artists, absorbed in the study of man, were attracted to Neoplatonic philosophy because it seemed to offer a means of interpreting the natural world, including human passions, in terms of man's highest potentialities. It enabled them to treat of love and beauty—and to embellish these perennial themes of art—while at the same time appealing to the intellectual and moral faculties; and by drawing upon the rich storehouse of pagan mythology they could invest subtle metaphysical concepts with a warm and radiant symbolism.

Straightforward as it appears to be, the art of the High Renaissance can be apprehended only superficially unless the deep influence of Neoplatonism is taken into account The abundance of nudes, for example, reflects—along with an undeniable fascination with the human body—the boldly expressed conviction that reality is independent of external trappings, that truth is unadorned. Erotic themes, while utilizing the traditional figures of mythology, were made to symbolize the Neoplatonic conception of love as a divine force leading its object upward from the earthly plane. Two different levels of love were commonly represented by two Venus figures. The higher or "celestial" Venus personified pure intelligence. The "natural" Venus stood for the generative principle which permeates the world of living creatures and which, by imparting the image of beauty to physical objects, kindles in the soul a desire for true beauty, beyond material form or appearance. The second Venus is not lust, not an evil temptress, not strictly speaking earthly, but a necessary link in the chain that unites the world of sense with the divine realm of absolute being and intellect. Mere sensuality, desire that remains on the level of physical appetite, was scorned by most artists as outside the pale and contemptuously classified as "bestial love" or even as a disease.

One of the most famous treatments of the twin Venus theme and one which strikingly illustrates the Neoplatonic conception of love is the painting by Titian popularly called *Sacred and Profane Love*, dating from about 1515. Of the two seated women, the nude figure is the more prominent. While with her left hand she raises a flaming lamp, representing divine light, she leans gently toward her companion, who is richly but tastefully clothed. The lovely robed figure is natural love, the necessary generative principle, while the unadorned Venus symbolizes pure intelligence. The painting is not a sermon on vice and virtue; it draws no invidious comparison between the sacred and the "profane." It pays tribute to both celestial and human love as complementary forces both inherently desirable. Artists under the spell of Neoplatonism did not negate the world. They accepted it gladly, recognizing it as a region incomplete and unsatisfactory in itself but penetrated by rays of celestial fire and capable of preparing man's soul for its upward ascent. Such a view of reality is far removed from that of classical or of modern man, and probably untenable in the long run. It is not, strictly speaking, ascetic; it does not enjoin celibacy or hair shirts; but it places a high premium on inward and spiritual qualities and bases its appeal on mysticism rather than on common sense. That such a philosophical groundwork could stimulate an exuberant flow of artistic creativity underscores the optimistic temper of the Renaissance. In a less confident age it would have dried up the springs of imagination. Artists of the High Renaissance were able to transform an elusive metaphysical concept into something visible and inspiring. Without denying the flesh, they did not so much glory in it as seek to glorify it. In their hands "the Word became flesh" and dwelt among men—a thing of beauty to delight the eye, and at the same time a reminder of a spiritual quest.

Sandro Botticelli is one of the major artists whose works were deeply influenced by Neoplatonism. Two of his most famous paintings—*The Birth of Venus* and the *Primavera* or *Allegory of Spring*—have sometimes been cited as examples of the triumph of paganism over the taboos of traditional Christianity. These two scenes portray not saints, angels, or madonnas, but Olympian deities and personifications of the forces of nature. In the *Primavera*, Flora—a full-fleshed, barefooted young woman in a billowy, flower-spangled gown, her face glowing with an adolescent reverie of early spring—strikes the viewer as an exquisitely sensuous creature. In their entirety, however, both works embody Neoplatonic idealism and are at the opposite pole from the cult of sensuality. The two scenes are complementary and Venus is the central figure of each. *The Birth of Venus* shows the goddess naked (she has been born of the sea and has no mother) because she symbolizes divine love, which has no earthly affiliation and belongs to a sphere more exalted than that of reason or intellect. The Venus of *Primavera*, fully clothed, represents human love. Although of a lower order than the celestial Venus, she is not in the least voluptuous: her posture and the arrangement of her garments are those traditionally associated with the Virgin of the Annunciation. And the figure of Mercury, personifying human reason or the probing intellect that guides the soul, has turned his back on the entire company—the chaste goddess of human love no less than the dancing Graces, Flora and Zephyr—and directs his gaze upward and beyond.[6] Far from repudiating Christianity, Botticelli transformed pagan mythological themes into moral and spiritual allegories.

Undeniably, examples can be found of works that are genuinely pagan, sensual, even gross, but these are not characteristic of the mainstream of Renaissance art. Also, unfamiliarity with the symbolism employed may easily lead one to misinterpret or to miss entirely the meaning of a work of art. A case in point is the *Allegory of Luxury* by Angelo Bronzino, painted about 1546 (now in the London National Gallery). This picture, which shows in the foreground a nude Venus offering her ripe body to a naked youth, seems to be unbridled sensualism, startling in its directness. The scene, however, was designed to illustrate both the allure and the torments of love, with emphasis on the latter. In the background lurk treacherous figures of Jealousy and Deceit together with an assortment of sinister objects, while wrathful Time and Truth draw back a curtain to expose vice to the light of day. Bronzino's *Allegory*, condemning sexuality indiscriminately, goes beyond the Neoplatonic tradition in its austere and negative morality. It signifies a waning of optimism, a growing doubt as to the compatibility of man's physical and spiritual natures. With its exaggerated sensuality and violent conjunction of vice and virtue, the picture reflects the spirit of the Counter Reformation rather than of the Renaissance.

THE GENIUS OF MICHELANGELO

The most profound of all the artists of the Italian Renaissance was Michelangelo Buonarroti. His enormous talent coupled with seemingly superhuman energy make him almost unique in the history of art. To some critics he appears to stand alone and therefore not really to belong to the Renaissance, although the dates of his life (1475–1564) coincide with the High Renaissance and extend beyond it. Like others of the rare breed of supreme geniuses, Michelangelo cannot be compressed into a school or a period. Nevertheless, he thought, triumphed, and suffered as a man of the Renaissance. If his

---

[6] *Ibid.*, pp. 191–200; see also Edgar Wind, *Pagan Mysteries in the Renaissance* (New York: Barnes and Noble, 1968), pp. 113–127.

personality was atypical and his genius unique, he, of all artists, provided the most penetrating comment on the age in which he lived—its premises, its aspirations, its frustrations and failures. Michelangelo was caught up in the currents of his age and assailed by its pressures. Not by temperament or choice a political man, he became embroiled in the stormy political fortunes of Florence and the papacy. Nurtured in Florence under Lorenzo the Magnificent, he served the republic during its brief period of independence and helped defend the city in its desperate stand against imperial troops in 1529. He also worked, however sullenly, for the Medici after they had reoccupied the Florentine republic and converted it into a despotism. He was scarred by the adversities of warring city-states and vexed by the caprice of imperious patrons, including the willful Pope Julius II and the two Medici popes. His childhood and youth had been clouded by such experiences as the discipline of a stern father, the early death of an adored mother, and the indignity of a broken nose inflicted by a bully in Lorenzo de' Medici's entourage. Michelangelo's penchant for unhappiness was also intensified by his own irritability, oversensitivity, and woeful deficiency of judgment, and he was destined to remain a lonely figure. Even his love affairs were strange and unsatisfying. He struggled against his homosexual nature and sought refuge in spiritualized relationships—finally, when he was past sixty, with one of the remarkable Italian women of the age, the talented and devout Vittoria Colonna, whose sonnets stimulated Michelangelo's outpourings of verse and whose friendship intensified his religious longings. He sublimated his passion for Colonna so completely that she became for him a symbol of divine love, a mystical figure like Dante's Beatrice.

Although Michelangelo's art and ideas were shaped by the currents of the time, they were not restricted to its immediate concerns. His works demonstrate with equal clarity the stimulus derived from the revival of antique classical forms and the still powerful influence of medieval Christianity. Whatever he drew from these sources he transmuted into something distinct and original through the force of his own imagination. He was fully cognizant—sometimes jealous— of the achievements of other artists, but although influenced by others he never imitated them and had no need to imitate. The disappointments and loneliness of his life, instead of withering his creative talents, drove him on to continuous and often furious activity which hardly abated before his death at the age of eighty-nine.

Michelangelo possessed a craving for beauty that remained unsatisfied even after he had tasted the fruits of fame. He found only limited satisfaction in physical beauty, in spite of a skill for portraying it that aroused the envy of his competitors. His artistic canons were grounded in Neoplatonic idealism and Christian dogma. The discerning critic Erwin Panofsky goes so far as to assert that only Michelangelo among his contemporaries adopted Neoplatonism "in its entirety," not merely as a philosophical system but as "a metaphysical justification of his own self." [7] According to Neoplatonic doctrine, physical beauty is evanescent, a mere image or echo; true beauty is an attribute of the soul, a spiritual state which the soul remembers from a precorporeal existence. On the mortal plane the soul is a prisoner of the body, and the soul's struggle to attain beauty and freedom is an agonizing process. No other artist pursued this paradox so relentlessly as Michelangelo. But dominating even the quest for beauty was his determination to fathom and assess the nature of man. In an age of humanism, he above all other artists made man's state and destiny his perpetual theme, to the exclusion of irrelevant or purely ornamental elements.

In view of the fact that Michelangelo's working years spanned three quarters of a century, it is not strange that his style and mood changed noticeably during the course of his career. Some critics designate the period of his youth as "classical," in contrast to the "religious" period of his later life. In fact, there is no fundamental opposition between these stages. The sculpture of his youth and early manhood indeed reflects an appreciative study of the examples of Greco-Roman statuary that were coming to light; but even his early works are markedly different in mood from the antique. They are invested with the tautness and the restrained energy that were to remain characteristics of his style throughout. And when he turned to religious subjects he imparted to them a vigor, a solidity and fidelity to human anatomy acquired from familiarity with classical models. In his Sistine Chapel fresco *The Last Judgment*—a painting so austere and otherworldly that it seems a renunciation not only of paganism but also of humanism—he chose to portray the figure of Christ the Judge as a muscular broadchested Apollo. Michelangelo's

---

[7] Erwin Panofsky, *Studies in Iconology* (New York: Harper & Row, 1962), p. 180.

creative output reveals growth and development but not the replacement of one set of values by another. It is unnecessary to assume that he underwent a "conversion" to Christianity. The deep emotional experiences of his life impelled him in a single direction. The end is implicit in the beginning. Particularly notable are a series of sculptures and reliefs of Madonna and Child executed in 1504 and 1505 when the artist was about thirty years old. They include the Madonna of Bruges, the Pitti Madonna in Florence, and the Taddei Madonna in the Royal Academy, London. These products of Michelangelo's allegedly classical or pagan period are arresting not for any antithesis to Christian teachings but for a combination of heroic dignity with a sense of foreboding. The harmony between Mother and Child is intimate and complete but troubled. The young Mother has the rapt gaze of a prophetess. The Child of the Taddei relief shrinks from a bird in the hands of his playmate John as if it were a nameless terror. In the Bruges statue the Child squares his firm little body to step down from the Madonna's lap, while he lowers his eyes and reaches back to cling to her hand. Completed even earlier, when Michelangelo was in his mid-twenties, was the great *Pietà* of St. Peter's, a supremely beautiful monument to the enduring compassion of human motherhood and also a perfect expression of the Christian doctrine of Christ's sacrifice, reflected in the profound but unprotesting grief of the Virgin—a "mute monologue of pain." [8] Almost from the outset of his career Michelangelo attempted to probe into man's nature and destiny. Pagan mythological motifs, Neoplatonic philosophy, the dogmas of Christianity were only means assisting to this end. When he applied himself to specifically Christian subjects, he did not hesitate to inject Neoplatonic elements, although in his case the effect was hardly calming. He was constantly torn between his passion for physical beauty and his yearning to go beyond it. He grew disillusioned and bitter over the failure of human beings to respond to the divine summons which he believed it was the artist's privilege to witness and his duty to make manifest.

One of Michelangelo's most ambitious projects, the tomb of Pope Julius II in the Church of San Pietro in Vincoli, would have provided a magnificent exposition of Christian Neoplatonism if its original plan had been carried out. The final product symbolizes not

---

[8] Wölfflin, *op. cit.*, p. 48.

only the frustration likely to be encountered by an uncompromising idealist but also the personal frustrations of the artist. Originally conceived in 1505, the plans were repeatedly revised and curtailed, and the tomb was not completed until 1545, more than thirty years after the death of the pontiff it was intended to honor. The Medici popes Leo x and Clement vii made other demands upon the artist, and the project was interrupted so many times that its final form embodied only pitiful fragments of the original conception. Michelangelo had envisioned a mighty complex of sculpture and architecture portraying the ascent of the soul from its earthly habitation to the highest realm of being. Man's animal nature enmired in the appetites was to be dramatically symbolized by a group of fettered slaves, while statues of victory represented the soul liberated from bondage. Figures of Moses and St. Paul, on a higher tier, were to personify respectively the virtues of the active and the contemplative life. An image of the pope supported by angels, at the apex of the structure, was intended to convey something more significant and universal than a dead man's transposition to heaven. (This crafty potentate's credentials for such a destination were dubious at best, as attested by Erasmus' pungent satire, *Dialogue of Julius Excluded from Heaven.*) The entire monument, like Dante's *Divine Comedy,* was conceived as an allegory of man's spiritual progress from the domain of beasts to the realm of angels. It was to treat human redemption and beatitude not as a miraculous event but as the final culmination of an orderly progression. In reducing his grand design to the modest limits of a wall tomb, Michelangelo had to sacrifice much of his symbolism and most of his figures. Besides, by the time the work was finished the glowing expectations of his youth had become somewhat dimmed. The tomb, as completed, remains a tomb, noble but motionless. The level depicting earthly struggle (including the bound slaves, examples of which can be seen in the Louvre and the Florence Academy) was eliminated entirely. Absent also is the essential motif of the soul ascending. The recumbent image of the pope rests secure on his sarcophagus, flanked by saints and beneath the feet of the Madonna. "A monument to the 'consonance of Moses and Plato' had developed into a monument to the Counter-Reformation." [9] But not completely—for the tomb retains the awesome figure of Moses. This Jovian horned creature, fingering his

---

[9] *Studies in Iconology, op. cit.,* p. 199.

flowing beard and gazing into eternity, is endowed with the *terribilità* of his creator. Contrary to a popular tradition, however, he represents not an angry Moses, about to rise and chastise the children of Israel for worshipping the Golden Calf, but a seer enraptured with a vision of the inward eye, transported by the splendor of divine light.

Neoplatonism also supplied the fundamental theme for another of Michelangelo's most famous works of sculpture, the Medici tombs in the chapel of San Lorenzo in Florence. This undertaking, like the tomb of Julius, was subjected to a series of revisions and reductions of the original plan. Michelangelo worked on it over a period of more than a decade (1521–34) and left it uncompleted. Even more than in the case of the papal tomb, the Medici chapel creations reflect the artist's growing sense of frustration and a melancholy approaching despair. His feelings toward his Medici patrons were ambivalent. When in 1529 Florence made its second ill-fated bid for freedom, he laid aside hammer and chisel to supervise the strengthening of the city's fortifications—in vain as the event proved. He may well have been depressed by the collapse of the republic and the restoration of tyranny under Duke Alessandro de' Medici, but his disillusion went deeper than concern for the success or failure of a political faction. The final choice of subjects for the statuary of the Medici chapel is ironical. Only two family tombs were included, one for Giuliano, Duke of Nemours, youngest son of Lorenzo the Magnificent, and the other for the great Lorenzo's grandson, Lorenzo, Duke of Urbino—two of the most insignificant representatives of the illustrious family of Medici. Their only qualification for the honor bestowed on them was that both had died recently. To compound the irony, Michelangelo chose the Giuliano figure as a symbol of the active life, although the Duke of Nemours had been notoriously indolent and his most strenuous activity the pursuit of women. And the figure of Lorenzo, whose health had been broken in the iniquitous campaign to seize the duchy of Urbino from the della Rovere family, was made to symbolize the life of contemplation. The sculptures, although realistically executed, are not in any degree portraits of the deceased but are representations of ideal qualities. Particularly notable are the nude figures—reclining on sarcophagus lids not big enough to hold them properly—associated with the four principal times of day. These twisted forms are both powerful and beautiful but most striking for the sense of sadness they convey. Beneath the chair of Lorenzo (Contemplation), Twilight, an old man, subsides into a stupor of exhaustion while Dawn, a comely young woman, arouses herself with painful reluctance. Under Giuliano (the active principle) Father Day glowers hatefully over his crunched shoulder and fertile Mother Night, with her head bowed in resignation, seems too hopelessly sorrowful for sleep. The dominant aspect of gloom is relieved somewhat by an unfinished freestanding statue of the Madonna and Child placed against the entrance wall of the chapel, which is a hymn in stone. Not a miraculous creature although she almost floats above the supporting base, the Mother, yielding her breast to the importunate Child, seems to embody all compassion and understanding.

Cheerfulness is not a characteristic of Michelangelo, but no Renaissance artist paid higher tribute than he to man's inherent potential for nobility and greatness. The period of his most confident humanism was that which produced the sequence of frescoes covering the ceiling of the Sistine Chapel in the Vatican. To these he devoted four years when he was in the vigor of young manhood (1508–12). As usual, this work of almost indescribable magnificence embodies paradoxes. Michelangelo accepted the commission from Pope Julius with reluctance, complaining that he was a sculptor rather than a painter. But he gave himself completely to the project, not only insisting on a free rein for the choice of scheme and subject matter but also filling in much of the tedious detail with his own hands. Grumbling and cursing his fate, toiling long hours on an uncomfortable scaffold, he created a succession of earthly and heavenly figures such as the eye of man had never seen before. His vision expanded as the work progressed, and he frequently disregarded his preliminary tracings as he strove for bolder effects.

The nine panels of the upper ceiling depict the Creation narrative of Genesis and dramatize the epic of man from his divine origin to his fall. The story is told in reverse order; the frame nearest the Chapel entrance shows man's fallen state in the guise of drunken Noah, while at the far end near the altar appear the scenes of God the Father calling forth light, the world, and the waters. The creation of man and woman and their expulsion from paradise are placed prominently in the center of the series. This nonchronological arrangement is perfectly in keeping with Renaissance Neoplatonism, which taught that man occupies a middle state in the hierarchy of being and has freedom to ascend or descend. The Sistine frescoes are freighted with ancient mythological and Neoplatonic symbolism, but it is not necessary to decipher the symbolism in order to feel their impact. While the Prophets and oracles pictured are figures traditionally interpreted as foretelling the advent of Christ, specifically Christian—that is, New Testament—elements are lacking. The whole panorama is a perfect fusion of Hebraic mythology and Neoplatonism transmuted into a moral allegory of tremendous strength and clarity. Although the theme of man's fall and degradation is a tragic one, the accent is on the positive vital forces of the cosmos, forces which gave birth to man and which man can himself employ. Life and strength, the glory of being and beholding are proclaimed by the Prophets and Sibyls of the border panels and by the seemingly superfluous but inspired nudes that Michelangelo placed on the corners of the central pictures. Special prominence is given to the figure of Adam, who, extending his arm to receive the spark of life, is stationed almost on the same level as his Creator. The Garden of Eden scene, with serpent and apple and angel of wrath, is neither depressing nor sinister. The recumbent nude figure of Eve—reaching languidly to accept the apple and thus bring sin into the world —is one of the most movingly beautiful representations of womankind in the annals of art. And unlike Leonardo's inscrutable *Mona Lisa,* her expression is perfectly transparent in its tender and innocent sensuousness.

Strikingly different in conception and mood is Michelangelo's great painting of the *Last Judgment,* which covers the wall behind the altar of the Sistine Chapel and was executed some thirty years later than the ceiling frescoes. If the earlier work is Old Testament and Hebraic, the wall scene is New Testament and Christian, but in a manner which reverses the traditional interpretations of the two Covenants. The ceiling narrative, with pagan Sibyls and athletes, the Flood and the Fall, glorifies man and offers hope. The *Last Judgment,* with Christ, the Holy Virgin, saints and martyrs, pronounces a doleful sentence on the whole human race, including the artist himself (his face appears in the folds of the flayed skin of St. Bartholomew). But even in this terrifying work with its harsh overtones of the Counter Reformation, the humanist theme is transposed rather than extinguished. If man is doomed, the Christ who metes out judgment and around whom the cosmos revolves is not an emaciated Galilean but a majestic, full-fleshed Apollo.

The changes in style evident in Michelangelo's later years are very marked, but the artist's retreat into conventional Christianity must be regarded as an accompaniment rather than a sufficient explanation of these changes. Toward the end of his life he withdrew from the mainstream of Renaissance art and seemed indifferent to his own earlier accomplishments. The sculpture of this late period shows a relaxation of tension, an abating of passion approaching, though never quite attaining, serenity. Abandoning both classicism and realism, he turned to mysticism in a series of dreamy, distorted, half-finished Pietàs, including the Deposition in the duomo of Florence, originally intended for his own tomb. While investing his art with an abstract spirituality, he intensified his quest for personal purity and reproached himself for attachment to "fables of the world." As a final offering of faith, he undertook to design the new basilica of St. Peter's. This demanding architectural project—although it evoked the usual jealous controversies—afforded a welcome opportunity to the world-weary artist to divert his attention from human imperfections to the ideal properties of space and form. In spite of the fact that Michelangelo's plan for St. Peter's was not carried out entirely, by surrounding the dome with columns and vertical ribs he was able to leave a Gothic imprint on a structure essentially baroque.

The quietism and otherworldly quality of Michelangelo's last work reflect a new personal orientation—a quest for peace after a lifetime of struggle—but not a fundamental change of faith. To interpret them as the result of a "conversion" to Christianity is to overlook the fact that Michelangelo had been a believing and practicing Catholic throughout his life. He responded earnestly to the various religious currents of his age. In his youth he was deeply impressed by the fiery prophetic sermons of Savonarola. Through his friendship with Vittoria Colonna he became attracted to the evangelical and mystical Catholic Reform movement, which espoused the Lutheran doctrine of justification by faith alone and was consequently condemned by popes of the Counter Reformation. But although sympathetic to the message of reformers, Michelangelo remained obedient to Rome, and he offered to build a church for Ignatius Loyola. Accepting unquestioningly the sacraments, decrees, and authority of the Church, Michelangelo had little interest in dogma. His was a broader and more penetrating vision than could be comprehended in an official creed. The Church militant could not claim him as a champion, although it could mute his voice and desecrate his art by ordering clothing to be painted over some of his heroic nudes. He took no part in the controversies that were enraging the clergy and splitting Western Christendom asunder. The split between Catholics and Protestants was symptomatic of a deep rupture that affected both camps—the growing separation between faith and works, between the realms of action and belief, between the actual world and the ideal world. It was this deeper dichotomy that afflicted Michelangelo and that he attempted in vain to resolve. If his final works no longer depict the titanic struggle of opposites—flesh and spirit, natural and divine—it is because his contemporaries were no longer listening to what he had to say. For the majority of them, Catholic or Protestant, the conflict had been resolved, by awarding an easy formal victory to Faith—accepted not as an instrument to spiritualize man's animal nature or the material world but as a vehicle of escape for his soul.

It is not strange that at the end Michelangelo sought to make his own private peace and quiet his turbulent spirit. But he remained to the end the great tragedian of the Renaissance, and he is one of the greatest tragedians of all time. The recurrent theme in his works, and which he could never relinquish, was man's inherent capacity for greatness and man's tragic refusal to accept the role for which he is eligible.

THE FINE ARTS IN NORTHERN EUROPE— THE FLEMISH SCHOOL

The period of the Renaissance witnessed an outpouring of artistic creativity not only in Italy but also in sections of northern Europe, particularly the Netherlands and Germany. Although influenced by Italian examples, artistic movements in the north differed from the Italian in fundamental respects. The art of the northern countries, where there was no deeply rooted classical heritage, was more directly a continuation of medieval forms. In architecture the Gothic remained dominant, inclining towards excessive complexity and ornamentation. Sculpture only timidly attempted to divorce itself from architecture, and, lacking the invigorating influence of classical models to draw upon, tended—with some notable exceptions—to degenerate from the crisp dignity of Gothic saints and madonnas into affectation and artificiality. Painting, the pioneer art where innovation was a necessity, showed the most vitality and attracted the

MICHELANGELO
Virgin of Bruges
PHOTO ALINARI

Below:
MICHELANGELO
Fall of Man
PHOTO ALINARI

MICHELANGELO
Medici Virgin
PHOTO ALINARI

DURER
Four Naked Women
NATIONAL GALLERY OF ART,
WASHINGTON, D.C.,
ROSENWALD COLLECTION

DURER
Adam and Eve
NATIONAL GALLERY OF ART,
WASHINGTON, D.C.,
ROSENWALD COLLECTION

DONATELLO
David
PHOTO ALINARI

greatest talents. However, even this versatile medium was utilized chiefly to provide new treatment for traditional themes.

Northern Europeans were not inferior to the Italians in artistic talent or inventiveness. They produced geniuses of the first rank, whose works are fully equal in merit to the masterpieces of Italy. In some particulars they scored success ahead of the Italians, notably in the development of oil painting by the fifteenth-century Flemish school. In music the Netherlands composers, masters of polyphonic style, led the Western world during the fifteenth and early sixteenth centuries. They dominated the musical capitals of northern Italy until the time of Palestrina (d. 1594), and even the noble Masses of this "Prince of Music" reflect Netherlands influence, as do the works of the English seventeenth-century madrigalists. However, the rich harvest of vocal—and, to a lesser extent, instrumental—music during the period of the Renaissance represents a fulfillment rather than a revival—living proof of the maturity of an art that had been nurtured by the Church for centuries and was now beginning to assert its independence. The visual arts on the whole, although yielding some extraordinary specimens, developed in a more restrained and less spectacular manner than those of Italy. While innovations in painting in fifteenth-century Flanders were as significant as those associated with Giotto and his Florentine successors, the northerners apparently did not conceive of their own artistic movement as a rebirth. During the course of the Renaissance they learned much from Italy, but what they borrowed they assimilated to their own tastes and idioms.

Regional characteristics stamped their imprint upon the art of each of the three principal centers of Renaissance culture. The artists of Italy had begun with an almost unconscious fusion of classical pagan and Christian elements. The happy result of this synthesis was—for a time—a reaffirmation of natural and especially human values, a declaration of faith in man's physical and spiritual destiny. In the Low Countries, a deeply implanted Gothic heritage, mellowed somewhat by the influence of humanism, attained a ripe perfection and then gradually dissolved into the countless genres suitable to an increasingly complex and cosmopolitan society. The sumptuous but conventionally pious masterworks of the great Flemish religious painters marked the ultimate stage of a tradition that could be carried no further and became increasingly irrelevant. In the sixteenth century Pieter Brueghel the Elder favored landscapes and realistic but sympathetic portrayals of the life of humble peasants. His successor, Peter Paul Rubens, turned to heroic subjects and the gratification of aristocratic tastes, producing the grandest paintings of the baroque era. Because the art of the Netherlands was never so completely absorbed in Renaissance themes as that of Italy, it could be adapted more readily to changing societal and cultural patterns, and Netherlands artists retained an ascendancy over other Europeans after the Renaissance era had passed. The soil of Germany was least hospitable to a flowering of the plastic arts, especially of the Italian variety. Germany lacked the fertile substratum of a classical heritage, and the morbid aspects of medieval Christianity were still potent enough to induce an obsession with death, phantasms of horror, and a dread of the approaching end of the world. In spite of these inhibiting factors, the Renaissance spirit did assert itself and evoked a profound response. German Renaissance art, like that of the High Renaissance in Italy, was characterized by seriousness of purpose and tragic tension, but it was destined to be short-lived.

The cities of Flanders and the Netherlands, like those of northern Italy, had become thriving commercial centers before the close of the Middle Ages and therefore were well able to foster the arts. A prosperous urban society, with rich burghers as well as princes and ecclesiastics, provided patronage and connoisseurs of discriminating taste. And the heritage of northern European medieval art was readily adaptable to the demands of the time. The skillful draftsmanship evident in the miniatures which adorn the pages of medieval illuminated manuscripts was now applied by Flemish painters to larger surfaces and to the production of portraits, landscapes, and interior scenes executed with remarkable realism, scrupulous detail, and pleasing color harmonies. The art of the fifteenth-century Flemish painters is warm and human, a faithful mirror of contemporary Flemish society both bourgeois and aristocratic, and also a testimony to the persistence of traditional Christian beliefs. It lacks the tension and dramatic quality so characteristic of the Italian schools, especially the Florentine. Whatever intellectual quickening it exhibits can be traced not to a revival of pagan antiquity but to the influence of the Brethren of the Common Life, whose *Devotio Moderna* inculcated a dignified and mystical pietism. Even in religious circles there was nothing comparable to the Italian firebrand Girolamo Savonarola, who both damned art and fired the imaginations of such great artists as Fra Bartolommeo and Michelangelo.

The work of the Flemish school, for all its emotional sincerity, reflects even less of the turmoil of the age than can be found in contemporary Italian art. Jan van Eyck's beautifully executed paintings, so tender and expressive, seem devoid of motion. His much admired portrait of the merchant Arnolfini and his wife—flawless both in its realism and its conscientious symbolism—is a perfectly posed photograph, a frozen moment of time. Neither husband nor wife, nor the little dog, shows the slightest desire to move. The van Eyck brothers' magnificent altarpiece for the Ghent cathedral (1432) is clearly religious yet equally striking in its realism. Adam and Eve appear not as conventional nudes but in the true likeness of man and woman. Nevertheless, this impressive work, both convincingly lifelike and intensely devout, is projected above the realm of human struggle and suffering. It is a monument, in pigment rather than wood or stone, to the mystery of Christ's sacrifice and atonement.

Roger van der Weyden (ca. 1400–64), in contrast to the van Eycks, imparted to his figures not only deep emotion but also a sense of movement and dramatic significance, as exemplified in the *Descent from the Cross* (now in the Prado Museum). Here ten figures compressed into a small area on a single plane are linked together in such a way that each gesture of grief or despair accentuates the shock evoked by the stark white body of the dead Christ. But if this is drama it is drama in which the action is finished, and only anguished contemplation and resignation are permitted. It cannot properly be called tragedy because it lacks protagonists. Christ's betrayer is not shown; there is no martyr earning his crown, nor even a sinner. Mary Magdalene, a graceful figure on the right, is as sanctified as the prostrate Virgin. The drama is God's, even though enacted for and among men. Van der Weyden was undoubtedly an innovator, notably in his economy of space, linear clarity, and the exclusion of symbolic and extraneous details for the sake of unity and heightened emotional impact. Because of his emphasis upon form and his tendency toward abstraction, he has been hailed as a modernist. But rather than reach forward to a new era his work crowned with fresh glory the dying Gothic tradition. His *Descent from the Cross*, despite its vibrant colors and undeniable realism, has a lofty solemnity not of this world. Like the spire of a Gothic cathedral, it directs the view of the beholder upward to the realm of the Almighty, which commands reverence but surpasses human understanding.

GERMANY—THE ART OF ALBRECHT DURER

In Germany the visual arts were already flourishing before the Renaissance began, but essentially as handicrafts, fostered and transmitted by successive generations of metalworkers, goldsmiths, woodcarvers and stone-carvers. German technicians took the lead in the development of engraving and in creating the press and movable type for printing books—probably the most important invention to come out of the whole era of the Renaissance. Artistic progress therefore, resting upon native foundations, moved in somewhat different directions from those followed in Italy. Renaissance currents, as they penetrated into Germany, affected more immediately not the artist's workshop but centers of learning, where they incited intellectual ferment and contributed to the religious schism of the sixteenth century. However, German art could not escape the impact of the Renaissance and was deeply shaken by it. Without abandoning their own traditions, German artists attempted to cope with the moral and philosophical problems that had engaged their Italian contemporaries. The uneasy balance, or overt antipathy, between the Gothic and the humanist spirit injected into their works a note of agitation, which subsided only when the German mind was caught up in the tide of the Reformation—itself the product of forces and ideas inherently hostile to the Renaissance.

Among the significant figures of the German artistic Renaissance, the name of Dürer towers above all others. Albrecht Dürer of Nuremberg (1471–1528), one of the supreme geniuses in the history of Western art, was at the same time emphatically a man of the Renaissance. Carefully nurtured in the traditions of German craftsmanship, he brought to perfection the technique of engraving on copper plates and made the unpretentious wood-block print a versatile and effective vehicle of artistic expression. Meanwhile he assimilated the lessons of Italian masters—Andrea Mantegna's firm line, austerity and masculine vigor; Giovanni Bellini's use of light and color as effective elements of design; suggestions from the styles of Leonardo and Michelangelo. He came to equal and in some respects surpass his teachers, and his example in turn left its mark upon Italian painters, notably Raphael. A prodigious worker, he strove constantly for greater excellence and sought out the new and unexplored. Absorbing classical and allegorical motifs, he transformed them into symbols enhancing the eloquence of his own ideas. A dying Orpheus is metamorphosed into Christ bearing the Cross; an apocalyptic engraving of Christ as the Sun of Justice combines classical and medieval astrology with the cult of the Roman Sun-Emperor (ultimately derived from Mithraism) and still remains an arresting vision of the Christian Day of Judgment. The range of his activity and of his restless imagination was enormous. He reveled in the colors of day, and he plumbed the black depths of night. His numerous portraits—including a series of introspective self-portraits —are infinitely expressive. His landscapes are clear and evocative, but frequently nostalgic, mystical, or macabre. He constructed elaborate displays of pageantry, monumental altarpieces filled with saints and apostles; he also depicted in accurate and loving detail trees, flowers, animals, even a piece of turf. He was both robust and devout, a realist who turned to allegory and symbolism and who exploited the fantastic in trying to capture all the facets of truth and experience.

As befit the age in which he lived, Dürer was something of a paradox. Although he found the atmosphere of Italy congenial and easily won acceptance among the proud and sophisticated Venetians, he chose to spend most of his working years in his native land and native town, where an artist's status was still only that of an artisan and where he was dependent on the patronage of his social superiors. Endowed with the perspicacity and diligence of a scientist—Panofsky calls him "a natural-born geometrician" [10]—he enlisted science in the service of art. Exhibiting a talent for design so precocious that it seemed to be sheer instinct, he nevertheless aspired to equate the principles of painting with the rules of mathematics, and he searched long and earnestly for a single formula to embrace the laws of perspective. A treatise on painting he left unfinished; but his *Treatise on Geometry*, first published three years before his death, won the respect of both Kepler and Galileo, and his *Four Books on Human Proportions* laid the foundations of scientific anthropometry. Besides a strong intellect, and despite a rather frail constitution, Dürer possessed a zest for life and healthy animal spirits. In his personality he seems to have been a singularly uncomplicated man—bearing up reasonably well under the strain of an incompatible marriage, capable

---

[10] Erwin Panofsky, *The Life and Art of Albrecht Dürer*, 4th ed. (Princeton: Princeton University Press, 1955), p. 254.

of laughing at himself, free from envy, warm in his friendships, and generous to a fault. Yet he was sincerely and thoroughly committed to a religion that was stark, if not primitive. He was beset with fears and haunted by portents. A dream that came to him three years before his death he interpreted as a revelation of the imminence of a second Deluge. In the midst of profound reflection he could not free himself from pangs of terror and visions of the wrath to come. His greatest masterpieces reflect the tensions of a restless and tormented spirit.

Although molded by his German environment, Dürer grappled with all the crucial themes of Renaissance thought. Receptive to the influence of the humanists (his closest and lifelong friend was the aristocratic social and literary lion Willibald Pirckheimer), he was interested in the whole man, insisted on fidelity to nature, and gave the body its due. In paintings like *Bathing Women, The Four Witches, Combat of Virtue and Pleasure in the Presence of Hercules,* and *The Abduction of Proserpine,* he produced a galaxy of nudes, amply proportioned, unabashed, and appetizing. But while he immortalized the enticing beauty of form and flesh he also served warning that pleasure is transitory and illusory. A multitude of drawings and engravings reflect his sense of the closeness of death. A grinning skeleton holding an hourglass leers from behind a tree at a handsomely dressed couple enjoying a stroll. Death as a ghastly old man greedily lifts the skirt of a helpless young woman. Dürer conjures up monsters, scenes of violence, rape, and abduction —succulent flesh in the grip of evil or demoniac forces.

While he did not celebrate unbridled carnality, it would be false to classify Dürer as morbid or as a puritanical moralizer. He sought to understand the full nature of man in all its complexities. Like so many of his contemporaries he was strangely indifferent to the harsh social realities of his day—the plight of the unfortunate peasants, for example—but he recognized and was tormented by the ambivalence of human nature torn between the rival claims of body and spirit, of intellect and intuition. In Dürer's inner being and in his works the planes of existence remained painfully separated; they could be brought together only by a juxtaposition which is forced, incongruous, and disturbing. An enigmatical study of about 1514, with a weird medley of figures and faces that has earned it the title of *The Desperate Man,* prominently displays a sleeping but flagrantly voluptuous nude. In an engraving of 1504 depicting the

Fall of Man—a theme repeated in a painting three years later—a classically modeled Adam and Eve, epitomizing natural human beauty at its ripest, are denied the slightest premonition of the fate into which they are about to plunge the race of mortals by yielding to the temptation of the serpent.

Dürer brought to his task the curiosity and diligent application of a scientist, the hypersensitive imagination of an artist, and a deeply rooted religious faith which tended to override all the rest. As he sought, vainly, for a formula to explicate the artist's craft, he probed for a solution to the riddle of man's distraught existence. Oppressed by superstitions, he yearned for rational explanations. His studies, which ranged widely in a Faustian quest for knowledge, gave him clues but no final answers. He felt, like Leonardo, that man's mind should be capable of penetrating the universal secrets of nature. And in spite of his northern primitivism he asserted, even more categorically than the Italians, that the role of the artist was not simply to reproduce but to discover, actually to create—that it was the artist's Godlike function to bring into intelligible form phenomena which were meaningless to the eye of an ordinary mortal.

Dürer has been called the Leonardo of the North, but he is more comparable to Michelangelo in his absorption with man's cosmic destiny. His methods, though, were decidedly different from those of the great Italian. While Michelangelo distorted and idealized, blending together male and female forms into a Platonic superbeing, Dürer remained the realist, with an eye for homely detail—the curious shape of an object, the mood of a country village, or the look of an abandoned stone quarry. The angel in *The Angel with a Lute*, in spite of his authentic wings, is still a wiry, strong-featured man of the people; a brush drawing for the head of an Apostle for the Heller altarpiece portrays the kindly, shrewd, weather-beaten face of an old German patriarch; an early miniature of the Infant Jesus holding a globe shows a real child's face, almost puckish. Regardless of differences of style, Dürer, like Michelangelo, created images calculated not merely to delight the eye but to illuminate the understanding—to inspire, admonish, or, at the very least, to crack the shell of complacency that insulates all of us.

Dürer's far-ranging insights into the nature and predicament of man came closest to a synthesis in his two most famous engravings: *St. Jerome in His Cell* and *Melencolia*, both executed in the year 1514 as part of a series. The contrast between the two works could hardly be more pronounced. The *St. Jerome* is "a *ne plus ultra* of consistency, clearness and, above all, economy." [11] The learned monk bends comfortably over his desk, absorbed in his writing. His cell is a cheerfully illuminated study, with all objects disposed in perfect order, including the skull on the windowsill and the sleeping lion in the foreground. In the *Melancholy* everything is in disarray. Broken and discarded objects are scattered about the floor, where a half-starved greyhound lies shivering. The light within the cluttered room seems only to deepen the gloom; outside a comet blazes fiercely within a frozen rainbow arching a lifeless sea. The central figure, a massive woman with drooping wings, one hand supporting her cheek and the other idly holding a geometer's compass, gazes into space with an expression more hopeless than angry or despairing. Both of these engravings are burdened with symbolism, but their central themes—opposing yet complementary—are forceful and direct. Dürer was exploring one of the most frequently debated topics of Renaissance speculation— the potentialities and limits of man's knowledge and of his capacity for action. The subject is related to the eternal argument over freedom of the will; more specifically, it deals with the respective claims of the active versus the contemplative life. This was a favorite Renaissance theme, but Dürer transformed a worn cliché into a fresh and insightful commentary.

The figure of Melancholy represents theoretical or speculative wisdom. She personifies the quest of science, as indicated by the hapless assortment of instruments strewn around her. St. Jerome, the ascetic monk, symbolizes the domain of faith. But in *St. Jerome* the contemplative state, energized by faith, has been converted into purposeful activity. Oblivious to self and surroundings, the scholar-saint writes with serene confidence, in the full light of day; while Melancholy, the strong-browed, probing thinker, is immobilized in the shadows of night and constrained to a profound but futile contemplation. Panofsky observes that Dürer "opposes a life in the service of God to what may be called a life in competition with God—the peaceful bliss of divine wisdom to the tragic unrest of human creation." But the artist was not pointing a simple moral, nor was he denigrating the scientific spirit. *Melencolia's* predicament

---

[11] *Ibid.*, p. 156.

stems from the fact that theoretical knowledge must be joined with action, that it is sterile unless it finds an outlet in achievement, just as practical skill or action devoid of thought is puerile and meaningless (as illustrated in *Melencolia* by an ignorant infant scribbling on a slate). Dürer also conveys the notion that natural reason alone is insufficient: it cannot generate the light necessary for its own successful functioning.

The figure of Melancholy is not an object of scorn. She represents both science and art, the two pursuits to which Dürer had given his life's blood. Furthermore, he believed that the true artist has the gift and the duty of apprehending truth, even divine truth —a conviction that explains the astounding self-portraits in which he portrayed himself in the likeness of Christ (once as the Savior and once as the Man of Sorrows). But he realized that the artist, like any technician, can founder in his own precocity. The scientist runs the risk of self-insulation. Lost in abstractions and mesmerized by his calculating machines, he may find that instead of penetrating to the heart of reality he has lost contact with it. And the artist— torn between a yearning to express the infinite and a recognition of his own finiteness—likewise knows the anguish of frustration, an anguish to which Dürer was no stranger. Thus the *Melencolia* is both a compassionate reminder of the fallibility of human reason and a personal testament—"a spiritual self-portrait of Albrecht Dürer." [12] Beyond that, in pointing to faith as the only avenue of escape, it signalizes the decay of the Thomistic tradition of optimistic rationalism and foreshadows the coming of the Reformation.

The unresolved inner tensions which Dürer projected into his art, though held in check by a disciplined and austere craftsmanship, led to an increasing preoccupation with conflict and suffering. His later works are dominated by religious themes of tragic import, such as the Passion of Christ and the Crucifixion. Driven by doubts and troubled by the upheaval of the times, he sought solace in the bedrock of faith and found it most assuredly in the version proffered by Luther. Writing in his diary in 1521, he referred to Luther as "this God-illumined man" and called upon Erasmus as a "Knight of Christ" to "ride forth" and "protect the truth": "Let thy voice be heard, and then the Gates of Hell, the Roman See, as Christ has said, will not prevail against thee." Dürer never formally broke

---

[12] *Ibid.*, p. 171.

with the Catholic church—he continued to go to confession and executed commissions for Cardinal Albrecht of Brandenburg—and he refused to prostitute his art by propagandizing for either side in the schism. However, there is no doubt that he became a convinced and unwavering Lutheran in his personal beliefs. Although he never met Martin Luther, he looked up to him almost as a personal savior, and he longed to paint his portrait "as a lasting memory of the Christian man who has helped me out of great anxieties."[13] The gospel of complete, self-abnegating acceptance of faith as the only hope for sinful man came as a balm to the weary and disconsolate artist.

Dürer could scarcely have recognized the gulf between himself and Luther, still less the gulf between the marvelous world of poetic fancy he had made his own and the harsh world of economic and political conflict that was to be ushered in with the Reformation. Nor could Luther appreciate the genius of a Dürer. Erasmus—although more attracted to Hans Holbein the younger, who painted several portraits of the humanist scholar—paid high tribute to Dürer's skill as a draftsman. Luther, on the other hand, in commenting on Dürer's death said not a word about the loss of a great artist but only that he should be mourned "as the most pious of men"[14]—surely one of the most inadequate epitaphs ever penned. The Reformation was to produce a multitude of pious men, but no Dürer to challenge them to unite piety with a relentless search for truth and beauty.

REFERENCES AND SUGGESTIONS FOR FURTHER READING

ITALY

The Autobiography of Benvenuto Cellini, trans. John A. Symonds (Garden City, N.Y.: Garden City Publishing Co., 1927). A fascinating psychological document. Cellini's braggadocio

---

[13] *Ibid.*, pp. 151, 198–199.

[14] Letter to Eobanus Hesse, quoted in Marcel Brion, *Albrecht Dürer*, trans. James Cleugh (London: Thames and Hudson, 1964), p. 278.

masked an insecurity that came close to paranoia and drove him to conduct by no means "typical" of the Renaissance life style. He does typify the passionate and inflexible dedication of the creative artist to his work.

· Berenson, Bernard, *The Italian Painters of the Renaissance* (London: Phaidon Press, 1952). Five esays by a distinguished art historian and critic, originally written between 1894 and 1907.

· Blunt, Anthony, *Artistic Theory in Italy 1450–1600*, 2nd ed. (Oxford: Clarendon Press, 1956). Excellent brief discussion of prominent artists and their aesthetic creeds.

⌐ Gombrich, Ernst H. J., *Norm and Form: Studies in the Art of the Renaissance* (London: Phaidon Press, 1966). A collection of essays on artists and Renaissance conceptions of art.

· Hauser, Arnold, *The Social History of Art*, trans. Stanley Godman, Vol. I (New York: Knopf, 1952). Comprehensive and informative.

Meiss, Millard, *Painting in Florence and Siena after the Black Death* (New York: Harper & Row, 1964). Examines the impact of fourteenth-century crises upon the Italian art of this generally neglected period.

Panofsky, Erwin, *Renaissance and Renascences in Western Art*, 2 vols. (Stockholm: Almquist and Wiksell, 1960). *Studies in Iconology: Humanistic Themes in the Art of the Renaissance* (New York: Harper & Row, 1962). "Artist, Scientist, Genius: Notes on the 'Renaissance-Dämmerung,'" in Wallace K. Ferguson *et al.*, eds., *The Renaissance: Six Essays* (New York: Harper & Row, 1962). Panofsky's works are learned and penetrating in analysis.

Sypher, Wylie, *Four Stages of Renaissance Style: Transformations in Art and Literature 1400–1700* (Garden City, N.Y.: Anchor Books, 1955). Offers a brief, provocative comparison of Gothic and Renaissance styles and stresses Renaissance indebtedness to Gothic "proto-humanism."

Vasari, Giorgio, *The Lives of the Painters, Sculptors, and Architects*, trans. A. B. Hinds, 4 vols. (New York: Everyman's Library, n.d.). *Vasari's Lives of the Artists*, abridged and ed. Betty Burroughs (New York: Simon and Schuster, 1946).

Wind, Edgar, *Pagan Mysteries in the Renaissance*, enlarged edition (New York: Barnes and Noble, 1968). Illustrates the symbolism of Italian Renaissance art through careful analysis of specific works.

Wittkower, Rudolf, *Architectural Principles in the Age of Humanism*, 2nd ed. (London: A Tirenti, 1952).

Wittkower, Rudolf and Margot, *Born under Saturn—The Character and Conduct of Artists: A Documented History from Antiquity to the French Revolution* (New York: Random House, 1963).

Wölfflin, Heinrich, *The Art of the Italian Renaissance* (New York: Schocken, 1963). A discriminating study of the aesthetic principles of great masters of the Florentine and Roman schools, valuable for interpretation of the High Renaissance.

MICHELANGELO

Clark, Kenneth, "The Young Michelangelo," in J. H. Plumb, ed., *Renaissance Profiles* (New York: Harper & Row, 1965).

de Tolnay, Charles, *Michelangelo*, 5 vols. (Princeton: Princeton University Press, 1943–1960). A monumental work, product of a lifetime of study. The gist of Tolnay's conclusions are presented attractively in his brief volume, *The Art and Thought of Michelangelo*, trans. Nan Buranelli (New York: Random House, 1964).

Schott, Rolf, *Michelangelo*, trans. Constance McNab (London: Thames and Hudson, 1964), The World of Art Library.

Symonds, John A., trans., *The Sonnets of Michael Angelo Buonarroti* (New York: Gramercy, 1960).

NORTHERN EUROPE

Benesch, Otto, *The Art of the Renaissance in Northern Europe: Its Relation to the Contemporary Spiritual and Intellectual Movements*, rev. illustr. ed. (London: Phaidon Press, 1965). Explores the influence of the Gothic tradition, humanism and religious change.

Friedländer, Max J., *Early Netherlandish Painting, from Van Eyck to Bruegel*, trans. Marguerite Kay (London: Phaidon Press, 1956). Brief sketches of artists, with illustrative plates.

Panofsky, Erwin, *Early Netherlandish Painting, its Origins and Character*, 2 vols. (Cambridge, Mass.: Harvard University Press, 1953).

DÜRER

Brion, Marcel, *Albrecht Dürer*, trans. James Cleugh (London: Thames and Hudson, 1964), The World of Art Library.

Kurth, Willi, ed., *The Complete Woodcuts of Albrecht Dürer* (New York: Crown, 1946).

Panofsky, Erwin, *The Life and Art of Albrecht Dürer*, 4th ed. (Princeton: Princeton University Press, 1955). An illuminating study.

MUSIC

Láng, Paul H., *Music in Western Civilization* (New York: Norton, 1941).

Reese, Gustave, *Music in the Middle Ages* (New York: Norton, 1940); *Music in the Renaissance* (New York: Norton, 1954).

Excellent and informative brief contributions are the articles by Edward Lowinsky, "Music in the Culture of the Renaissance," in Paul Oskar Kristeller and Philip P. Wiener, eds., *Renaissance Essays* (New York: Harper & Row, 1968). "Music of the Renaissance as Viewed by Renaissance Musicians," in Bernard O'Kelly, ed., *The Renaissance Image of Man and the World* (Columbus: Ohio State University Press, 1966); and Paul Oskar Kristeller, *Renaissance Thought II* (New York: Harper & Row, 1965), Chaps. VIII and IX.

VII

VIEWS OF MAN
AND THE COSMOS

Man is the most fortunate of creatures and consequently worthy of all admiration . . . to be envied not only by brutes but even by the stars and by minds beyond this world.
—Pico della Mirandola, ORATION ON THE DIGNITY OF MAN

The world would not endure if everyone were theoretical.
—Pietro Pomponazzi, ON IMMORTALITY

DIRECTION AND LIMITATIONS OF RENAISSANCE THOUGHT

Fascinating in its indomitable personalities, its flair for eloquent expression, its monumental art, the Renaissance does not stand out as a great epoch in the history of ideas. It failed to produce an original and distinctive body of thought. This defect certainly cannot be attributed to a prevailing current of anti-intellectualism. On the contrary, Renaissance culture had been inaugurated by intellectuals —scholars and writers—and every leading field of activity was laden with ideas that were provocative of debate. Renaissance art, in addition to its compelling beauty, is an inexhaustible storehouse of philosophical, religious, and moral concepts. Furthermore, Renaissance thinkers made a conscious effort to unite theory and practice, to bridge the gap between the speculative and the active faculties. And finally, the perennial subject of discussion and inquiry was nothing less than the nature of man and his place in the universe.

In an overall view of Western intellectual history the Renaissance seems deficient in two key areas—philosophy and science. The "scientific revolution," without which our modern age would be inconceivable, came at the very end of or after (some would say in spite of) the Renaissance; and it nullified ideas and assumptions that had been articles of faith for representative thinkers of the Renaissance. Instead of producing an original school of philosophy suitable to a new age of geographical discovery, secular orientation, and political sophistication, the Renaissance revived antiquated philosophical cults and—worse still—tried to graft these onto the medieval Scholastic tradition. To some observers the poverty of Renaissance philosophy is sufficiently demonstrated by the vogue of Neoplatonism, dismissed by George Sarton as "a superficial mixture of ideas too vague to be of real value."[1] But the fact that the Renaissance made little progress in science and formulated no new philosophical school does not negate the value of its thought. More than in most eras—including those celebrated in the annals of philosophy—its thinkers attempted to draw upon the wisdom of the past for the purpose of heightening man's awareness of his own nature and enriching his experience. Although they fell short of their hopes and failed to provide final answers, they focused attention upon issues of central and lasting importance. It is impossible to measure the full dimensions of the Renaissance without taking the stream of ideas into account.

THE ARISTOTELIAN TRADITION—PIETRO POMPONAZZI

The fabric of Renaissance thought was woven from three main strands which, at the risk of oversimplification, may be labeled the humanist, the Aristotelian-Scholastic, and the Platonist—the last two of which stretched through the Middle Ages back to classical antiquity. Humanist scholars and writers contributed the newest strand, although they also claimed antiquity for their inspiration. While championing Greek and Latin letters, the humanists concerned themselves with the question of values and claimed moral philosophy as their special province. The Aristotelian-Scholastic strand, developed in the thirteenth century by Albertus Magnus and Thomas Aquinas into a closely reasoned system, had established itself in university curricula. Besides underpinning the late medieval theology, it also constituted the basis of orthodox scientific beliefs and thus dominated the whole world view of the

---

[1] In James Westfall Thompson et al., *The Civilization of the Renaissance* (New York: Frederick Ungar, 1929), p. 79.

late Middle Ages—religious, philosophical, and scientific. At the same time, because it combined elements of Aristotelian rationalism with dogmatic Christianity, it carried the seeds of incipient heresy, skepticism, and materialism. The third strand, least conspicuous but in some ways most significant of all, derived from Plato and pre-Aristotelian thinkers who had influenced Plato, especially Pythagoras. The revival of Platonic and Pythagorean thought, and the increasing interest in mathematics which accompanied it, provided a fresh approach to the study of nature and eventually a challenge to Aristotelian physics. Just as readily, it opened the door to poetic vision and religious mysticism. Renaissance Neoplatonism represents one variation of this theme.

Each of these contrasting intellectual currents contained within itself diverse and mutually incompatible elements. Also during the Renaissance still other philosophical traditions, pagan and Christian, were brought into play. It was a time of questing and experimenting, an age of adventure in the world of ideas. Most of the contributors to Renaissance thought were eclectics rather than fanatical devotees of a single creed, and some were hopeful of achieving a reconciliation or synthesis of the various schools, a task which Pico della Mirandola undertook with the greatest enthusiasm.

The Aristotelian philosophical system, colored by the interpretations of Averroes and other Arabic commentators, had been cultivated in the universities of northern Euorpe from the eleventh century onward and was utilized by Aquinas for his tremendous synthesis of faith and reason, the *Summa Theologica*. Aristotelianism, solidly entrenched by the close of the Middle Ages, was not as stereotyped or rigid as has been alleged. During the fourteenth century, students of physics at both Paris and Oxford showed an inquisitiveness irreconcilable with a blind acceptance of Aristotle's laws of motion. However, the combined authority of Aristotle and scholasticism was so overwhelming in the northern universities that it stood as a bulwark against the encroachment of humanistic studies. In the Italian universities, on the other hand, where Aristotelian philosophy did not gain a secure foothold until near the end of the thirteenth century, it developed simultaneously with the rise of Italian humanism and was influenced by it, especially as humanist scholars made fresh Latin translations of Aristotle's works. Both Aristotelianism and humanism gained a place within the arts faculty of the northern Italian universities and, in spite of inevitable rivalry, a fruitful cross-fertilization took place between the two disciplines.[2] The Aristotelians were particularly concerned with logic and with natural philosophy—that is, science—which held little interest for the humanists, dedicated as they were to the advancement of Latin and Greek literary studies. But both groups occupied themselves with moral philosophy, with the definition of human nature and human values. At the universities of Bologna, Padua, and Pavia, no less than at such humanist centers as Florence, thinkers wrestled with the problems of God, freedom, and immortality. The University of Padua became during the fifteenth century the leading center of Aristotelian philosophy in all of Europe, while its teachers also drew upon a host of ideas from various sources. Proud of its reputation in the field of medicine, the university was secular and anticlerical in tone, anti-Thomistic, and scornful of the humanists. Determined to arrive at an understanding of nature, the Paduan professors groped their way toward the scientific method and came as close to finding it as was possible while still clinging to their master Aristotle's belief that the universe was composed of fixed substances qualitatively distinct and arranged in an ascending order of excellence. Their labors proved useful to the sixteenth- and seventeenth-century revolutionaries who finally performed the Herculean task of overthrowing the Aristotelian physics.

The Paduan scholars did not conform to a single pattern, and their debates, on psychological and moral as well as scientific topics, produced repercussions throughout Italy and beyond. The ablest representative of this school was the controversial Pietro Pomponazzi of Mantua (1462–1525), who held professorships in philosophy at both Padua and Bologna. Pomponazzi sought to purify Aristotle's teachings by stripping away the Christian and Arabic accretions of Platonism and Averroism, but in the process he assimilated elements from both humanism and the Thomistic tradition. Among Aristotelians he is outstanding not only for his syncretism but also for his preoccupation with the nature and limits of human knowledge and his attempt to establish a purely naturalistic system of ethics. In spite of the vigor, clarity, and oc-

---

[2] Paul Oskar Kristeller, *Renaissance Thought* (New York: Harper & Row, 1961), pp. 35–47.

casional nobility of his thought, however, its direction was toward a dead end in the Renaissance philosophy of man. This is not because he rejected the doctrine of personal immortality—which in theory he did, without injury to his professional career. It is, rather, because he attempted to combine irreconcilables—idealism and materialism, faith and skeptical rationalism, humanist values and inflexible logic—and bring them all within the framework of Aristotelian-Scholasticism. The result was not a closer harmony between rival schools of thought but an irremediable dichotomy, pointing to the conclusion that a choice must be made between reason and faith. Pomponazzi's cogent work *On the Immortality of the Soul* [3] (published at Bologna in 1516) illustrates in the philosophical field the same troubling doubts, the same retreat from a proud confidence in man's place in the cosmos that was beginning to affect political theory, literature, the arts, and religion at the very climax of the High Renaissance.

Pomponazzi's treatise *On Immortality* undertakes to explain phenomena in terms of natural causes and to subject ideals to the light of actual experience. Not a radical empiricist or rebel against authority—he never doubts the authority of Aristotle properly interpreted—the author insists that his propositions agree with reason, maintaining "nothing mythical, nothing depending on Faith." He scorns superstitions, dismisses the belief in ghosts as an illusion—incited perhaps by the exhalation of gases from cemeteries—and affirms that anyone seeming to be possessed of demons is "suffering either from bile or insanity." But he startles the modern reader by accepting without question a whole world of prophecies, soothsayings, portents heralding the birth of great men, the foreknowledge proffered in dreams, and other prodigies. He claims that all these have natural causes; his apparent credulity stems from his absolute faith in astrology, which he thinks should be—though admittedly is not—an infallible science. In conformity with Aristotle, he believes the stars are composed not of the dross of earth but of incorruptible matter, moved in their spheres by immaterial Intelligences. The celestial Intelligences are God's mediating agents, and if they can guide the eternal stars, reasons Pomponazzi, they can control events on the humble plane of

---

[3] Ernst Cassirer *et al.*, eds., *The Renaissance Philosophy of Man*, trans. William H. Hay II (Chicago: University of Chicago Press, 1948).

earth. The same natural causation is invoked to cover the marvels that stud the history of religions. Pomponazzi denies that God moves in a mysterious way His wonders to perform, while he freely credits the wonders. Miracles, he says, are not miracles in the popular sense but merely striking examples of the operation of cosmic forces, entirely consistent with the eternal law that governs the universe, including man's domain. A large part of Pomponazzi's treatise is devoted to demolishing the doctrine of the immortality of the soul. Rejecting categorically the Averroistic concept of the unity of the intellect—which held that a single intellect or soul is present in all men and therefore can be separated from any one of them without itself being destroyed—he insists that every man is endowed with an individual soul that gives him his distinctive character and personality. And the human soul, although sharing to a limited degree the immaterial quality of pure intelligence, is dependent on the body, not for its origin but for the object of its activity. It is the form that permeates, molds, and moves the body by means of its own subordinate faculties (the "vegetative" and "sensitive" principles). Pomponazzi does not evade the necessary conclusion that the soul must perish along with the body, although he is loath to contradict "the Blessed Thomas" ("for what is a flea against an elephant?"); and he buttresses his anti-Christian deposition with several lines of argument, including the logical dictum that the finite and the infinite are incommensurate terms (man's time-bound mortal life cannot be part of eternity, which is infinite).

With his vision cleared of all superstitions except those blessed by Aristotle, Pomponazzi coolly regards man's place in the cosmic scheme and finds it a not very exciting one. As is befitting in an age of humanism, he does the best he can for his species, but his definition of the human condition is hardly optimistic and far from a declaration of independence. Like the Neoplatonists he places man in an intermediate position between the temporal and eternal, "halfway between the gods and the beasts," and he concedes that the soul or intellect "partakes in some fashion of immortality"—it is *unqualifiedly* mortal and *relatively* immortal. Unlike the Neoplatonists, however, he does not believe that man can alter his position—or, to be more accurate, that he can improve it. He cannot move upward into the heavenly sphere although he can easily sink to a lower level.

For all its bold display of rationalism, Pomponazzi's outlook is deeply tinged with pessimism. He constantly reminds himself and his readers that man belongs to the order of things corruptible, that his soul is *generated,* not *created.* Though man is the noblest of all material things and his intellect—akin to the divine Intelligences—his crowning glory, still the human intellect is "hardly the shadow" of true intellect, which "perceives all things by a simple intuition" rather than "reasoning by composition, discourse, and time." And even this inadequate intellect, a grudging gift from the higher powers, is hardly conspicuous in man. "Almost an infinite number of men seem to have less intellect than many beasts," and "those who are rational are most rare."

Nor does this line of argument permit religion to compensate for the weakness and fallibility of the mental faculties. Subjected to the spotlight of reason, religion reveals itself as a feeble contrivance, necessary perhaps because the majority of men require tangible incentives to morality and fables may serve a useful purpose. The faiths of mankind, like all else in the corruptible sphere, follow a cycle of generation, corruption, and decay. Developing this theme more explicitly in a book written a few years after *On Immortality,* Pomponazzi cited Christianity as an example of the decaying state: "Whence now too in our own faith all things are growing frigid, and miracles are ceasing, except those counterfeit and simulated, for it seems to be near its end." [4]

Turning to the world of experience, Pomponazzi can find little to offer consolation. He may oppose the ignorance spawned by bigotry and superstition, but he has no inkling of the potentialities of science—the plodding route of "composition, discourse, and time"—for the expanding of knowledge. The human intellect he regards as such a poor instrument for the conquest of truth that our knowledge even of natural objects can be nothing more than "a two-fold ignorance." Neither is there comfort in contemplating man's role in the community of his fellows, where the guiding principle is to oppress or be oppressed: "Almost always those established in power are mad, ignorant, and filled with every sort of vice." In the political realm at least, it would seem that man is

---

[4] Quoted by John Herman Randall, Jr., in *The Renaissance Philosophy of Man, op. cit.,* p. 278.

the most unfortunate of creatures, "since no race of animals is thus oppressed by one of its own species."

Pomponazzi did propose a way out of the morass, a way which is neither Aristotelian nor Christian, neither scientific nor humanist, although it may legitimately be called philosophical. It reflects character and wisdom, but wisdom born of disillusionment. His prescription is none other than the Stoic attitude of submission to a universe which man cannot control or recognize as just but which he accepts as good in its totality. The universe, he asserts, is greater than any of its parts, and the race of mankind is more important than any individual. The individual must be content with his assigned role, however humble or inglorious. The human community needs—and gets—few philosophers, but many weavers, spinners, craftsmen, and farmers. Inequality, hierarchy (and the natural subjection of women) are inherent in the cosmic and social order. Pomponazzi exhorts men to be good for the sake of mankind and also to gain happiness for themselves, recognizing that virtue is its own reward and vice its own punishment. By virtue he means steadfastness, moderation, temperance—the ability to be content with what is suitable to one's condition: "This power can make almost everyone blessed. For farmer or smith, destitute or rich, if his life be moral, can be called happy, and truly so called, and can depart contented with his lot." But happiness identified with virtue—and virtue identified with conventional mores and acceptance of the status quo—assumes a rather pallid complexion. It is limited, theoretical, and proportional to man's ambivalent position midway between the mortal and the immortal. Thus Pomponazzi at the end of his carefully spun argument reveals himself as a Stoic in the garb of a Scholastic.

Actually he presents still another way out of the impasse, but one which suddenly appears like a deus ex machina and oddly negates the whole of his thesis. The final chapter of *On Immortality* is a retraction, an abject obeisance to the authority of the Church. He concludes—although the conclusion is illogical and unsupported —that the question of the immortality of the soul is philosophically "a neutral problem"; that the immortality of the soul is a divine truth revealed by Christ; and that any argument to the contrary is inherently false. He adds, quite consistently however, that the doctrine cannot be established by rational proof and must be received exclusively as an article of faith. Even in this strange coda to his work—which may have been conceived as a formal gesture to forestall censure—he jealously guards the distinction between the realm of faith—"revelation and the canonical Scripture"—and that of natural reason. There is no doubt that his intellectual allegiance remained with the latter, even though his own logic forced him to describe it as restrictive and cold compared with the realm of faith. Whether wistful or ironic he was at any rate prophetic when, contrasting the certainty of Christian truth with the obscurity of natural philosophy, he observed: "The wise men of this age . . . when they call themselves wise, have become fools. For whoever goes this way, I think, will waver always uncertain and wandering."

THE PYTHAGOREAN-PLATONIC REVIVAL—
NICHOLAS CUSANUS

The Aristotelian tradition, inherited by the Renaissance and treated with considerable respect, embodied a closed system, comprehensive and carefully reasoned but rigid. Even such an energetic thinker as Pomponazzi could not break out of its confines. Meanwhile other influences and tendencies were welling up from the remote past. Plato was studied afresh as his works became available in Greek editions or reliable Latin translations, and interest was attracted to pre-Socratic philosophers, especially Pythagoras, the mathematician and mystic who had interpreted reality in terms of number. The role of this stream of influence in the thought of the Renaissance has received less attention than it deserves, partly because it did not lead to a distinctive philosophical school and partly because it tended to sink into the quicksands of fantasy. In its entirety, the revival of concepts drawn from pre-Aristotelian Greek thinkers and reshaped in the crosscurrents of Renaissance speculation yielded results both fruitful and distracting. On the one hand it encouraged the belief that the universe is mysterious and magical and stimulated a tendency toward mysticism, essentially irrational (the Scholastic-Aristotelians were custodians of the rationalist tradition). On the other hand it suggested the possibility of apprehending reality through direct and intimate experience rather than through abstract a priori concepts. Thus, by offering a new approach to the study of nature it helped prepare the way for the modern scientific method.

The most remarkable exponent of the Pythagorean-Platonic tradition, and a great genius by any reckoning, was the Italianate German Nicholas of Cues or Cusa—whence his Latin surname Cusanus. In some ways Cusanus was the most medieval of Renaissance philosophers. He employed the vocabulary of scholasticism— no other vocabulary had yet been invented for the type of speculation in which he was most interested. But the direction of his thought differed fundamentally from that of the Scholastics and enabled him to break through the constrictive formulas of Aristotle. Although modest in demeanor, devoutly religious, and outwardly conventional, Cusanus was a system smasher. He sought to open a new door to understanding, to provide a method that squared with experience. Theologian, moralist, and natural philosopher all in one, he aimed at defining human nature, human knowledge, and the relationship between man and God. These intellectual objectives were shared by most philosophers of the Renaissance, but, in contrast with the majority, he believed the transcendental goal of comprehending the infinite was not only compatible with but actually dependent upon an understanding of the world of matter and finite experience.

Cusanus (1401–64) had the advantage of a very broad training for his task. Educated first at Deventer by the Brethren of the Common Life, where he absorbed the mystical piety of the *Devotio Moderna*, he studied Scholastic science and theology at the University of Heidelberg. Most decisive for his intellectual development, both in what he appropriated and in what he rejected, was his Italian period, which began with his enrollment at the University of Padua in 1417. While exposed to the Aristotelian and Averroistic rationalism of Padua, where he studied canon law, mathematics, and astronomy, he did not neglect humanistic subjects, although his interest in antiquity inclined more toward mathematics and philosophy than poetry and rhetoric. His intellectual achievements were performed amidst the pressures of a strenuous career in the service of the Church. Ordained priest at the age of twenty-five, he displayed from the outset a singular independence of mind. He questioned the authenticity of the *Donation of Constantine* before Valla had exposed the notorious document as a forgery. He played a prominent part in the Conciliar movement that attempted to limit papal authority, although he represented the pope at Constantinople in 1437 in connection with abortive efforts to reunite the Eastern and Western churches and, after the failure of the Council of Basel, lent his weight to the side of papal supremacy. He was papal legate to Germany, Bishop of Brixen, and finally, in 1445, Cardinal. Summoned to Rome by Pius II (Aeneas Sylvius Piccolomini), he served virtually as prime minister to this shallow and unappreciative pontiff.

Unwaveringly loyal to the spiritual idealism of the Middle Ages, Cusanus was one of the most original thinkers of the entire Renaissance. His contributions, insufficiently noticed by his contemporaries and by posterity, were not extraneous or tangential but directly relevant to the central problem of the Renaissance— "the discovery of the world and of man." Ernst Cassirer, emending Burckhardt, renders this tribute:

Cusanus played an important role both in the re-awakening of objectivity and in the deepening of subjectivity. His greatness and his historical singularity consist in his having brought about this change not in opposition to the religious ideas of the Middle Ages, but from the standpoint of these ideas themselves. His "discovery of nature and of man" was accomplished from the very heart of religion, where he sought to base and to anchor that discovery.[5]

Cusanus provides a striking example of the fact, demonstrated in almost every area of achievement, that the Renaissance was indebted to the Middle Ages not simply for background and genesis but for its dynamic forward thrust.

The medieval Scholastics, adhering to Aristotelian formulas, had visualized a finite and closed universe, with all its parts linked together in ascending hierarchical order ranging from the corruptible sublunar sphere upward to the ethereal fires of the fixed stars and the invisible incorporeal Intelligences. In this scheme all matter, including living creatures, was acted upon, through intermediate agencies, by the outer Intelligences, which in turn were directed by God the absolute Being, perfect Intelligence, and First Cause. Man could comprehend the universe, it was held, because the universe is rational, orderly, and perfectly circular, and therefore amenable to the reasoning faculty implanted in man. But understanding depended on a process of deduction, inference, and

---

[5] Ernst Cassirer, *The Individual and the Cosmos in Renaissance Philosophy*, trans. Mario Domandi (New York: Barnes and Noble, 1963), p. 36.

analogy. Man could know God only through the observed effects of His subordinate agents, never "face to face." Even when fleshed out by Christian doctrines of the Incarnation and the immortality of the soul, such a cosmology was frustrating emotionally if not intellectually, and it had been challenged or sidestepped by the great medieval mystics.

Himself a mystic by inclination, Cusanus rejected the mystic's intuitive approach to truth. Truth, he insisted, can be reached not through an emotional experience but only through mastery of the symbolic language of nature; it is a conquest of the intellect, attained by the route of investigation rather than formal logic. He also drew a sharp distinction between the kind of reality accessible to human understanding and that which lies beyond man's grasp. In this respect his philosophy is dualistic; but he maintained the distinction in the interest of eliminating ambiguities and establishing sharper definitions, an essential step toward the acquisition of reliable knowledge. And while separating the finite world from the infinite, he affirmed not only that man can profitably investigate the former but that the knowledge he acquires, and the very limitations of that knowledge, can provide him with insight into final truth.

Cusanus' assault on the Aristotelian cosmology began with his revival of the Platonic concept of the antithesis between Idea and matter, which supported the conclusion that God—the ultimate Idea—is not part of the universe, as Aristotle had taught, but remains outside it. The Aristotelians and Scholastics had assumed an unbroken chain of relationships reaching from the lowliest element or creature to the absolute Being. Cusanus disposed of this nebulous chain at one stroke by denying that the finite material world can be part of the infinite eternal reality. There can be no identity, he argued, between a form and its shadow, between a transcendental Idea and the matter which bears its imprint, and anyone who attempts to find the connecting link between these contraries will fail to grasp either of them. But far from ruling out the possibility of human knowledge, Cusanus was attempting to ground it on a sound basis. The finite world, subject to the same laws and made of the same substance as man, could, he maintained, be investigated and comprehended in terms of man's own experience and capacities.

The tools essential for ordering and analyzing natural phenomena are already at man's disposal, Cusanus pointed out, because these tools are constructs of the mind itself. He had the insight to perceive and the temerity to assert that knowledge represents not a mere reproduction of static reality but an act of creation. He cited the example of the sciences which are created by the mind—arithmetic, geometry, and astronomy. Such universal concepts as space and time are not actually "universals," not absolutes or eternal archetypes, but ideas *developed* by the human reason out of concrete experience. It follows, therefore, that man, although admittedly of limited and imperfect intellect, can acquire valid knowledge, because the terms and intelligible patterns through which he clarifies his experience are inherently relevant to experiential data.

The validity of factual, demonstrable knowledge was only one side of Cusanus' intrepid speculation. He held, with equal emphasis, that man could also penetrate the realm of eternal truth, by a curiously indirect route. Developing the Platonic hypothesis, he argued that because the material and finite is separate from the nonmaterial and infinite—is in fact its opposite—the characteristics of the infinite can be deduced from their reverse manifestations in the finite. The human mind can know the eternal by virtue of "the coincidence of opposites"—a theory suggestive of the antithesis between matter and antimatter in modern theoretical physics. Man, reasoned Cusanus, cannot take the Heavenly Kingdom by direct assault, but he can nevertheless gain admission by recognizing his own ignorance and making the most of it—by using his intellect to plumb the finite world to its depths and then beholding, in its reverse image, the world of the infinite. He can reach *nonknowledge* of the Absolute, which is beyond his grasp, and thereby know the unknowable. Thus human knowledge comes to understand its own otherness. Such is Cusanus' doctrine of the "learned ignorance" *(docta ignorantia),* an apparent contradiction in terms but more penetrating and provocative than the learned credulity of Pomponazzi.

On the surface Cusanus' epistemological formula seems like a game played with pieces of Scholastic dialectics. Actually, its implications were revolutionary and far-reaching. His assumptions shook the foundations of Aristotelian physics, to which Pomponazzi was clinging resolutely two generations later. He rejected Aristotle's finite concentric universe, arguing that any part of the universe could with equal justice be regarded as its center. He repudiated the dogma—embedded in the European mentality until the time of Galileo and beyond—that the region of matter is characterized by qualitative differences between the "higher" and "lower." He doubted that the earth was at rest, although he had only hazy ideas as to its motion. Again in contrast to Aristotle, he grasped the concept that motion and rest are relative states and affirmed that a state of absolute rest would be identical with infinite motion. To him every part of the universe was important and worthy of study, because "the Maximum is in each thing and in no one thing in particular," because God is both the center and the circumference of the universe and in every part of it, not as a presence in the pantheistic sense but as the implied perfection of every imperfect object.

The medieval intellectual scheme, bound to the Aristotelian tradition, had assigned an inferior place to the mathematical sciences. Excluded from the theory of physics and astronomy, mathematics served as hardly more than a counting mechanism, useful mainly for calculating the position of the planets and constructing navigation tables. Cusanus, although he couched his ideas in the language of theology, hailed mathematics as the science of the infinite and identified it as the proper tool for the investigation of nature. He believed it held the key to the symbolic language in which nature's secrets are written—a belief cherished by Leonardo da Vinci half a century later and acted upon by Kepler and Galileo in the seventeenth century. Cusanus' specific contributions to science were nil; he lacked the conceptual tools, including an adequate mathematics. But he did, however murkily and intuitively, point the way to the province and the method of the scientific discipline. Perhaps because he was ahead of his time, he seems to have had little effect in hastening its development.

Despite its Scholastic cast and obscurity, Cusanus' thought embodied an affirmation of basic ideals of the Renaissance. A theologian rather than a humanist, he nevertheless upheld human dignity and freedom. He proclaimed the autonomy of man in the sphere of values: "Wherewith we see how precious is the mind, for without it, everything in creation would be without value." He interpreted the Christian doctrine of redemption not as the liberation of man from the world but as a process whereby the world and the whole finite universe, including man, are joined to the infinite. According to Cusanus man is not merely the object of salvation but its active agent; with him and through him the whole natural order is redeemed; although created, man is also creator. The incipient revolutionary tendencies in Cusanus' theology relate to his quest for a scientific method. Parallel to his "learned ignorance" are his "sacred ignorance" and his "negative theology." We cannot know God, he says, either in this life or the life to come—God alone knows Himself—but we can come closer to an understanding of God as we eliminate specific qualities from our conception (nonknowledge is a way of knowing). "According to this negative theology, He is neither Father nor Son nor Holy Ghost." The respected churchman concludes that religion itself belongs to the realm of finite things and cannot convey absolute truth or direct knowledge of God. And just as every point in the universe may be regarded as its center, so in the cosmology of religions each one is equally near God and equally far from Him. It is no wonder therefore, and no matter, that there are such wide differences in rites and beliefs among the several faiths of mankind. Cusanus is not voicing skepticism nor wavering in his own loyalty to Christian revelation, but he is exposing the senselessness of a claim to finality for any dogma. The implications of his point of view for religious toleration are obvious, and equally obvious is the gap between his approach and the conventional wisdom that precipitated the destructive fanaticism of the Reformation era. Cusanus' searching mind cast a light deep into the darkness, but darkness is not easily dispelled.

RENAISSANCE NEOPLATONISM

Stemming from the same sources as the thought of Cusanus, but developing in a different direction, was the philosophical movement known as Neoplatonism. The leading exponents of Renaissance Neoplatonism were the group of scholars associated with the Florentine "Academy," a Medici foundation originating with Cosimo de' Medici, who in 1462 endowed the young Marsilio Ficino with a villa near Careggi, a library of Greek manuscripts, and a life income. In the course of his lifetime (1433–99) Ficino produced Latin translations not only of the Dialogues of Plato but also of the writings of Plotinus and of the considerable body of medieval texts traditionally associated with Neoplatonism. Ficino and his colleagues performed a useful service in making the Platonic writings readily accessible and in stimulating interest in Plato's philosophy not only in Italy but in northern Europe as well. Ficino influenced such German humanists as Johann Reuchlin and Willibald Pirckheimer and the artist Dürer, and he had an effect on the thought of Thomas More and the Oxford Reformers in England. The so-called Academy, however, was less an institution for research or instruction than a cult of Plato worshipers. Members of the group celebrated Plato's birthday, burned a lamp before his bust, and sang hymns in his honor, accompanied by Ficino playing the lyre. They addressed Ficino as "father" and greeted one another with the motto "Salvation in Plato." Doubtless the renowned Florentine Academy was also an asset to the rule of Lorenzo de' Medici—patron, pupil, and "brother" of Ficino— because it encouraged intellectuals to contemplate the heavenly beatitude of a liberated soul rather than scrutinize the sordid politics of an earthly city.

The syncretic Neoplatonism of the Florentine Academy claimed to represent a continuous philosophical tradition that included Zoroaster, Orpheus, and Pythagoras, as well as Byzantine, Arabic, and Western medieval Platonists. At the same time it was neither anti-Aristotelian, nor anti-humanist, and emphatically not anti-Christian. Colored by the ideals of the humanists, it sought in turn to reinforce these ideals with a metaphysical underpinning. Because its rational aspects were interlaced with, and sometimes smothered by, poetical symbolism and mysticism, it readily lent itself to imaginative treatment, and it received its most eloquent evocation in works of Italian artists of the High Renaissance.

Despite the intelligence and high-mindedness of its practitioners, Neoplatonism failed as a philosophy. It attempted to synthesize incompatible elements and was flawed by logical contradictions. As originated by Plotinus and adapted to early medieval Christianity—in the writings of Dionysius the "pseudo-Areopagite" and others—it was a mixture of disparate elements drawn from Aristotle as well as from Plato. Lacking a coherent and logically defensible base, Neoplatonism had always been more of a religion than a philosophy, with an emotional appeal centering in the mystical goal of the soul's release from matter. The Renaissance variety also had much of the character of a religion. Ficino's major work expounding his own teachings he appropriately entitled *The Platonic*

Theology. Although the Florentine Neoplatonists venerated Plato and apocryphal or pseudo-Platonic works as the embodiment of divine truth, they believed them to be completely in harmony with Christian revelation, and they conceived it to be their mission to strengthen the Christian faith by providing a bulwark against skepticism. Despite an experimental attitude and a catholicity of tastes, their ultimate allegiance was to an otherworldly ideal. And if the fragile philosophical edifice they erected should prove unsafe, they were prepared to retreat into Catholic orthodoxy. Ficino at the age of forty entered the priesthood.

Tinged with asceticism and mysticism, Renaissance Neoplatonism nevertheless emphasized the worth and dignity of man. It taught that man is the focal center of the universe, a microcosm in which the streams of influence converge. Although he belongs to the material sensible world, man's immortal soul is part of divine Being. Imperfect, separated from the higher spiritual realms, he has the capacity to advance toward perfection without losing his humanity—directed by his reason and impelled upward by love, which in its higher form is a yearning of the soul for God. Sensitive to the role of beauty in guiding the imagination, and probably also influenced by the teachings of Cusanus, the Neoplatonists developed the theme that man has the power to transform his experience, clothe it with meaning, and become an active participant in the process of creation. If he is not the divine event toward which the whole creation moves, he is the medium through which it must move to reach its goal. While winning the redemption he sorely needs and yearns for, man, affirmed Ficino, can transform the natural order and reveal its true significance, just as the artist creates beauty that transcends the loveliness of his model and of the media he employs.

A cardinal tenet of Renaissance Neoplatonism proclaimed man a free agent, who through his autonomous will can chart his own course, upward or downward. To defend this thesis was a bold undertaking for a philosophy that always identified "upward" with the nonmaterial and accepted unquestioningly the cult of astrology, an essentially deterministic system. Ficino declared that every man is joined to his planet from the moment of his birth (and lamented that he was melancholic Saturn's child), but he maintained that while the stars circumscribe one's sphere of action they cannot determine the direction of his will. Every man, he insisted, can exercise choice within the limits prescribed for him; his will remains free.

It must be admitted that Ficino labored valiantly to defend human freedom and dignity even against the implications of his own philosophy. The Florentine Neoplatonists, drawing inspiration from the widest variety of sources venerable and occult, brought all into focus upon the theme of man's unique position in the cosmos. Responding enthusiastically to the challenge of the humanists, they described a glorious vista stretching from this world to the next. Some passages from Ficino—taken out of context—suggest the most inflated view of human nature, implying that man is lord of creation and darling of the universe, with a grasp fully equal to his reach. The microcosm apparently has the power to swallow the macrocosm:

And what does the will strive to do if not to transform itself into all things by enjoying all things according to the nature of each? . . . the effort of the soul is directed . . . toward this end: that the soul in its own way will become the whole universe.[6]

But in the context of Ficino's thought such passages appear less extravagant. The quest for which he so confidently predicts success is a supraterrestrial one. He means that the soul can absorb and transform the universe in the sense of grasping its spiritual essence, not as a means of establishing man's dominion over nature. The world of nature with all its beauty is of only incidental importance, a tarrying point in the soul's upward ascent. For Ficino the true end of man is to know God, and this end can be attained only by separation from the world and the flesh. It is incompatible with man's natural life since it is conceived as a state of quiescence—"rest without change." Ficino postulates the same goal for man as did the medieval Scholastics, and he shares the medieval mystic's contempt for the world:

We seek the highest summits of Mount Olympus. We inhabit the lowest valley. We are weighted down by the burden of a most troublesome body . . . outside the sublime fatherland, we, unhappy people, are confined to the lowest places, where nothing presents itself which is not exceedingly difficult, where nothing happens which is not lamentable.[7]

---

[6] "Five Questions Concerning the Mind," trans. Josephine L. Burroughs, in *The Renaissance Philosophy of Man, op. cit.,* pp. 200–201.

[7] *Ibid.,* p. 209.

And reason—"always uncertain, vacillating and distressed"—can only add to man's misery as long as it remains in the body, where it is torn between the rival claims of appetite and intellect without being able to satisfy either. Consolation is found in an article of faith— the immortality of the soul—to which Ficino adds the notion that the immortal soul will acquire an immortal body after being freed from earthly toils.

The Neoplatonism of Ficino and his circle entered the lists as ally and champion of Christianity and was therefore vulnerable to any attack launched against it from that quarter. There was little to fear from the Renaissance popes, but toward the close of the Quattrocento Savonarola cast a heavy shadow over the leading figures of the Florentine Academy, impelling them in the direction of overt piety, asceticism, and self-doubt. Not all of them became active disciples of the Dominican; Ficino, after Savonarola's execution, composed the apology of the city of Florence for having been deceived by the "antichrist of Ferrara." Savonarola's influence, however, is seen in the growing feeling, even among followers of the Neoplatonic tradition, that religion and philosophy had come to a parting of the ways, with religion dependent upon divine revelation rather than accessible to human reason.

PICO DELLA MIRANDOLA, PRINCE OF CONCORD

Associated with the Florentine Neoplatonists, although "pledged to the doctrines of no man," was that bright but evanescent star in the firmament—Giovanni Pico, Count of Mirandola. Pico della Mirandola (1463–94) seemed to be Fortune's favorite—born of a wealthy noble family, easily winning friends by his good looks and gracious personality, and stunning his contemporaries with his nimble and versatile mind. Actually he was a tragic figure. Hounded by the Church to which he remained faithful, shaken by the dire message of Savonarola, he died of a fever at the early age of thirty-one. Nevertheless he cut a wide swath during the short span of his lifetime. He claimed to have found the key to universal wisdom, and he delivered the most glowing tribute to the human race in all of Renaissance philosophy.

Endowed with a precocious intellect and an omnivorous appetite for knowledge, Pico, after mastering Latin and Greek, turned to the study of Hebrew and Arabic. He soon reached the conclusion that all systems of thought embody the same fundamental truth. Not content with the synthesis of Platonism and Christianity effected by the Florentine Academy, he would enlarge it to include the Scholastic and Aristotelian dispensations, all religions, the musings of legendary seers and oracles, and the collection of medieval magic and mysticism preserved in the Jewish Cabala. He aimed at a synthesis of syntheses. In 1486, when only twenty-three years old, he published in Rome a list of nine hundred *Conclusions* (theological and philosophical propositions) and invited all interested scholars to join in a public debate on this staggering agenda. The disputation, suspended by Pope Innocent viii, never took place. A papal commission condemned several of the theses as heretical, and Pico fled to France for safety. After returning to Italy at the urging of Marsilio Ficino, he spent the few remaining years of his life in a villa near Florence given him by Lorenzo de' Medici.

Pico's far-ranging mind swept everything into its net and attempted to fit all the pieces into a coherent system. He was the great reconciler of all strands of the Western tradition together with the lore of the East, factual or fanciful. "What were the gain if only the philosophy of the Latins were investigated," he asked, "if the Greek and Arabian philosophers were left out—since all wisdom has flowed from the East to the Greeks and from the Greeks to us?" The "Prince of Concord," as his friends liked to call him (punning on the name of his ancestral estate, Concordia), was the antithesis of parochialism. His prodigious breadth of view went beyond—too far beyond—the toleration of faiths differing from one's own. Actually, it was not toleration that he strove for but, rather, a proof of the identity of the one Universal Truth so variously disguised in the multiple sacred and secular literatures of the world.

Pico was an enthusiast, not a disciplined thinker. His energetic and eager intellect was, unfortunately, undiscriminating. His writings are a bewildering blend of rare insights and popular prejudice, of erudition and myth mongering, of sublime poetry and tortured dialectics. His thought rises to majestic heights but also sinks to banality, pettiness, and petulance.

The most obvious weakness in Pico's reasoning was his obsession with the idea of double meanings in every text he perused. He was convinced that all ancient writings of any importance conveyed, hidden under the veil of symbol and allegory, the precepts of Greek philosophy and the doctrines of Christianity (which he believed to be one and the same), and the truths of science as well. Homer, he said, had concealed the science of the Divine beneath the wanderings of his Ulysses. As for the Pentateuch: "It is the firm opinion of all the ancients, unanimously asserted as beyond doubt, that the five books of the Mosaic law contain the entire knowledge of all arts and wisdom both divine and human." [8] And the occult Cabalistic writings, however tangential to the spirit of Judaism, Pico regarded as a fountainhead of wisdom and Christianity's secret weapon. The Cabala, he said, had been delivered by God to Moses on Mount Sinai together with the Law, but at God's command had been kept out of reach of the common herd until after the Exile, when "the mysteries of the heavenly teachings" were finally collected into seventy volumes. Having himself purchased and studied the books "with unwearying toil," Pico found in them

not so much the Mosaic as the Christian religion. There is the mystery of the Trinity, there the Incarnation of the Word, there the divinity of the Messiah; there I have read about original sin, its expiation through Christ, the heavenly Jerusalem, the fall of the devils, the orders of the angels, purgatory, and the punishments of hell. . . .[9]

Instead of thanking the Hebrews for this treasure, however, Pico boasted that the Cabala could be used to refute them out of their own mouths, leaving them "not even a corner" to hide in.

Pico devoted the whole of one small book, the *Heptaplus*, to explicating the occult significance of the Genesis account of creation. The treatise well illustrates how he could manipulate a text to extract the meaning he wanted. Confident that the Book of Moses contains an explicit prophecy of the advent of Christ, and of the rise and mission of the Church, by elaborate calculations he determined that Christ had come exactly 3508 years after the creation of the world. His exposition of the phrase "In the beginning" runs to four pages. By rearranging the letters of a single Hebrew word he produces a sentence. And what a sentence! "The father, in the Son and through the Son, the beginning and end or rest, created

---

8 Pico della Mirandola, *Heptaplus*, trans. D. Carmichael (Indianapolis: Library of Liberal Arts, 1965), p. 170.

9 "Oration on the Dignity of Man," Par. 36, trans. Elizabeth L. Forbes, in *The Renaissance Philosophy of Man, op. cit.*

the head, the fire, and the foundation of the great man with a good pact." His labored exegesis converts the terse and stately prose of the Old Testament into a mishmash of philosophical jargon.

In spite of naive and fanciful elements, Pico's thought embodied much that was noble and original. Sharing with the humanists and the Neoplatonists the belief in man's capacity for spiritual growth, he went beyond most of them in exalting man's potentialities, his inviolable freedom, and his central role in giving meaning to the whole natural order. In contrast to his Neoplatonic friends he flatly rejected astrology, and wrote a polemic against it in the last year of his life. He condemned it as practically useless (predictions seldom come true), as a hopelessly clumsy approach to the problem of causation, as contrary to Christianity, and above all as a denial of human freedom. It is monstrous, he reasoned, to consider as subject to the stars a creature who in the realm of values is *above* the stars: "The wonders of the mind are greater than the heavens. . . . On earth, nothing is great but man."

Intuitively, rather than systematically or purposively, Pico sometimes approached the borders of empirical science, but never with any clear apprehension of the essence of the scientific discipline. He sensed a distinction between science and pseudoscience (astrology and demonology), but both false and true science were to him species of magic. Although he applauded the true variety, which "brings forth into the open the miracles concealed in the recesses of the world," his "natural magic" bore only the faintest resemblance to modern science. Instead of an objective investigation of nature, it was "a higher and more holy philosophy" and had, he believed, long since been known to Christian theologians, Greek thinkers from Pythagoras to Plato, Zoroaster, the Magi of Chaldea, and numerous others of dubious credentials. Pico accepted unhesitatingly the medievalized Aristotelian cosmology with its empyrean heaven presiding "like the commander of an army over nine heavenly spheres" and with the gift of circular motion denied to the baser material elements, including man.

Pico's most famous work and the one in which he pronounced his boldest panegyric is his *Oration on the Dignity of Man*. Composed in the full tide of youthful exuberance, it was intended as an introduction to the ill-fated nine hundred theses, and was not published until after his death. The *Oration*, particularly its opening section, is a magnificent and moving hymn of praise to the creation and to man, who is the creation's supreme object and also its heir and successor. Often quoted is the imaginative description of how God, after forming the world and filling it with creatures, bestowed upon man the role of creator:

Neither a fixed abode nor a form that is thine alone nor any function peculiar to thyself have we given thee, Adam, to the end that according to thy longing and according to thy judgment thou mayest have and possess what abode, what form, and what functions thou thyself shalt desire. The nature of all other beings is limited and constrained within the bounds of laws prescribed by Us. Thou, constrained by no limits, in accordance with thine own free will, in whose hand We have placed thee, shalt ordain for thyself the limits of thy nature. We have set thee at the world's center that thou mayest from thence more easily observe whatever is in the world. We have made thee neither of heaven nor of earth, neither mortal nor immortal, so that with freedom of choice and with honor, as though the maker and molder of thyself, thou mayest fashion thyself in whatever shape thou shalt prefer. Thou shalt have the power to degenerate into the lower forms of life, which are brutish. Thou shalt have the power, out of thy soul's judgment, to be reborn into the higher forms, which are divine.[10]

This poetic myth obviously goes beyond an affirmation of freedom of the will in the usual sense. Man, declares Pico, is the "chameleon" of creation, and his potentiality for change is not limited to the range of material things. He can surpass the stars and become like unto the angels—Seraphim, Cherubim, and Thrones. "If we have willed it, we shall be second to them in nothing." Here the Renaissance view of man attains its boldest and most ideal expression. However, it is only an expression; and the ideal is qualified even in the *Oration*, the discourse that represents the pinnacle of Pico's aggressive optimism. Taken in the context of his thought as a whole, his creation myth loses much of its force. In spite of his emphasis on the autonomy of the will, Pico in fact believes that the only valid option open to man is the rugged one of a spiritual ascent, and this inexorably leads him along the road of asceticism, mysticism, and dogmatic Christianity. He views with contempt the lower functions of the soul—"the tinder of lust." With the Neoplatonists he laments "the desert loneliness of this body," the soul's prisoner. Who,

---

[10] *Ibid.*, Par. 3.

he asks, would want to lose the light of truth "in filth, in the darkness of pleasures?" "Let us therefore flee here . . . let us fly to the Father" to escape "the law of the flesh." Natural philosophy, he confesses in the *Oration,* is but the handmaiden of "holiest theology," and the end of scholarly research is to confirm "the inviolable Catholic faith." His most powerful words are uttered not with the accents of a humanist but in the tone of a Christian mystic:

The moving spirit knocks unremittingly at the door of your soul. . . . If you let it in, you will be carried back at once, full of God, along the orbit of religion to the Father. . . . This is our whole reward, this is the eternal life, this is the wisdom which the wise men of this world do not know, that from every imperfection of multiplicity we are brought back to unity by an indissoluble bond with him who is himself the One.[11]

In Pico's vision, no less than in the vision of the Florentine Neoplatonists, the motif of renunciation triumphed over the impulse toward affirmation. In the case of Pico, hailed as a "phoenix among minds," the reversal is the more startling. The precocity and zest of his early youth hardly pointed to a life of ascetic self-denial. At the age of twenty he had run off with the wife of a tax official from Arezzo, and to avert the consequences of this escapade he needed the help of his friend Ficino, who composed on his behalf an "Apology for the Rape of the Nymph Margarite by the hero Pico." Within the space of two or three years after this affair, however, Pico experienced a religious conversion, so intense that it gradually estranged him from the more temperate Ficino. In the Florence of Lorenzo the Magnificent he began to live like a monk, expressed a desire to preach barefoot in the towns of Italy, and became preoccupied with the imminence of death. It was at Pico's urging that Lorenzo invited Savonarola to return to Florence in 1490 and resume his preaching. Pico was drawn to Savonarola by his own disposition and convictions, not, as has been alleged, by the fanatical preacher's hypnotic powers or terrifying threats. Although he resisted Savonarola's entreaty to enter the Dominican order, Pico died clothed in the garb of a preaching friar and was buried in the convent church of San Marco. Perhaps, as Cassirer contends, Savonarola had won the fight for Pico's soul.[12]

---

[11] *Heptaplus, op. cit.,* Seventh Exposition, Proem.

[12] Cassirer, *Individual and the Cosmos, op. cit.,* p. 62.

THE HUMANIST CONCEPT OF THE WHOLE MAN

Although the influence of the humanists was so pervasive and their leadership so prominent in every branch of culture that the Renaissance has been called the Age of Humanism, there is no distinctive or coherent body of ideas that can be set apart as "humanist." Representatives of a movement that was literary in origin, the humanists were not philosophers in the formal sense. They derived their ideas eclectically—not exclusively from classical texts but from various philosophies and beliefs, most frequently from the Christian religious tradition. Ill suited to develop a system of their own because their approach to truth was aesthetic and intuitive rather than by the route of logic or metaphysics, they nevertheless dealt with the subject that must engage any philosophy of more than trivial significance —the nature of man and his position in the cosmos. Their central emphasis on the importance of man, together with their freedom from the confines of any single school of thought, gave them a unique opportunity to bring intellectual resources to bear on the problems of the age. Moral problems especially interested them and, considering the passionate conflicts and confusion of values that marked the Renaissance, there could hardly have been an area more deserving of attention. Their speculations ranged over many fields, including politics, ethics, manners and etiquette, and the substance of the good life. In none of these, however, did they break very decidedly with traditional patterns. The intellectual positions they defended provide an index to the direction of Renaissance thought. Only to a limited degree did they determine it.

Italian humanists—revering the example of Petrarch and going beyond him in their defense of secular pursuits—propagated the doctrine of the whole man. They sought to extend the dimensions of experience and develop the full potentialities of the human being. Their approach was both subjective and objective, attentive to the claims of individual personality and to the role of the individual in society. But while wishing to remove inhibitions that stood in the way of man's perfection, they lacked equipment for making a realistic analysis of the human psyche, the structure and operation of society, or the natural environment. They relied on precepts and maxims garnered from ancient or medieval thinkers, and their perspective was affected by prevailing metaphysical dogmas. They acclaimed the gospel of the whole man but visualized man as a dual creature, whose contrary parts could with difficulty—perhaps never —be made compatible. The humanists inclined more to Stoicism than to Epicureanism, to Augustine than to Aquinas, and their adaptation of Aristotle was colored by the mysticism of Plato. Even though successful and influential humanists gave every indication of enjoying the goods of this world, most of them upheld the superior excellence of the mind or soul over the body and accepted as an article of faith that supreme happiness can be attained only in the life to come.

The concept of the whole man, enthusiastically advanced by the humanists, encouraged the belief that the legitimate scope of human activities could be enlarged. The "civic humanists" of Florence during the early fifteenth century celebrated the merits of the active life as opposed to a life of solitary contemplation or monastic withdrawal. They asserted that man's vocation lies on this earth and that the purpose of philosophy is to prepare him for useful endeavor. They stressed the need for a broad education to inculcate a sense of civic responsibility, praised the institution of marriage and the family—ties that bind the individual to a larger community where his involvement will enable him to realize his full potential. They called—in writing at least—for hard work, for toil and sweat. Leon Battista Alberti inquired, "Who could believe himself to have any dignity or value . . . without sweat in order to attain to laborious and manly goals?" and he declared, "Man is born in order to be useful to other men." [13] The humanist chancellors—Coluccio Salutati (1331–1406), his pupil Leonardo Bruni, and Poggio Bracciolini—saw in dedicated service to the Florentine republic the noblest earthly calling and the road to freedom and happiness.

The humanist ideal of self-realization through active involvement not only found an outlet in literary scholarship and the cultivation of eloquence but also attached itself to existing institutions. Contemporary institutions, although admittedly imperfect, were accepted as true patterns of the ideal and not subjected to thorough and critical examination. The approbation of the humanists added an aura of dignity to the interests and position of privileged members

---

[13] Eugenio Garin, *Italian Humanism*, trans. Peter Munz (New York: Harper & Row, 1965), pp. 61, 64.

of society. If they advocated patriotic participation in government, they also glorified the pursuit of wealth and honored those who obtained it. The concept of the whole man was too readily altered to fit the profile of the fortunate man—one who was able to stand above the mob, relieved from the pressure of a daily struggle for existence. Although they showed perceptive insights and sometimes issued clear warnings, the humanists largely conformed to the age in which they lived. They fought with determination and heroism for the cause of letters; on social and moral issues they were far less innovative and far less bold.

The troubles arising from the armed invasions, economic crises, and religious controversies that besieged Italy in the later Renaissance dimmed the humanist vision of the complete person who enters wholeheartedly into the world's work and directs it toward the realization of man's higher aspirations. But long before this period of crisis the ideal civic humanism propounded by Bruni and Poggio had disintegrated under the Medicean hegemony. The confident attitude of the early humanists had never rested on a very sure foundation and was always hedged with reservations. Coluccio Salutati, who at the end of Petrarch's century vigorously championed the active life and condemned monasticism, regarded religion as the highest and noblest form of activity—"the strenuous path which leads, through the cliffs of this world, to the sweet peace of heaven." [14] With the decline of republican liberties in the late fifteenth and early sixteenth centuries, Italian humanists, while not repudiating the concept of the whole man, found it less relevent to the sphere of political action, which seemed to be dominated by forces beyond the control of men whether wise or foolish. As the humanists occupied themselves increasingly with lofty and harmless theoretical propositions or with the perfecting of the art of expression as an end in itself, they widened the gap between culture and the society which had given it birth. Some attempted to withdraw from worldly entanglements and revived the concept of the superiority of a life of contemplation to one of active engagement.

The intellectual vigor of the humanist movement suffered erosion from the tide of disillusionment and pessimism that swept over Italian society during the High Renaissance. It was affected not only by external events but also by general changes in outlook and

---

[14] *Ibid.*, p. 28.

mood—manifest in the arts and in the vogue of Neoplatonism with its depreciation of the flesh—and finally by the jolting challenge to human pride hurled by a series of religious reformers from Savonarola to Luther. Before this onslaught there were few who did not retreat. While honoring man's reason, the humanists had more typically affirmed the supremacy of his will. In the sixteenth century the loudest voices were those crying the poverty of the intellect, the feebleness of reason, and—most insistently—the bondage of the will.

THE NATURAL MAN'S CHAMPION—PIETRO ARETINO

Pessimism was by no means universal or complete at any stage of the Renaissance. The contrary is indicated by a notorious but ebullient figure who was born in Arezzo about the beginning of the Italian High Renaissance—Pietro Aretino (1492–1556). Although sometimes dismissed by historians as inconsequential, he was taken seriously by his contemporaries, both friends and enemies, and at the height of his career, when he was living in the luxurious city of Venice, he enjoyed a considerable reputation in the field of letters. A representative of what might be called the literary underworld, Aretino laid no claim to philosophy or scholarship or even a formal education, and he is chiefly remembered as an unscrupulous adventurer. In his own peculiar way, however, he achieved distinction as an exuberant champion of human nature. The humanists had extolled the whole man in theory but weakened the concept in practice by inflicting upon it the traditional dualism that relegated the body and its urges to an inferior plane. They usually identified man's spiritual progress, if not with extreme asceticism at least with a continual struggle between passion and reason, between the instinctual and the intellectual faculties. Aretino did not restore or perfect the doctrine of the whole man—he was no metaphysician— but he met head on the challenge of a restrictive asceticism.

Pietro Aretino stands, if not as the devil's advocate, as a kind of Sancho Panza to whatever of the Renaissance was hopelessly ethereal or quixotic. Of lowly birth, he wriggled his way into aristocratic society, took its measure, and exposed it pitilessly with his self-tutored but telling pen. He lived by flattery and blackmail— lying, wheedling, railing, or inflating as the occasion demanded. A brilliant and versatile scamp, openly for hire, he infuriated and fascinated his contemporaries, and moved in and out of the company of famous figures of the day. In later life he became a close friend and boon companion of the great Titian of Venice. Sometimes known as "the divine Aretino," he was more appropriately called "brigand chief of letters" and "the scourge of princes." The sworn enemy of cant, hypocrisy, and sham—although quite willing to use all of these for his own purpose—he conferred on himself the title of "truth-teller."

Aretino deserves no place in formal intellectual history, nor did he seek it. Even in the field of letters, which provided his liveli-hood, he was a maker of verses rather than a poet. But he was piercing in judgment and a remarkably astute art critic. His function was to shatter pretense and burst dream bubbles. In an age that often took itself too seriously, indulged in utopian visions, and at the same time threatened to destroy itself in senseless fits of fury, he would bring men back to earth and to their senses, not through sermon or syllogism but with a Gargantuan belly laugh. He could be coarse, reckless, obscene, but it is unjust to call him amoral or even immoral in the sense that a Cesare Borgia was. Capable of terrifying verbal attacks, he would not strike a fallen adversary, was more inclined to forgive than to nourish a grudge, allowed people to impose shamelessly on his generosity, and, while almost drowning in sensuality, loathed violence. He would have heartily approved the slogan, "Make love not war."

The most original aspect of Aretino's thought (if it may be dignified with such a name) was his exaltation of the natural man. He celebrated the body and all its urges—not as etherealized through Neoplatonic apologetics and symbolism—as a naked physical and sufficient reality. He dedicated himself to lust as if it were the pursuit of the Holy Grail. To him all natural acts and functions were blessed, sacramental, thank offerings to God; and he would gladly serve as high priest. Love, which the Neoplatonists distilled into the beckoning light of divine spirit, was for Aretino not only the most ecstatic physical delight but the beginning and end of man's exis-tence (he claimed himself to require sexual gratification forty times a month). His explicit and unblushingly erotic writings transform animal sensuality into something almost mystical. Aretino was such a single-minded apostle of the flesh that he found it hard to under-stand why his tastes shocked the susceptibilities of polite society. Early in the pontificate of his friend Clement VII (Giulio de' Medici)

Aretino composed a group of sizzling sonnets to
album of engravings that must have been one of th
do-it books ever printed: "The Twenty-six Modes (
When the ensuing scandal forced Pietro to flee fro
brief period, in a letter to a physician friend he complained of the
"hypocrites": "I am out of patience with their vile judgment and the
nasty custom that denies the eyes what most delights them. What
wrong is there in seeing a man possess a woman? Why, the very
beasts are freer than we!" [15]

Aretino was right about the hypocrisy. It is no secret, and it
was no secret during the Renaissance, that laxity in sex matters extended far enough to tolerate a high incidence of prostitution,
adultery, illegitimacy, and perversion. But whatever the private
practice, Renaissance society publicly upheld the proprieties, and its
professed moral code was colored by the ascetic view of man's
physical nature inherited from the Middle Ages. In the wide-open
city of Venice, sodomy was listed officially as a crime punishable
by death. Strict enforcement of the law would have brought a mea-
surable decline in the city's population. Aretino, the consummate
liar, possessed more fundamental honesty than his detractors. He was
one of the few radical enough to challenge artificial restraints and
moral standards in the name of human nature in its entirety.

Although this brash champion of the natural man repeatedly
flouted the prevailing mores, he offered no serious proposal for reforming them; still less did he articulate a genuine philosophy of life.
His espousal of a sensuality too strenuous for any but the most
athletic represents an apology for his own life rather than a reasonable creed. It provided a refreshing antidote to prudery and to a
too precious transcendentalism, but it recognized only one facet of
the human psyche. Aretino could not fully emancipate himself from
the predilections and value judgments of his era even though he
defied them, and his bravado failed him in the face of bitter personal misfortune. When deserted by one of his mistresses, a particularly unscrupulous young adventuress, he cursed himself for having
succumbed to "the vile, vain, and rank pleasures of the flesh," and
wondered "whether woman, the root of all evil, is not the likeness

---

[15] Ralph Roeder, *The Man of the Renaissance* (New York: Viking, 1933),
pp. 428–429; see also James Cleugh, *The Divine Aretino* (New York, 1966),
pp. 68–72.

the Fiend more than man is the image of God." [16] And when an illegitimate daughter was born to him, his grateful solicitude matched that of any respectable father. To a friend he rejoiced in the thought that the sweet little girl might comfort his old age, underlined the importance of guarding her virtue (he who had played fast and loose with the virtue of so many women!), and prayed that he might live to see her safely married.

THE PROBLEM OF FREEDOM

The knotty problem of human freedom intruded itself into every sphere of Renaissance activity and occupied a prominent place in speculative discourse. Humanists attacked the problem both in the philosophical context of the relation between freedom and necessity and on the theological plane of free will versus predestination. In attempting to vindicate and clothe with meaning the concept of human freedom, the humanists set themselves a formidable task. The classical tradition was of little help. The Greco-Roman world view had been bounded by the notion of eternally recurring cycles, affecting man's condition but outside his control, and by a belief in the immutability of fate. True, the golden age of Greece had engendered and briefly demonstrated the ideal of political liberty, but this was the liberty of free citizens in a self-governing, homogeneous, well-ordered community. The Italian Renaissance city-states, closer to the ancient pattern than anything else in Europe, were heterogeneous, despotically governed, and in a chronic state of disorder. During the Renaissance, which paid homage to the ideal of freedom, the individual found most avenues to its expression blocked, and he was forced to seek it within himself rather than through participation in society. His inner resources needed to be stout to stand against the tide of popular superstitions, which embraced palmistry, witchcraft, sorcery, and demonology. Even many educated people regarded Fortune not playfully as "Lady Luck" but fearfully as a capricious and implacable deity, and few doubted the influence of the stars in molding human destiny.

Neither could the humanists coax much reassurance from their occasional allies the philosophers. Cusanus (who was half medieval) was the only philosopher of the first rank who consistently vindicated

---

[16] Roeder, *op. cit.*, pp. 529–530.

the principle of human freedom at every stage of his thought, and his abstruse reasoning had little tangible impact. The Neoplatonists and Pico della Mirandola, in spite of their paeans to the dignity of man, conceived of freedom as a transcendental goal—the transmuting of human nature into something else—and were too ready to retreat into a negative asceticism. Pomponazzi, the champion of reason, could offer only the cold comfort of Stoic resignation. It is not strange, therefore, that the humanists, in company with the majority of their contemporaries, looked hopefully to the Christian dispensation and measured the concept of freedom against the frame of religious teaching and experience. In so doing they were turning in the direction men must inevitably turn when grappling with the biggest and most persistent questions. But they were not fully equipped for the task—already abandoned by professional theologians—and they became caught in the cross fire of partisan controversy.

In every age the concept of freedom takes on meaning only in the context of the physical and social environment, in relation to the range of activities and choices open to the members of society. The structure and operation of Italian society in the late Renaissance seemed to be beyond the control of human will. The individual could act and might achieve success within the structure but could neither change it nor escape from it; and the prospect of drastically altering the physical environment through the application of scientific knowledge was hardly glimpsed. The fine moral judgments of philosophers were not the guiding principles of the marketplace, the council chamber, or the *condottiere's* camp. The whole European community was showing signs of strain. As Charles Trinkaus observes, it was beginning to exhibit "the consequences of a divorce between ethics and economics, between the moral and the expedient, between the spiritual and the material." [17] The humanists were forced to come to terms with this schism, this tantalizing disparity between the ideal of freedom and the opportunities for its exercise. A few of them managed to cling to the thesis that man is a free moral agent even though powerless to shape the material world or regulate his own conduct within it.

---

[17] Charles Trinkaus, "The Problem of Free Will in the Renaissance and the Reformation," in P. O. Kristeller and P. P. Wiener, eds., *Renaissance Essays* (New York: Harper & Row, 1968), p. 187.

The moral dilemma confronting philosophers—and also the path destined to be followed in attempting to get around it—had been spotted by one of the keenest minds of the first half of the Quattrocento, the humanist scholar and critic Lorenzo Valla (1405–57). Valla has won a sinister and undeserved reputation as the incarnation of an obstreperous paganism. Equipped with razor-sharp critical faculties, he turned his sometimes venomous pen against spurious texts, sacred as well as profane; and in spite of the fact that he was employed for years as apostolic secretary to Pope Nicholas v he seemed quite willing to war against the whole ecclesiastical apparatus. No paragon of piety, he relied on his wits for his personal safety as well as for his livelihood. Summoned before a church court of inquisition in Naples, he could coolly confront his inquisitors with the disarming but unflattering defense: "I believe what Mother Church believes, even though she knows nothing." The accusation of paganism brought against Valla derives largely from a book written in 1431, entitled, in its first version, *On Pleasure*, and in a later version, *On the True Good*. In this work, which presents the arguments of a Stoic, an Epicurean, and a Christian in support of their respective philosophies, the Epicurean spokesman makes a remarkably strong case, exalting pleasure, both sensual and intellectual, as the chief end of man's existence—the true good. Valla did not really consider Epicureanism an adequate guide to life; he used its tenets—distorted somewhat—to refute the gloomy, austere, and negative teachings of Stoicism. Scorning all philosophies ancient or modern, he chose the "worst" of the ancient creeds as a club with which to demolish the "best" and so left the way open for a fresh approach to the question of values. Valla developed more fully and unequivocally than most of the humanists their doctrine of the inherent goodness of man. He viewed man's instincts and appetites—bestowed by nature—as necessarily good and not to be denied, and he affirmed that pleasure was the consequence and reward of following nature.

The key to Valla's discourse *On the True Good* lies in his separation of pleasure from virtue. Instead of accepting the traditional notion—common in varying degrees to Stoicism, Platonism, Aristotelianism, and Christian theology—that virtue can be won only by suppressing desire, he placed virtue and pleasure in different categories, with pleasure occupying the higher position. Unlike Aretino a century later, Valla was not the apostle of unbridled sensuality, although his treatment of virtue was decidedly cavalier. He acknowledged it as useful insofar as it promoted happiness, but he remained skeptical on this point, observing that the rich are more likely to be happy than the virtuous. Still, Valla was undoubtedly sincere in professing himself a believing Christian. He attempted to translate the message of Christianity into the humanist doctrine of the whole man—interpreting the one true religion not as a metaphysical explanation of the mysteries of the universe nor as a prescribed code of conduct but as a vindication of man's essential nature and a seal of approval upon his aspirations. The bliss of the soul in heaven he conceived of neither in terms of release from the body nor as the contemplation of God but as the *enjoyment* of God. Such a radical application of the pleasure principle would, if carried out fully, inevitably run counter to the teachings of the Church, and this Valla had no intention of doing. Upholding the claims of flesh and spirit, he also defended both reason and faith. Determined to free faith from intellectual encumbrances, he removed it from the confines of reason and defined it as a spiritual form of eloquence. But just as he ranked pleasure above virtue, so did he place faith above reason. Far from rejecting faith, he appears to have regarded it as man's staunchest bulwark and final court of appeal.

The most profound of Valla's writings, essentially a theological disputation, throws light on his conception of the limits of human knowledge and human freedom. The *Dialogue on Free Will*, written about 1440, upholds the doctrine of predestination. Its argument leads to the conclusion that, although God's *foreknowledge* of events does not bring them about, nevertheless His *will* does ordain them; the fixity of God's will annuls man's freedom of will. Valla quotes with approval the Pauline doctrine that God elects some to salvation regardless of their works, that "he hath mercy on whom he will have mercy, and whom he will he hardeneth," and he declares that even the grace of Christ, which freed man from the taint of original sin ("the disobedience of the first parent in which all of us have sinned"), is of no avail to those not chosen by God. And when the justice of such an arbitrary decree is challenged by Valla's imaginary disputant, the answer given is that God's reason is hidden, a mystery revealed not even to the angels and quite beyond the scope of human inquiry. Valla's *Dialogue* has been cited as a proof of an emerging critical spirit which brought the problem of freedom "before an entirely secular forum, before the bench of 'natural reason,' " [18] but such a liberal interpretation is not borne out by the text. It is true that Valla defends the free play of reason within its proper sphere, but he is equally emphatic in forbidding it to intrude upon matters of faith. Faith, he implies, stands above reason and needs no support from it: "We do not know the cause of this matter; of what consequence is it? We stand by faith not by the probability of reason. Does knowledge do much for the corroboration of faith? Humility does more." He excoriates philosophy as "a seedbed of heresy" and singles out Aristotle as the chief of those damned by God for their "arrogance and boldness" in "raising their own mouths to heaven, and wishing to scale it."

It is ironic but entirely logical that Lorenzo Valla—the *enfant terrible* who attacked the secular authority of the Church, ridiculed sacred texts for their errors and bad Latin, and went so far in his espousal of hedonism as to say a prostitute is better than a nun— should have become a source of inspiration not to skeptics and freethinkers but to a new tough breed of champions of the supremacy of faith over reason. Both Luther and Calvin acknowledged their indebtedness to him.

When in the late Renaissance the doctrine of freedom of the will came under attack from the Reformers, neither philosophers nor humanists could stage an effective defense. Erasmus, a somewhat timid but incorruptible crusader in the cause of sanity and tolerance, did enter the lists with his anti-Lutheran *Diatribe on Free Will* (1524). Acknowledging the dogma of Original Sin and the necessity of redemption through Divine Grace, Erasmus took the modest position that man's free will is at least a "secondary cause" in effecting his salvation; and he warned against the excesses of doctrinal disputes, whence "the lightnings and thunders arise which today violently shake the world." A rumble of the thunder came the following year in Luther's reply, *On the Bondage of the Will* (literally *On the Enslaved Will—De servo arbitrio*). Here Luther declared: "This is the highest degree of faith—to believe that He is merciful, who saves so few and damns so many; to believe Him just, who according to His own will makes us necessarily damnable." To believe such things, Luther acknowledged, was not possible through reason but only through the faith vouch-

---

[18] Cassirer, *Individual and the Cosmos, op. cit.*, p. 78.

safed to the Elect: "the Elect shall believe it; the rest shall perish." In their quest of freedom, Renaissance intellectuals piloted their frail craft through rough waters only to strand them eventually on the reefs of religious controversy. In the last analysis, however, the deficiencies in Renaissance thought are to be found not in any single defeat. They stem from the fact that its protagonists set themselves a staggering task and underestimated its difficulties. They aimed at a total understanding of man, as a physical, psychological, and moral being, and also of the cosmos insofar as it relates to man. Moreover, they sought this knowledge not merely for intellectual satisfaction but as a means of enabling humanity to rise to its full stature. The goal of philosophers was the good life—not as theoretically conceivable but as actually livable in the world accessible to Renaissance man, who was defined neither as a lonely creature lost in an indifferent universe, nor merely as a link in the great chain of being, but as the central reality of the whole of creation.

In undertaking a pragmatic synthesis of the microcosm and macrocosm, Renaissance thinkers drew upon all the resources available to them, and these were rich indeed. Foremost was the Judaeo-Christian tradition, which in spite of supernatural trappings embodied a view of humanity more dynamic than any known to the classical world. It nourished the hope of man's ultimate release and triumph—a hope which could be translated into temporal and earthly terms. To many idealists it seemed that man was ready, or nearly ready, to enter upon his long promised inheritance.

Philosophical and religious systems, no matter how rich, must be reshaped to meet changing conditions if they are to be continuously effective. This is especially true when the basic norms and the economic structure of society are shifting, as they were during the Renaissance. The noblest ideals remain colorless abstractions unless made operative in the arena where men work and struggle. The Christian ethic, which humanists and philosophers invoked in support of their cherished values, could not adequately defend these values unless it were brought to play in the realm of business, politics, and social relationships. Renaissance thinkers, while not exactly armchair philosophers, gave insufficient attention to the character of their society and appeared oblivious to many of its glaring abuses. To read some of the idyllic treatises penned during the Renaissance is to wonder whether their estimable authors had ever looked around them to see what men were doing to one another. Too many leaders remained political innocents, if not merely gifted snobs—taking little notice of the horde of common folk, victims rather than molders of their destiny, who made up the majority of the species lauded by the humanists. This unsung multitude—too lightly regarded by scholars and philosophers—was not neglected by leaders of the Reformation and Counter Reformation, who found it a fertile recruiting ground.

THE SLOW EMERGENCE OF SCIENCE

A twentieth-century observer of the Renaissance scene is impelled to ask where science was hiding. In an age of discovery and inquiry, why did people of obvious intelligence and courage not utilize the instrument that has proved so efficacious in illuminating areas of darkness and ignorance? The scientific tradition is the fruit of a long and obscure evolution reaching into the mists of antiquity. There had been no suppression of science, no conspiracy against it during the Middle Ages, as has sometimes been supposed; the medieval period made important contributions to the advancement of science. Granted that science did not burst into bloom during the Renaissance nor Europeans suddenly acquire a scientific temper and outlook. However, the assertion of overly enthusiastic medievalists that the Renaissance actually inhibited scientific progress is dubious to say the least. Renaissance thinkers undoubtedly made some wrong turns, but this has happened often in later and more "scientific" eras. It would be fairer to say that practically all roads of inquiry during the Renaissance led in the direction of science but that none of them was clearly marked or free from detours. The Ptolemaic-Aristotelian-Scholastic tradition, which flourished at such universities as Padua, Bologna, and Paris, stoutly supported the principle of causality, as illustrated by Pomponazzi's conscientious attempt to rationalize astrology. And if Renaissance schoolmen were still enthralled by veneration for their master Aristotle, Cusanus had shown that the rigid Aristotelian categories could be broken and had nominated mathematics to lead the way to more exact knowledge. The humanist-architect Alberti, and even the Neoplatonist Ficino, had also regarded mathematics as the clue to universal secrets.

The Renaissance displayed more interest than the Middle Ages in the workings of nature. As nature ceased to be regarded as demonic or hostile, the feeling grew that the sympathetic study of natural phenomena could lead to an understanding both of the physical world and of man himself. At the same time, the approach of even most intellectuals to nature was naive and intuitive rather than analytical. While direct experience began to be valued as a door to knowledge, it was typically the experience of the senses or of the undisciplined imagination and bordered on the world of miracles. Nature was sensed, felt, and consequently personified, endowed with animistic forces. No longer forbidden territory, she remained the enticing domain of mystery and magic. She could be absorbed, enjoyed, and understood through an immediate spiritual experience that did not require laborious analysis. The prevalence of such assumptions—rather than the humanists' preoccupation with classical manuscripts—delayed the adoption of a discipline based on exact description and experimentation. The natural philosophy of the Renaissance, lacking a critical method and essentially poetic and mystical—"natural magic" as Pico called it—pointed the way not to the scientific method but to a new metaphysics of idealism and subjectivism.

While the Renaissance philosophy of nature tended to stray into the bypaths of fancy, a discipline which might conceivably have been the domain of still wilder imaginings afforded at least a glimpse of the true road. Renaissance artists, seeking to master the technique of precise observation in order to attain what Leonardo da Vinci called "exact fantasy," came closer than most of their contemporaries to the essence and the spirit of investigative science. Leonardo da Vinci, who provides the most illustrious example, was the true successor of Cusanus in this respect, although he worked from the bias of a creative artist rather than a theologian. Whether or not directly influenced by Cusanus, Leonardo shared the cardinal's distrust of Scholastic premises and, in his extensive empirical observations, exemplified the scientific temper much more fully.

Largely self-educated, proud, and sensitive to the slurs of humanists and schoolmen, Leonardo heaped scorn on those who followed the conventional routes to knowledge of the physical world. He condemned the natural philosophy of his day as a species of idle dreaming, its illusion of dominance over nature unjustified because it did not rest on a mathematical foundation.

"There is no result in nature without a cause," he wrote in his *Notebooks;* and "There is no certainty where one can neither apply any of the mathematical sciences nor any of those which are based upon the mathematical sciences." He recognized a kinship between the mathematician and the artist, both of whom must deal with exact quantities, relationships, and proportions. He believed it was the duty of the artist not merely to depict beauty but to *see* reality with his outer and his inner eye and to reveal it to others, not through literal imitation but by means of an "exact fantasy" which brings to light the hidden meaning of things.

There has been extensive and largely unprofitable dispute over Leonardo's proper place in the history of science. His famous inventions—many of which were purely theoretical and not intended for construction—are probably the least important aspect of his activity and interests. Neither Cusanus nor da Vinci can be called a scientist in the full sense; but, for that matter, neither can many of their honored successors. Copernicus was in some ways more conservative and "medieval" than Leonardo, and Kepler was half religious mystic. Leonardo's *Notebooks* are cluttered with fragmentary jottings, disjointed and enigmatical. His knowledge of mathematics, which he revered so highly, was feeble even by the standards of his day. Although he stressed the importance of mechanics—"the paradise of the mathematical sciences, because by means of it one comes to the fruits of mathematics"—he made no original contributions to it except in the field of hydrodynamics. Nevertheless, in spite of his limitations—and even aside from his brilliant pioneer work in anatomy—he demonstrated essential traits of the scientist. He looked for particular causes rather than an ultimate First Cause, underlined the importance of exact quantitative measurement in investigating phenomena, and while accepting the universality of natural law—"the necessity of nature"—insisted that nature's workings are based on reason and can be understood if man will apply his powers of observation and analysis.

Not until after the Renaissance did the new heliocentric cosmology and the implications of the scientific method affect the public consciousness even of the educated classes. The reason for the slow pace of scientific advance was not, as has been alleged, the hostility of the Church. The Renaissance Church has much to answer for; it can be blamed for the decay of both morality and religion, but it cannot be fairly charged with the throttling of science. The real explanation is that it is always difficult for people to divest themselves of cherished beliefs or to look at familiar data from a new perspective. Copernicus hesitated to publish his great work—and finally did so only at the urging of fellow churchmen—because he feared the ridicule of other astronomers for questioning a system that had worked satisfactorily for centuries and that seemed to square with everyday experience and common sense. Even Kepler, one of the most heroic spirits in the annals of scientific thought but by no means free from the prejudices of his day, wasted years trying to fit the orbits of the planets into an arbitrary sequence of Pythagorean geometrical figures and only reluctantly parted with astrology.

By the time science had matured to the stage exemplified by Galileo, Harvey, Boyle, and Newton, it had largely broken from its medieval and Renaissance moorings and embarked on an uncharted course. Renaissance science, however inadequate and halting, was never a separate discipline but always interwoven with other fields of knowledge and inquiry. Nicholas Cusanus, groping toward a scientific world view, searched most deeply into man's relation to God and his moral and spiritual destiny. Leonardo, although he exalted mathematics, illustrated perfectly the union of science and art. Like the Neoplatonists, with whom he had very little in common, he believed the true artist penetrates to the heart of reality and transforms it. Both art and science were for him creative functions: "Science is a second creation made with the understanding; painting is a second creation made with the imagination." Galileo a century later repeated Leonardo's admonition to learn the ciphers in which "the great book of nature" is composed, but he relegated both poetry and art to the realm of fiction. As science emancipated itself from the thraldom of ancient dogmas and attained its own sure footing, it abandoned the domain of aesthetics, religion, and morality.

If science had attained its majority somewhat earlier, it is doubtful that it could have rekindled the fading Renaissance dream of man's unique place in the universe; almost certainly it would have given the dream somewhat different contours. The cosmology erected during the two centuries between Copernicus and Newton completely overthrew the earth-centered order that had formed the backdrop for both medieval and Renaissance speculation. While the new heliocentric system, revealing a far vaster universe than had hitherto been imagined, did not necessarily disparage or debase man, the course of modern science did suggest that his future success might lie in mastering and manipulating cosmic forces rather than in attempting to bring his own little world into conformity with them. This was—and still is—a challenging, exciting, and potentially rewarding prospect but one quite distinct from "the end of man" as defined by theologians and philosophers.

Leonardo da Vinci, one of the few Renaissance figures to sense the rationale and the implications of reliable scientific knowledge, was both enamored and repelled by what he foresaw. It troubled him that the most ambivalent and unpredictable of nature's children had the power to appropriate her secrets. Conceivably, in the process of transforming nature to his liking, restless man might discover his own higher destiny. But in a mood of revulsion at the human propensity for wanton destruction, Leonardo invoked a prophetic curse on the race:

There shall be nothing remaining on the earth or under the earth or in the waters that shall not be pursued and molested or destroyed, and that which is in one country taken away to another . . . O Earth! what delays thee to open and hurl them headlong into the deep fissures of the huge abysses and caverns, and no longer to display in the sight of heaven so savage and ruthless a monster? [19]

REFERENCES AND SUGGESTIONS FOR FURTHER READING

THE HUMANISTS, AND GENERAL ASPECTS OF RENAISSANCE THOUGHT

Bainton, Roland H., "Man, God, and the Church in the Age of the Renaissance," in Wallace K. Ferguson *et al.*, eds., *The Renaissance: Six Essays* (New York: Harper & Row, 1962).

Baker, Herschel, *The Image of Man: A Study of the Idea of Human Dignity in Classical Antiquity, the Middle Ages, and the Renaissance* (New York: Harper & Row, 1961).

---

[19] Leonardo da Vinci, *The Notebooks*, quoted in Giorgio de Santillana, ed., *The Age of Adventure* (New York: Mentor Books, 1965), p. 87.

Garin, Eugenio, *Italian Humanism: Philosophy and Civic Life in the Renaissance,* trans. Peter Munz (New York: Harper & Row, 1965). One of the finest studies of Italian humanists and their influence. Garin stresses the positive aspects of humanist thought but acknowledges the inhibiting effects of the crisis of the late Renaissance.

Kristeller, Paul Oskar, *Renaissance Thought: The Classic, Scholastic, and Humanistic Strains* (New York: Harper & Row, 1961). *Renaissance Thought II: Papers on Humanism and the Arts* (New York: Harper & Row, 1965). "Changing Views of the Intellectual History of the Renaissance Since Jacob Burckhardt," in Tinsley Helton, ed., *The Renaissance: A Reconsideration of the Theories and Interpretations of the Age* (Madison: University of Wisconsin Press, 1964). Representative and extremely useful selections from Kristeller's writings.

O'Kelly, Bernard, ed., *The Renaissance Image of Man and the World* (Columbus: Ohio State University Press, 1966).

Rice, Eugene F., *The Renaissance Idea of Wisdom* (Cambridge, Mass.: Harvard University Press, 1958). Depicts a gradual "secularization" of wisdom, accompanied by a parallel current of spirituality and religious reformism.

Salvadori, Max, "The End of the Renaissance in Italy, 1530–1559," in *The Renaissance Reconsidered: A Symposium,* Smith College Studies in History, Vol. 44 (Northampton, Mass., 1964).

Spitz, Lewis W., *The Religious Renaissance of the German Humanists* (Cambridge, Mass.: Harvard University Press, 1963). Includes a discussion of the influence of Cusanus and of Neoplatonism and a chapter on the relations between Erasmus and the Reformers.

Taylor, Henry Osborn, *Thought and Expression in the Sixteenth Century,* 2 vols., 2nd rev. ed. (New York: Frederick Ungar, 1959).

Trinkaus, Charles E., *Adversity's Noblemen: The Italian Humanists on Happiness* (New York: Octagon Books, 1965). Finds little celebration of happiness among either early or late Italian humanists.

PHILOSOPHY

Cassirer, Ernst, *The Individual and the Cosmos in Renaissance Philosophy,* trans. Mario Domandi (New York: Barnes and

Noble, 1963). The most profound study of Renaissance philosophical thought; difficult but rewarding.

Kristeller, Paul O., *The Philosophy of Marsilio Ficino,* trans. Virginia Conant (New York, 1943). *Eight Philosophers of the Italian Renaissance* (Stanford: Stanford University Press, 1964). "Renaissance Platonism," in William H. Werkmeister, ed., *Facets of the Renaissance* (New York: Harper & Row, 1963).

Kristeller, Paul O., and P. P. Wiener, eds., *Renaissance Essays* (New York: Harper & Row, 1968); especially Ernst Cassirer, "Giovanni Pico della Mirandola," and Charles E. Trinkaus, "The Problem of Free Will in the Renaissance and the Reformation."

Robb, Nesca A., *Neoplatonism of the Italian Renaissance* (New York: Octagon Books, 1968).

Seigel, Jerrold E., *Rhetoric and Philosophy in Renaissance Humanism: The Union of Eloquence and Wisdom, Petrarch to Valla* (Princeton: Princeton University Press, 1968).

Weinstein, Donald, *Savonarola and Florence: Prophecy and Patriotism in the Renaissance* (Princeton: Princeton University Press, 1970). For the influence of Savonarola on the Neoplatonists and on Pico della Mirandola.

Whitfield, John H., *Petrarch and the Renascence* (New York: Haskell House, 1969). Includes good discussion of Valla.

SCIENCE

Boas, Marie, *The Scientific Renaissance, 1450–1630* (New York: Harper & Row, 1962), The Rise of Modern Science series.

Bronowski, J., "Leonardo da Vinci," in J. H. Plumb, ed., *Renaissance Profiles* (New York: Harper & Row, 1965).

Butterfield, Herbert, *The Origins of Modern Science, 1300–1800* (New York: Collier, 1951). A highly perceptive introduction to the subject.

Panofsky, Erwin, "Artist, Scientist, Genius: Notes on the 'Renaissance-Dämmerung,'" in Ferguson *et al.,* *The Renaissance: Six Essays.*

Randall, John Herman, Jr., "The Development of Scientific Method in the School of Padua," in Kristeller and Wiener, eds., *Renaissance Essays.* A significant contribution.

Rosen, Edward, "Renaissance Science as Seen by Burckhardt and His Successors," in *The Renaissance: A Reconsideration.*

Sarton, George, "Science in the Renaissance," in James W. Thompson *et al.,* eds., *The Civilization of the Renaissance* (New York: Frederick Ungar, 1929). A negative view. *Appreciation of Ancient and Medieval Science during the Renaissance (1450–1600),* (New York: Perpetua Book, 1961). A study of Renaissance awareness and knowledge of old scientific classics as revealed in early printed books. "The Quest for Truth: Scientific Progress during the Renaissance," in Ferguson *et al.,* eds., *The Renaissance: Six Essays.* A lecture given in 1952— his most favorable appraisal.

Thorndike, Lynn, *Science and Thought in the Fifteenth Century* (New York: Columbia University Press, 1929).

Truesdell, C. A., "Leonardo da Vinci, The Myths and the Reality," *The Johns Hopkins Magazine,* XVIII, 2 (1967).

SOURCES IN TRANSLATION

Cassirer, Ernst, *et al.,* eds., *The Renaissance Philosophy of Man* (Chicago: University of Chicago Press, 1948). Contains key works of Valla, Ficino, Pico della Mirandola, and Pomponazzi, ably translated and edited and supplied with introductions.

de Santillana, Giorgio, ed., *The Age of Adventure: The Renaissance Philosophers* (New York: New American Library, 1965), The Mentor Philosophers series. Brief, interesting selections from a wide range of figures, with incisive editorial commentary.

MacCurdy, Edward, trans. and ed., *The Notebooks of Leonardo da Vinci,* 2 vols. in one (New York: George Braziller, 1958).

Pico della Mirandola, *On the Dignity of Man, On Being and the One, Heptaplus* (Indianapolis: Library of Liberal Arts, 1965).

VIII

DESCENT
FROM THE SUMMIT

*How often, do you think, did I turn back and look up to
the summit of the mountain today while I was walking
down? It seemed to me hardly higher than a cubit
compared to the height of human contemplation,
were the latter not plunged into the filth of earthly
sordidness.*
—Francesco Petrarch, THE ASCENT OF MONT VENTOUX

*Too long have you been an exile from your fatherland
and from yourself. It is now time to return, for "evening is
falling and night is friend of the despoiler."*
—Francesco Petrarch, THE SECRET

THE RENAISSANCE—SUNRISE OR SUNSET?

The revolutionary changes that have altered the character of society
and the course of history in modern times have not erased the memory of the Renaissance. The reason for its enduring importance is
not the intrinsic worth of Renaissance culture, although this was
remarkable, even in areas displaying little originality, and although
its art ranks with the finest products of any earlier or later age.
Neither is it because the Renaissance inaugurated the modern era.
If defined as a segment of time the Renaissance does serve as a
convenient bridge between medieval and modern, but when understood as a set of cultural phenomena it cannot be called the proto-
type of modern Western civilization; it prepared the way for our
age chiefly in the sense that the disintegration of the Renaissance
culture pattern carried away the medieval and classical patterns as
well, allowing development in new directions and necessitating a
search for new guiding principles. The real significance of the
Renaissance is that it represents a turning point in the course of
Western civilization. It stands forth as a high plateau, the culmination of a long and irregular evolution extending from classical

246

antiquity through the Middle Ages. It was the final statement of an age both erudite and naive, embracing a world view compounded of scholasticism and humanism, pagan and Christian, that postulated a finite man-centered and God-directed universe; an age of much wisdom and eagerness for more but innocent of science and the scientific method; an age of credulity and of faith. Modern civilization, shaped so predominantly by science and by the technology provided by science, finds the assumptions and ideals of Renaissance thinkers not only unsubstantiated but of little relevance. But, in spite of almost incredible revelations by physicists, chemists, and biologists concerning the structure and behavior of matter and of the life process itself, the scientific age has evolved no adequate interpretation of man and no body of principles for him to live by in place of those that inspired the Renaissance.

The Renaissance was a testing time for beliefs that had been held, sometimes very feebly, for many centuries. It was also a period when new ideas and forces were beginning to come into play. Hence the Renaissance was both modern and medieval—as is, for that matter, the "modern" age, which exhibits some emotional attitudes and beliefs that go back to medieval, ancient, even prehistoric times. The Renaissance material base was a late medieval heritage—urban populations, a money economy, and the beginnings of capitalist enterprise, with small but thriving cities to foster and disseminate culture. These socioeconomic factors, so essential to the whole modern era, were not originated by or in the Renaissance. In fact, to some extent they were temporarily impaired during the fourteenth and fifteenth centuries by a drastic decline in population following the Black Death and by a contraction of industry and commerce in Italy and portions of northern Europe, accompanied by severe financial crises. If modern society is dependent on the prominence of a middle class—the origins of which can be traced to the late Middle Ages—the trend in the leading centers of Italian Renaissance civilization was retrogressive. Between the thirteenth and the late fifteenth centuries the urban middle class in Italy—the most advanced region of European civilization—shrank in numbers and influence as commercial oligarchies gained ascendancy. Italian society was more aristocratic in tone at the end of the Renaissance than at the beginning, and in Europe as a whole the democratic tendencies implicit in the growth of self-governing towns during the late Middle Ages—in France, the Netherlands, and Germany as well as Italy—had been largely suppressed. It is true that some important changes in interests and activities pointed in a modern direction, notably increased travel, the introduction of printed books, and fumbling but essential efforts to unlock the secrets of nature. But it is true that other equally important aspects of Renaissance society and culture were still oriented toward the past.

In the nonmaterial area the debt of the Renaissance to the Middle Ages was most profound. To say that Renaissance civilization was not modern does not mean, however, that it was merely a continuation of the medieval or—least of all—that it represents an inferior or decadent phase of the medieval. The Renaissance was unique in that it restated and reshaped medieval concepts and aspirations—fortifying them with an infusion of ancient Greek and Roman thought—and undertook to give them heroic expression in works of creative imagination and also to make them operating principles in the human community and in the lives of individuals. For all its classicism and for all its worldliness, the Renaissance through its greatest artists and thinkers reiterated the theme that man is the central figure in the universe and capable of attaining both dignity and happiness—not because of his superior cunning or manipulative powers but because he is a moral agent, endowed with the ability to discriminate between good and evil. This affirmation, without which Renaissance culture would have been empty breath, was the logical—if startlingly bold—fulfillment of the Christian medieval tradition. It is also a measure of the tremendous distance between Renaissance man and modern man.

Although marking a high peak in cultural evolution, the Renaissance was not a period of tranquillity and contentment. It was an age of political conflict within and between states and of often ruthlessly competitive economic and social struggle. Not only on the physical plane but on the cultural and intellectual level also it was afflicted by crises, and it suffered from a dichotomy that pervaded the musings of scholars and philosophers. The dichotomy in Renaissance civilization—difficult to pinpoint—was essentially the gap between theory and practice, which remained wide, even though intellectuals of the period conceded in principle the necessity of bridging it. The stimulating and liberating concept of the universal man, the fully developed and whole man, they exploited for the benefit of a small privileged minority, without extending it to the generality of mankind; and they made almost no attempt to apply the ideal to improvement of the social and political order. Older institutions such as the guilds, the feudal contract and manorial regime, and the administrative machinery of a universal Church, which were now breaking up, had never adequately met the needs of society; but the Renaissance supplied no better ones. For all its range of interests, its brilliant resourcefulness, it produced no new formula for a healthy political and social body. Admittedly, during this era the modern political institution of the state assumed more definite form. But the origins of the national state derive from the late Middle Ages, and the contribution of the Renaissance, though substantial, reflects very distinctly the dichotomy of Renaissance mentality. While humanists and philosophers were insisting that man is a moral agent, not only the theorist Machiavelli but practicing rulers and governments demonstrated that politics can be removed from control of the ordinary citizen and freed from any moral restraint whatsoever.

The crisis that confronted and finally impaired Renaissance civilization arose both from external events and from the schism inherent in Renaissance thought and ideals. Armed invasions that converted large portions of the Italian peninsula into appendages of European dynasties, the decline of a once robust civic life, the economic effects of the loss of maritime and financial supremacy by the Italian cities—all of these factors contributed to the crisis of the Italian Renaissance. A more insidious cause was the withering of hope and confidence that had invigorated the mind and spirit, a growing realization that men and events did not conform to the ideal, and a growing doubt as to whether man was actually free to set his own course. Assailed by the fear that man may be only a helpless puppet of cosmic forces, Renaissance intellectuals retreated from their venturesome outpost, seeking such consolation as they could find in submission to fate or the dictates of Heaven. Their retreat facilitated the triumph of the Reformation, Protestant and Catholic.

It would be difficult to overemphasize the contrast between the Renaissance and the Reformation, even though the two movements were closely intertwined and although the Renaissance may not accurately be interpreted as anti-Christian. Paralleling and deeply influencing the secular manifestations of the Renaissance flowed a strong current of religious feeling. Religious enthusiasm and a zeal for positive reform of the Church became especially active in the late fifteenth and early sixteenth centuries, as the Renaissance approached its climax. The movement not only enlisted religious professionals like the prophet Savonarola but also attracted prominent laymen in Italy and in northern and western Europe, humanist scholars, and such a colossal artistic genius as Michelangelo. Inclining toward a mystical piety, its drew inspiration largely from the doctrines of St. Paul and St. Augustine—key figures in Protestant theology—but it aimed to purify and preserve the Church Universal. If this Renaissance religious reform movement had succeeded, it might conceivably have made the Reformation of Luther and Calvin unnecessary and prevented the splitting of Europe into rival theological camps. As religious conflict intensified, however, dividing the countries of Europe from one another, it also obliterated the Renaissance vision of the whole man, replacing it with the image of fractional man. Henceforth both Catholics and Protestants, while plotting slightly different courses to salvation, depicted man as a creature who could be redeemed from his innate worthlessness only through the intervention of supernatural agencies. And both theologies, although investing human actions and life on earth with moral significance, accepted man's inability to mold his destiny or to alter the social environment the better to serve his needs.

The complexity of physical and social changes—increasing from the Renaissance to the present at compound interest or like a nuclear chain reaction—still poses obstacles to the understanding, let alone the improvement, of the human condition. The Renaissance view of man and the cosmos failed to take such changes into account. Renaissance thought at its loftiest, although identifying the potentialities of man and warning against his liability to error, assumed the perpetuation of a simple and already outmoded pattern of society: the prince surrounded by his courtiers; the merchant, with ink-stained hands, remaining in his shop; humanist scholars spreading the gospel of light; the "rabble" performing the necessary drudgery without disturbing their betters. In spite of a display of energy, the Renaissance overview was static rather than dynamic. Like that of the late Middle Ages which it had adapted and embellished, it offered a majestic cosmic picture and inspiration for self-fulfillment. Embodying one of the richest collections of ideas ever credited to invention or revelation, it might have remained an adequate guide to human endeavor if the medieval world had remained constant. But this world was dissolving into another alien and uncharted. Hence the disjunction between the ideal goals of Renaissance thinkers and the crass realities of the hour, and hence the growing mood of disenchantment reflected in most areas of expression, notably in art. For all its gaiety and spontaneity, the Renaissance carries the tragic overtones of an agonizing struggle that was beginning to be abandoned without having been resolved. Rather than a rebirth or a new birth, it was the final testament of an exhausted age—less the dawn of a new day than the magnificent sunset of one that was dying.

THE NEXT STAGE: THE REFORMATION

The religious upheaval known as the Reformation made a different response to the changes agitating society in the fifteenth and sixteenth centuries. Although in conception more reactionary than the Renaissance because it resurrected the old Augustinian doctrines of human depravity, predestination, and the bondage of the will, the Protestant Revolution and its Catholic counterpart came to grips with contemporary realities. If the Reformation did not remove the defects or solve the problems of society, it at least confronted them and helped the individual to make his peace with them. In spite of its intense religiosity and the revival of primitive dogma, it summoned its disciples to action, while warning them that the arena of action was not one fashioned to the heart's desire. It proclaimed, and perhaps exaggerated, the imperfections of the world of the flesh and the devil; it recognized the hopelessness of man's struggle against evil; but at the same time it called upon him to apply his energies to the tasks within his competence, confessing his sinful nature and leaving to God the question of judgment.

The religious reformers proved themselves greater realists than the secular humanists. Not only did they acknowledge the evil in human society and institutions; for the most part they accepted the evil as ineradicable, urging their followers to strive for an inner purity while living in the midst of corruption. To see how the expansive idealism of the Renaissance could yield to a resolute and stoical resignation, compare Luther's views on government with those of Erasmus and More or even of Machiavelli, and compare Luther's and Calvin's definition of "Christian liberty" with Pico della Mirandola's tribute to the dignity and freedom of man. The goals and dreams that quickened Renaissance minds were not otherworldly, but they did tend to disregard the brute facts of existence. They reveal a longing for the good, the beautiful, and the harmonious, but the images of an idyllic society were typically set in some distant time or place—in the classical past, in Arcady, or Utopia. The Reformation tore the veil from men's eyes and forced them to look at the world, forced them to confess that it was, alas, a wretched and dirty place.

No doubt this was a necessary service that had to be performed. A civilization cannot thrive on ideals alone, especially if the ideals reflect the interests or blissful detachment of an aristocratic elite. However hierarchical the social structure, it must give the multitude some sense of belonging and must provide the common man with moral and psychological as well as material incentives. On this test the Reformation, despite its emphasis on transcendental values, was more pragmatic than the Renaissance. While directing its appeal to the heart of each individual, no matter how humble, it accepted and utilized the centrally organized state, supported the claims of princes and the nascent spirit of nationalism, and exalted human productive powers. But the mainsprings of action were strengthened at the sacrifice of a sense of wholeness, not only for society at large but for the individual personality as well. The Reformation dogmas upheld a dichotomy more incorrigible than the dichotomy in the creed of the Renaissance—an antithesis between the eternally elect and the eternally damned, between the inner and the outer man, between the private world where morality operates and the public world where morality, if not inoperative, is beyond human control.

This dualism between the planes of human experience was neither absolute nor unprecedented. Nor was it without compensations. While it represents the dissolution of an optimistic view of man and society it coincided not with an ebbing of vitality but with a surge of energy and the expansion of the orbit of European civilization. Just ahead lay the great age of discovery, and beyond that a scientific revolution, destined to offer its participants unprecedented equipment for widening their understanding and enhancing their resources. It is possible—and tempting—to argue that the tremendous achievements of the modern age, psychological as well as material, were made possible only by abandoning a unified and spiritualized conception of the environment. Even to begin to penetrate the secrets of the universe, it was necessary to cast off anthropomorphic preconceptions, to recognize that the universe cannot be explained as a projection of man's own needs or aspirations. An attitude of objectivity toward external reality was both a prerequisite for, and a consequence of, the advance of scientific knowledge. The philosophic doctrines of the Reformation, however, could hardly be said to reflect the scientific temper. Teleological and still anthropocentric, they pictured a universe dominated by the unalterable will of an inscrutable Deity. The Reformation dichotomy arose not from any dilemma imposed by scientific determinism; it was not the problem of the negation of man's subjective feelings and will by objective reality; rather, it split the human psyche in two by removing the moral law from man's jurisdiction and at the same time holding him subject to its dictates. It freed him to work in the world, even to develop and transform the world, but it required him to surrender his autonomy in the domain of values. In the long run this demeans rather than emancipates man. Nicholas Cusanus, who was as devout as the sixteenth-century Reformers, underlined a truth of the highest importance when he declared, while glimpsing the possibilities of scientific discovery, that man's unique prerogative and responsibility is the definition of values. This responsibility applies to social and political as well as private and personal goals.

THE RENAISSANCE AND OUR TIME

Every age develops its own frame of reference for interpreting the past and views historical periods from its own perspective. Historical "periods" are actually only convenient fictions, created by projecting judgments back into the past for the purpose of gaining insight into or imparting a sense of direction to the present. The Renaissance has long been regarded as embodying a set of changes particularly relevant to the genesis of the modern era. Though still useful, the concept is subject to reappraisal because it is no longer possible to regard the modern age—in the Western world or anywhere else— as a single entity. Panegyricists of the school of Burckhardt and Symonds hailed the Renaissance as the dawn of freedom, the first significant step on the road to the glorious world of the nineteenth century. Today that nineteenth-century world no longer seems so glorious; we know that it bore the seeds of our most intractable problems and frustrations; furthermore, it has disappeared and could no more be restored than could the world of antiquity. Confronted with the problems of today and tomorrow, we cannot escape into the past, cannot retrace our steps. But we can try to determine in which direction we are traveling. A discerning backward glance sees in the Renaissance a proving ground both for liberating forces that have carried man forward and for disruptive tendencies that have threatened him with the loss of his humanity.

The varying and unpredictable direction of the liberating currents traceable to the Renaissance is illustrated by the evolving concept of individualism. Both the Renaissance and the Reformation contributed to the discovery of the individual, but neither movement demonstrated how he may successfully relate to his society. The Renaissance accent on individual personality is seen as early as Petrarch, who reveled in introspection, and reaches a climax in the sixteenth-century French literary philosopher Montaigne, whose fertile and far-ranging *Essays* celebrate the self as the center and arbiter of experience. And if the Renaissance encouraged self-expression, the Reformation sprang from a personal self-assertive defiance of tradition and authority. However, none but the hardiest can stand alone, and the early modern period of emancipation from medieval bonds betrays a troubled sense of insecurity and a search for new pillars of authority. Italian citizens, whose ancestors had won municipal independence by standing fast against popes and emperors, submitted tamely to despotism nurtured in the bosom of their own communities. Partisans of religious sects bound themselves to princes who promised to uphold the church and the community of God's anointed, or followed their own religious leaders in furious onslaughts against those of opposing faiths.

It remained for later centuries to rediscover the individual and attempt to make him the cornerstone of a fairer and happier social dispensation. The notion of the inherent dignity of every person, wrested from its aristocratic base, became a buttress to support democratic institutions. Out of a brave struggle for the recognition of fundamental rights emerged the doctrine of the natural equality of men. During the nineteenth century this doctrine exerted effective pressure not only in the political field but also on living standards, education, recreation, and every important aspect of life. But the very success of the program has stripped it of much of its meaning. Paradoxically, the age that achieved the triumph of individualism has also witnessed the rise of totalitarian collectivism. And countries with the deepest liberal and democratic traditions are troubled by a growing fear that the individual may be overwhelmed by massive impersonal forces over which he has no control but which he lacks the will to resist. This modern social dilemma represents the opposite side of the coin, the reverse of the one that flawed Renaissance society. Renaissance man respected tyrants but despised conformity. Contemporary man hates tyrants but accepts the yoke of conformity.

The attempts of idealists to reconcile conflicting purposes and to bring again into a common focus the divergent aspects of experience, although never entirely successful, have provided the modern centuries with some of their finest hours. Particularly exhilarating were the efforts of the seventeenth- and eighteenth-century philosophers of the Enlightenment, who freely acknowledged the prevalence of wretchedness and corruption but also—in clear contrast to the leaders of the Reformation—denied that man's inherent vileness condemns him to remain in a degraded state. The *philosophes* believed and openly proclaimed that this anguished world could be transformed into a decent abode, by clearing away encrusted superstition and abusive privilege and subjecting all institutions to the scrutiny of reason. In the flush of enthusiasm they grossly oversimplified the task; the benevolent cosmopolitan "Heavenly City" of their imagination, although it claimed its charter from Newtonian physics, proved too fragile to withstand the shock of the French Revolution, virulent nationalism, and the travail of the early Industrial Revolution. Major scientific advances of the nineteenth century offered the promise of a more durable synthesis, but in actuality the new science in perverted form reinforced a narrowly materialistic interpretation of society and human nature. Forgetting that in the sphere of morals and in the defining of social goals man can and must retain his autonomy, false prophets allowed the concept of biological evolution, through a sort of feedback action upon philosophy, to produce a picture of man as nature's predator-in-chief and of the human community as a gladiators' arena.

The task of squaring the realities of the physical world with the latent potentialities of the human animal remains as a challenge to contemporary men of good will and good intellect. If they can achieve such a synthesis, they may, while rendering even greater homage to the discipline and the fruits of science, draw strength from the vision that impelled humanists and artists of the Renaissance. A summit once climbed can be scaled again.

CHRONOLOGICAL
GUIDE

CHRONOLOGICAL GUIDE/ITALY

	Political and Economic	Cultural
1282–93	Basic constitution of Florentine republic adopted; political power vested in guilds, excluding lower classes from office	Dante 1265–1321 *Divine Comedy* ca. 1307–21
ca. 1300	Supremacy of mercantile aristocracy in republic of Venice	Beginning of naturalism in painting Giotto ca. 1266–1336
1343–78	Limited progress toward democracy in Florence; broad middle-class representation in government	Dawn of humanism Francesco Petrarch 1304–74
1345–46	Failure of leading Florentine banking houses	Giovanni Boccaccio 1313–75 *Decameron* 1353
1348	Black Death inaugurates a century of economic contraction	
1378	*Ciompi* revolt in Florence: unsuccessful attempt of unorganized workers to gain economic and political rights	Impetus toward naturalism and revival of classical forms in architecture and sculpture
1382–1494	Florence, still republican in form, is controlled by a financial oligarchy	Filippo Brunelleschi 1377–1446
1380	Venice defeats Genoa and dominates Near Eastern trade	Lorenzo Ghiberti 1378–1455 Donatello 1386–1466
ca. 1390–1402	Florence leads resistance against expansion of Milan under Visconti despot	
1397	Medici bank founded in Florence	Manuel Chrysoloras, Greek scholar from Byzantium, comes to Florence 1397
ca. 1400–30	Florence subjugates all of Tuscany except Siena and Lucca	"Civil humanism" in Florence C. Salutati (Chancellor 1375–1406) L. Bruni (Chancellor 1427–44) P. Bracciolini (Chancellor 1453–58)

CHRONOLOGICAL GUIDE/ITALY

	Political and Economic	Cultural
1417	Pope Martin v (1417–31) elected by Council of Constance, ends the Great Schism and begins to strengthen Papal States	Flavio Biondo, archaeologist and historian 1387–1463
1434–64	Cosimo de' Medici dominates the oligarchy and the government of Florence	Florentine Academy founded 1462 Marsilio Ficino 1433–99 Leon Battista Alberti 1404–72
1435	Spanish House of Aragon displaces French Angevins as rulers of Naples	Prolific development of Italian painting Masaccio 1401–28 Fra Filippo Lippi 1406–69 Benozzo Gozzoli 1420–97 Giovanni Bellini ca. 1430–1516 Andrea Mantegna 1431–1506
1438–39	Pope Eugenius iv (1431–47) attempts to reunite Greek and Roman churches by Council of Ferrara and Florence	Pope Nicholas v (1447–55) patronizes humanists; founds Vatican library
1450	Francesco Sforza replaces Visconti as ruler of Milan	Lorenzo Valla 1405–57
1458–64	Pope Pius ii (Aeneas Sylvius Piccolomini)	
1463–69	Venice's commercial position weakened by defeat in war with Turks	Nicholas Cusanus 1401–64
1469–92	Lorenzo de' Medici "the Magnificent" rules Florence	Domenico Ghirlandaio 1449–94
1471–84	Pope Sixtas iv centralizes rule in Papal States; flagrant nepotism and corruption	Sandro Botticelli 1444–1510 Angelo Poliziano 1454–94
1478	Pazzi conspiracy against Medici foiled, but leads to war with papacy and crisis for Medici bank	Pico della Mirandola 1463–94 Oration on the Dignity of Man 1486

CHRONOLOGICAL GUIDE/ITALY

	Political and Economic	Cultural
1492–1503	Pope Alexander VI (Rodrigo Borgia) Cesare Borgia conquers territory in the Romagna	High ("Classical") Renaissance in art ca. 1490–ca. 1530 Fra Bartolommeo 1475–1517 Leonardo da Vinci 1452–1519 *Last Supper* ca. 1495 Raphael 1483–1520 Andrea del Sarto 1486–1531 Titian 1477–1576 Michelangelo 1475–1564 *Pietà* of St. Peter's ca. 1500
1494–95	French invasion of Italy by King Charles VIII	Aldine press founded in Venice (Aldus Manutius) 1493
1494	Expulsion of Medici from Florence; Medici bank is ruined	
1494–1512	Florence an unstable republic 1494–98 Dominant influence of the prophet Savonarola 1498–1512 Machiavelli in office	Niccolò Machiavelli 1469–1527
1499	French invasion under King Louis XII; occupies Milan	Francesco Guicciardini 1483–1540
1503–13 1512	Pope Julius II (Giuliano della Rovere) "Holy League" formed by pope, expels French from Italy. Florence, allied with French, defeated by Spanish troops	Julius II Tomb (Michelangelo) 1505–45 Sistine Chapel ceiling frescoes 1508–12
1512–27	Restored Medici regime in Florence	

CHRONOLOGICAL GUIDE/ITALY

	Political and Economic	Cultural
		The Prince 1513
		Pietro Bembo 1470–1547
		Lodovico Ariosto 1474–1533
		Orlando Furioso 1516
		Pietro Pomponazzi 1462–1525
		On Immortality 1516
		Baldassare Castiglione 1478–1529
		The Courtier ca. 1518
		Medici Tombs in Florence (Michelangelo) 1521–34
		Gasparo Contarini 1483–1542
		Pietro Aretino 1492–1556
		Benvenuto Cellini 1500–72
		Michelangelo's Last Judgment, Sistine Chapel, 1534–41
		Giorgio Vasari 1511–74
		Lives of Great Painters, etc. 1550
1513–21	Pope Leo x (Giovanni de' Medici) Climax of Renaissance Rome; splendor, reckless extravagance	
1515	French invasion under King Francis I reconquers Milan	
1523–34	Pope Clement vii (Giulio de' Medici)	
1525	French defeated at Pavia by imperial forces and again expelled from Italy	
1527	Sack of Rome by Spanish and German (imperial) troops	
1527–30	Medici driven out of Florence; last years of the republic	
1530	Florentine republic defeated by papal-imperial alliance	
1532	Republican constitution abolished; Alessandro de' Medici becomes first Duke of Florence	
1534–49	Pope Paul iii; beginning of the Catholic Reformation	

CHRONOLOGICAL GUIDE/NORTHERN AND WESTERN EUROPE

	Political and Economic	Cultural
1309–77	Avignon papacy ("Babylonian captivity")	Geoffrey Chaucer ca. 1340–1400
1337–1453	Hundred Years' War between England and France	Brethren of the Common Life formed at
1348–50	Black Death, followed by a century of retarded economic and population growth	Deventer 1384
		Imitation of Christ (Thomas à Kempis) ca. 1415
1378–1417	Great Schism in Church	Flemish school of painting flourishing
1414–49	Conciliar movement: unsuccessful attempt to establish supremacy of General Church Council over papal authority	Jan and Hubert van Eyck ca. 1370–1440
		Roger van der Weyden ca. 1400–64
1438	Albert II of Hapsburg Dynasty elected Holy Roman Emperor	Pre-eminence of Netherlands composers ca. 1420–1520
1440–93	Frederick III Holy Roman Emperor	Beginning of printed books ca. 1450
ca. 1450–1600	Voyages of overseas discovery, shifting trade routes away from Mediterranean ports	
1455–71	English Wars of Roses	
1461–1547	Strengthening of French monarchy under Valois kings	
1461–83	Louis XI king of France	
ca. 1470–1500	Severe banking crises and decline in number of private banking houses	Desiderius Erasmus ca. 1466–1536
		Sir Thomas More 1478–1535
ca. 1471–1603	Strengthening of English monarchy	
1479–1516	Unification of Spain under houses of Aragon and Castile; expulsion of Jews and Moors	
1483–98	Charles VIII king of France	Nicolaus Copernicus 1473–1543

CHRONOLOGICAL GUIDE/NORTHERN AND WESTERN EUROPE

	Political and Economic	Cultural
1485–1509	Henry VII (Tudor) king of England	"Oxford Reformers" ca. 1490–1520 (Linacre, Colet, More, Erasmus)
1493–1519	Maximilian I Holy Roman Emperor	Albrecht Dürer 1471–1528
		St. Jerome, Melencolia 1514
1498–1515	Louis XII king of France	Hans Holbein the younger 1479–1543
		Willibald Pirckheimer 1470–1530
1509–47	Henry VIII king of England	Praise of Folly 1511
1515–47	Francis I king of France	Education of a Christian Prince 1516
1516	Concordat of Bologna: Church subjected to state control	Utopia 1516
		Erasmus' Greek New Testament 1516
1516–56	Rule of Charles of Hapsburg	
1516–56	King Charles I of Spain	Letters of Obscure Men 1516–17
1519–56	Holy Roman Emperor Charles V	
1517	Luther publishes Ninety-five Theses, beginning of Protestant Revolt	
1534	Act of Supremacy separates English Church from Rome	Michel Montaigne 1533–92

INDEX